Library of
Davidson College

Three Decades of the French New Novel

Three Decades of the French New Novel

Edited by
Lois Oppenheim

Translated by Lois Oppenheim
and Evelyne Costa de Beauregard

University of Illinois Press
Urbana and Chicago

© 1986 by the Board of Trustees of the University of Illinois
Manufactured in the United States of America
C 5 4 3 2 1

This book is printed on acid-free paper.

LIBRARY OF CONGRESS CATALOGING-IN-PUBLICATION DATA

Main entry under title:

Three decades of the French New Novel.

   Proceedings of a colloquium held in the fall of 1982 at New York University.
   Includes bibliographies.
   1. French fiction—20th century—History and criticism—Congresses. 2. Fiction—Technique—Congresses. 3. Literature, Experimental—History and criticism—Congresses. I. Oppenheim, Lois.
PQ672.T48   1986   843'.914'09   85-20902
ISBN 0-252-01158-9 (alk. paper)

to my family

Contents

Introduction
   Lois Oppenheim   3
Opening Remarks
   Tom Bishop   13

Alain Robbe-Grillet   21

Alain Robbe-Grillet: At Play with Criticism
   Michel Rybalka   31
From the "New Novel" to the "New Novelist"
   François Jost   44
Publishing the New Novel
   Barney Rosset   57
Discussion   63

Claude Simon   71

Toward a Simonian Mimetics
   Ralph Sarkonak   87
Discussion   104

Nathalie Sarraute   119

The Place of the Action
   Monique Wittig   132
Discussion   141

Robert Pinget   143

Is There a New Novel Today?
   Leon S. Roudiez   152
Discussion   174

**The New Novel — Past, Present, Future:
A Roundtable** *179*
*Alain Robbe-Grillet, Claude Simon,
Nathalie Sarraute, Robert Pinget,
Monique Wittig, François Jost,
Michel Rybalka, Tom Bishop*

American Parallels: An Afterword   *195*
*John Barth, Jonathan Baumbach,
Robert Coover, John Hawkes*

Index   *211*

Three Decades of the French New Novel

Introduction

Lois Oppenheim

Today, some three decades later, a reexamination of the revolutionary aesthetic that so quickly came to represent the French New Novel (or Nouveau Roman) in the 1950s, 1960s, and 1970s is in order. The New Novelist, all too often assumed to have come to the novel armed with a theoretical awareness of the limits of narrative convention and the irrelevance of aesthetic tradition to the experience of modernism, is readily considered according to an ideological exaggeration, one that distorts the primary creative impulse and developmental history unique to the individual writer. Characterized, collectively, as rivals of the kind of realism that branded the nineteenth-century novels of Balzac, Stendhal, and Flaubert, the New Novelists have been declared subversive, mutinous disclaimers of plot, character, chronology, and the stability of social norms. They are viewed as repudiators, in short, of the very structures that traditionally gave credence to fiction and defined the scope of the novel's potential to be "well made."

In the fall of 1982, a colloquium was held at New York University to explore, in retrospect, the expressive anima of the New Novel as a movement, to celebrate the continuing artistry of several of the writers whose names are linked under the rubric of the Nouveau Roman, and to assess the impact on writing outside of France of those most unorthodox works of the novelists in question. The present collection includes the majority of the presentations made and discussed at that gathering. Some of the papers reflect the thinking on literary language as autonomous and self-reflective that has been the framework for many of the most important critical positions taken in recent years. Others are marked by a valuation of the New Novel as a narrative process intimately connected with a philosophically (existentially and epistemologically) informed worldview, thereby withdrawing from the exegetic arena any priority of language as the interrelation of signs over the innate subjectivity of meaning. All papers, however, reveal—either through critical appraisal or personal account—that what impelled the transformation of narrative forms was *not* a congruence of a priori theoretical determinations, a coming together of conscious dialectical thinking on the novel as it was and as it should be. The transformation was, rather, an effort to render more intelligible our experience of the world, to embody—on the level of what might be considered, given the uncertain and inconsistent circumferences of the postmodern age, a more valid "realism" than that of descriptive verisimilitude—perceptual chaos in narrative order.

In the essays of Alain Robbe-Grillet and Nathalie Sarraute, for example (I use the word "essay" in the sense of a trial or attempt because both writers offered, spontaneously, very speculative words on their beginnings as novelists), any notion of a theoretical revolutionizing of novelistic forms as a motivation for the New Novel is laid to rest. While Robbe-Grillet does, indeed, acknowledge a somewhat "naive" preliminary intent on his part to obliterate conformity in the structure of the novel, he maintains that a literary revolution as such never took place. And Nathalie Sarraute's remarks attest not only to the absence of any intent even vaguely akin to that of Robbe-Grillet, but also to a profound awareness of narrative form as an inherently flexible phenomenon able to be worked and reworked in accordance with the particular exigencies of a given novelistic material. In the presentations of both writers, therefore, the reader will witness a preoccupation with the fictional possibilities (social, metaphoric, and other) for the fullest realization of the generative power of language, as opposed to a subservience of language to the forms of its expression.

We recognize in Robbe-Grillet a deeply felt respect for language as constitutive of its own reality above and beyond that engendered by assumed links with the world of everyday experience. (His recent novel, *Djinn*, comes first to mind.) In the novels of Sarraute, on the other hand, it is the delicate interplay between the activity of the mind in relation to the quotidian world and the language used to articulate this interplay that is of greatest interest. In both writers, however, a delimitation of the *expressivity* of language is preeminent: Whether we hold, as some critics of recent years have been known to do, that the primary impulse of the Nouveau Roman was linguistic (one word inciting the next, one verbal image evolving from another) or that it tended to be more or less impressionistic (the language of the New Novel emanating from sensation), the profoundly creative achievements of these writers unveil, above all else, the *simultaneity of conception and execution* in their literary practice. Hence, if the New Novels of Alain Robbe-Grillet and Nathalie Sarraute, as well as those of their colleagues, may be said to be revolutionary, it is not that they—by way of a unified conceptual or theoretical position — succeeded in overthrowing that with which they are most often contrasted, the novelistic order that preceded them, but, far more significantly, that they uncovered the need for an awareness of the fundamental malleability of narrative forms that this simultaneity implies.

Robert Pinget is another writer in whom the long-standing preoccupation with renovation of the novel is manifested entirely on the level of the text, in the practice of writing, obviating any need or inclination to construct an independent theory. In his eloquent contribution to this volume, Pinget, like Robbe-Grillet and Sarraute, focuses on the dynamic interrelation of narrative form and the literariness of fiction, its language, tone, and texture, as the origin of a distinctly personal voice. In Pinget's essay, however, the reader will find evidence that the self-critical attitude inherent in the fiction, the self-consciousness intrinsic to the homogeneity attributed to the New Novelists, leads to the affirmation of experimentation as a necessary aesthetic response to the diversity and potentialities of verbal expression; it also leads to the very intimate relation between the fundamental nature of art (as the totality of mutually dependent forms and feelings) and technique: "Once a work of art has assimilated all possible complexities of expression, its aim must be to say only one simple thing which, I think, is called poetry."

Claude Simon's literary accomplishments offer insight into possibilities for renewal not only of novelistic forms but also of historical narration and the entire notion of historicity. Simon denies any conjectural or presumptive original thinking about the novel. He, in fact, goes so far in disclaiming any theoretical point of departure for his work as to declare that it has never even occurred to him that "he should write to fight against the established order to criticize it." Written in a markedly modest and perhaps even somewhat self-effacing tone, Simon's essay, a most sensitive examination of his "cultural 'baggage' " and literary formation, further contributes to what constitutes, from the beginning to the end of this book, a firm disavowal on the part of these writers of any revolutionary or tactical motivation for the New Novel. Situating in a temporal relation to *our* modernity (for, as Simon maintains, each period has its own) the coming to blows with "realism" characteristic of the efforts of the Nouveaux Romanciers, Simon evokes the substitution in painting of impression for an apodictic knowledge of reality. Insisting that every true artist, regardless of medium, is necessarily innovative, Simon judiciously adjusts our perspective on the New Novel by relating, in addition to those writers commonly acknowledged as its precursors, a decisive break from "realism" in the graphic arts to that in literature. In doing so, he, too, emphasizes the indivisibility of ideation and effectuation in artistic productivity.

What is particularly striking in the remarks of all four contributors, therefore, and what would appear to unite them more than any theoretical point of departure, is their need to defend themselves against a decidedly nonempirical image of the origin of the New Novel. If, indeed, the Nouveau Roman is to be conceptualized as a movement in the first place (and that this is a contestable issue was made ever more obvious by this colloquium), its practitioners rightly implore that it be valued not as a monolithic effort to free the novel of convention, autonomy, and its tradition of narrative equanimity, but as a contiguity of novelistic concerns arising from a fundamentally *interrogative* (experimental) creative posture, one diversely rooted in the imaginative (and perhaps idiocratic) visions peculiar to the individual writers. If we detect in these presentations, and in the discussions that ensued from them, an eagerness to be rid of the theoretical prescriptive prototyping imposed on literature by the onslaught of scientism to which the criticism of the 1960s and 1970s fell prey, we would do well to remember that this colloquium at New York University was the first major gathering of New Novelists and their critics since that held at Cerisy-la-Salle in 1971. As such, its significance was enhanced by the possibilities for retrospective thinking on the *critical evaluation* of the New Novel, as well as on the New Novel itself. Thus the desire for criticism to return to the praxis of literary language, to the primary context of the *creative* initiative of the author, a desire evidenced in all four of these essays, is substantiated by a defense against *any* tendency toward critical presupposition or determinism, whether that owing to the "scientific" orientation of

Introduction

particular critical approaches or that deriving from the assumption of a formative revolutionary aesthetic.

If a defense against deterministic thinking on the New Novel appears to set the tone for the presentations of these four novelists, in the critical essays that accompany these lectures a related effort is evident. A renewed interest in both the continuity of the individual creative endeavor—in the reliance of textual meaning on a consistent organization of a semantic universe—and in the practical (as opposed to theoretical) relation of the text to the world appears, in several of the critical papers, to supplant the recently popular conception of the text as a stratified composite of meanings isolated from any particular sensibility of their author and from any but a purely hypothetical mode of linguistic experience. This change in perspective has its greatest impact on the assumption of neutrality, of the suspension of narrative judgment, all too often held to be among the most significant characteristics of the Nouveau Roman. In reintroducing a primary authorial gestalt into the interpretative process, the critic serves to demystify an anonymity of the text that now seems to have been more apparent than real. This reevaluation of narrative viewpoint is not to be understood, however, as a favoring of some form of subjectivity over objectivity in the narratological dichotomy perpetuated by so much of the criticism written on the New Novel. Rather, the reassessment of authorial function, and hence of the ideological function of the text as expressive of an author's valuation of, and primordial situation in, the world, should be viewed as the result of a heightened awareness not only of the possibilities of literature to influence, but also its responsibility to reform, cultural and sociopolitical reality.

Michel Rybalka demonstrates this reinsertion of the author into the text and that of the text into the world in centering his study of the interplay between theory and creative practice in Robbe-Grillet around an extremely coherent fictional project or truth, one "whose presence is so strong from beginning to end that it resists the theories of others and even those of Robbe-Grillet" himself. And François Jost, affirming the need for criticism to redirect itself away from the New Novel toward the New Novelist, focuses his attention on "semantic cores" that constitute the very logic or internal organization of Robbe-Grillet's fictional world. Monique Wittig stresses textual worldliness in arguing that the primary modes of the human being's relation to language, as embraced by Sarraute in her highly intuitive and profoundly philosophic novelistic material, bear witness to the *potency* of each and every individual having language, that "paradise of visible, audible, palpable, palatable words," at his disposal. Language can kill, Wittig affirms, not only symbolically but also literally, through words of oppression. All three critics identify within the context of a given author's narrative universe, therefore, a singular holistic author-text-world configuration in which literary meaning is not only constituted but also sustained by the dialectical interrelation of language and the world that it expresses.

This methodological uniformity, in which the apprehension of a textual reality is dependent upon that of a perceptual praxis, is not, however, uncontested in the present volume. Ralph Sarkonak, for one, argues that a primacy of mimetic function determines the specificity of linguistic reference in a given work. Responding to what he perceives as a consistent " 'antimimetic' prejudice" implicit in Simonian criticism, Sarkonak attempts an explanation of the verbal and graphic production of meaning in Simon's work according to the premise that the reality of language is the *only* reality discernible in the text. Language, as such, is both self-replicating and originative for Sarkonak (through new syntactical arrangements, new linguistic or graphic modalities), but not perceptually referential. And Leon Roudiez, in proposing the notion of the "gynetext" (or "woman text") as a possible frame of reference for the interpretation of meaning, deviates from the perspective of nondeterministic thinking, although he remains significantly closer to the view of textual worldliness as the perceptual (rather than representational) functioning of literary activity. From Barney Rosset's overview of his initial association with the New Novel as the American publisher of Samuel Beckett and Robbe-Grillet to Roudiez's provocative analysis of the current status of the New Novel and a round-table discussion that includes all of the aforementioned participants, therefore, the diversity of viewpoints that characterizes any collective work offsets the homogeneity of critical trends. Over and above the presentation of new and differing critical perspectives on the New Novel, however—though it hardly needs to be said—it is in the interaction of New Novel critics and New Novel authors, and in the sorting out of the increasingly ambiguous circumferences of

Introduction

critical and novelistic discourse advanced by this interaction, that the real interest of a book such as this lies.

An afterword to this collection consists of excerpts from a roundtable among four American novelists of such distinction that their work is well known to most, if not all, readers of contemporary American fiction. The participation of John Barth, Jonathan Baumbach, Robert Coover, and John Hawkes in a colloquium on the French novel was invaluable for the opportunity it afforded those present to appreciate not only the mutual indebtedness of artists throughout the world, but also their common concerns. Although hardly forming as cohesive a group as that of the Nouveaux Romanciers, these writers do share with one another, as with their colleagues in France, preoccupations whose exploration at this roundtable inspired a variety of provocative questions. Highlights from that session are reproduced here.

Apart from participation of the American novelists—whose presence at a colloquium on the French New Novel was determined both by an interest in exploring their aesthetic and technical affinities with the French writers and by a desire to pay tribute to their colleagues from abroad—this book is undeniably reminiscent of the two-volume publication by the Union Générale d'Editions (10/18) that resulted from the 1971 Cerisy-la-Salle colloquium. In form as well as in content (the faithful reproduction of the discussions accompanying the prepared presentations and critical analyses complementing the self-descriptive accounts of the novelists), it appears as an extension of those earlier tomes. In fact, however, while such a view of this work is indeed a valuable one (insofar as it highlights the historicity of the Nouveau Roman and of its criticism, and insofar as it further accentuates the specificity of the authors in question by forcing us to trace the individuality of their evolutions), it is not an entirely accurate perspective in which to read the present work. It should be remembered, for instance, that the colloquium in France was undertaken on a much larger scale than that which took place in this country. It lasted a full week longer than the symposium at New York University, and it included, therefore, a far greater number of participants. The conference in New York, moreover, did not derive from an intent similar to that of the colloquium at Cerisy. Rather than the exploration of both general problems relating to the Nouveau Roman (the relation of the New Novel to film, criticism, phenomenology, politics, and so on) and that of the particular fictional corpus of each of the novelists present, the more recent colloquium aimed to delineate, within a retrospective framework, the present situation of the Nouveau Roman, what might be referred to as a third stage in the maturation of this fiction.

In its early years, the New Novel represented the first step toward liberation of the reader from a utilitarian epistemology, from a positivism rooted in the privileged referentiality of fiction to the bourgeois values of the quotidian world. The impetus for this first period of the Nouveau Roman, however, was not, as already stated, an eagerness on the part of the New Novelists to overstep the boundaries of realism in preference for some metaphysical interpretation of human life. Indeed, the early novels of the 1950s clung to verisimilitude (and a highly exaggerated verisimilitude at that) as *the* primary means of expressing the fundamental nature of life experience; so much so, in fact, that conventionality truly functioned as the *modus operandi* for disclosing its own insufficiency. In Robbe-Grillet's *La Jalousie,* Nathalie Sarraute's *Le Planétarium,* and Michel Butor's *La Modification,* for example, the fiction is resolutely anchored in representation of the cultural environment familiar to author and reader alike, allowing for the fullest externalization or objectivation in a worldly context of the subjectivity of experience. What *was* rejected in the first period of the Nouveau Roman was the effort to unify in a single literary work *all* aspects of life, *all* facets of the nonfictive world, and this in favor of disclosing, as opposed to interpreting, various modes of reference, by means of their magnification, of the ego to the world.

In its second stage, that associated in the late 1960s and 1970s with Jean Ricardou and the Nouveau Nouveau Roman, this fiction became linked, through the ensemble of theoretical formulations surrounding it, with the antireferential motif that sought to abstract narrative realism from its perceptual ties with the world and to resituate it on the level of its mechanical construction. The New New Novel, no longer steeped either in the positivist epistemology of nineteenth-century realism or in the epiphanous mode of understanding to which the realism of the earliest works of the New Novelists (descendants of Proust and Joyce) had given rise, pushed the epistemological function of this literature to its limit by identifying its semantic structures with the increasing deteriorization of pure subjectivity (be it that of author or character). The Barthesian "zero degree" of literary discourse then corresponded, in short, to the anonymous ego of a "speaking subject" to whom the visionary narrator of old had finally deferred.

In recent years, in this third period of the French New Novel, preoccupation with the structure of the novel genre that was the unifying aesthetic and epistemological force of the Nouveau Roman throughout its first and second stages has been replaced by a new set of problems. The primary question no longer focuses on expressing knowledge of the objective world through the referential relation of subject and object in perception or on the reduction of that referential relation to the linguistic structures that, over and above any hypothetical notion of their "profoundeur," *are* the text. Rather, the most recent fiction of the New Novelists reflects the general preoccupation of literary theorists, since the waning of structuralism on the critical horizon, with the revalorization of the author, as opposed to the referential or nonreferential mode of his or her work. Indeed, those works published in the past half-decade, works in some cases more autobiographical than fictional, are implicitly concerned with questions of authorial "voice," the transparency of language onto empiricism and the dissemination of meaning in personal usage. Specifically, in Robbe-Grillet's *Le Miroir qui revient* (1984) and Marguerite Duras' *L'Amant* (1984) (the latter being the most recently published work of an author often associated with the New Novelists, although she has chosen to remain on the periphery of the "movement"), it is the relation of prior experience to the recounting of that experience, the relation of childhood to the writing of autobiography, that provides material for the epistemological research toward which the New Novelist, impelled by the mystifying interrelation of truth and falsehood, reality and fiction, certainty and uncertainty, is forever inclined. In some respects, this interest in personal narrative (Nathalie Sarraute's *Enfance* is the only real autobiography among these works) comes as less of a surprise than the readers of the New Novel might imagine, for, if we remember that the New Novelist has aimed, these last thirty years, at eliminating all but the most primary elements necessary for disclosing the real nature of life experience, we will see that characterization, that most commonly cited *bête noire* of the Nouveau Roman, has, in a sense, merely been reduced to the author him- or herself. Hence Robbe-Grillet's (fictional) autobiography states: "Je n'ai jamais parlé d'autre chose que de moi" [I have never spoken of anything other than myself], and Duras' best-selling (autobiographical) fiction states: "Ce que je fais ici est différent, et pareil" [What I am doing here is different, and the same].

A word about the translation is in order. The papers of Tom Bishop, Barney Rosset, and Leon Roudiez were originally written in English. The essay by Robert Pinget was rendered in English by the eminent translator Barbara Wright. The remainder of the book was translated by Evelyne Costa de Beauregard and me.

Our effort was to remain as faithful as possible to the original texts. While some relied more heavily on the use of personal constructions, others were grounded in prevailing critical terminology. Stylistic uniformity being irrelevant to a collective work, however, the primary challenge of the translation lay in the need for maintaining—throughout the presentations and the discussions which followed them—a consistent awareness of a variety of literary and expressive sensibilities. As translation is governed by far more than the laws of an exact science, the risks of ambiguity and poor judgment were endemic to the task. We are thus exceedingly grateful to those authors who gave generously of their time to elaborate on their thinking and confirm our interpretations for the sake of translation accuracy.

I am extremely grateful to Tom Bishop, organizer of the colloquium, for his invaluable assistance in the planning of this book. I wish to thank as well Myriam Pinto, for taking the time to consider with me questions of translation, and Ann Lowry Weir of the University of Illinois Press, for her attentiveness and professional expertise.

Opening Remarks

Tom Bishop

Why a colloquium on the Nouveau Roman? Why at this time? And why at New York University? For those gathered here and for many others elsewhere who are readers of modern fiction, "le Nouveau Roman" is THE major emanation of the French novel in the second half of the twentieth century, an ertswhile avant-garde that has become for many the major mode of novelistic production not only in France, but in other European and American cultures as well.

For some, the New Novel remains avant-garde and therefore (for those same readers, or nonreaders) reviled and incomprehensible. But then that sort of reactionary position vis à vis innovation, the hallmark of the retrograde esthetic sensitivity or world view, accompanies every form of experimentation.

Referring to "three decades of the New Novel," this colloquium is termed a retrospective. If a retrospective appears justified in the early 1980s, three decades is a somewhat arbitrary time reference. To mention only the most obvious discrepancy in the time frame, Nathalie Sarraute published *Tropismes* as far back as 1939! Still, it was the early 1950s that brought the authors of what was to become known as the Nouveau Roman to the attention at first of a small public in France and then to a far larger public both in France and around the world.

The year 1953 marked publication of Alain Robbe-Grillet's *Les Gommes* [*The Erasers*] and Nathalie Sarraute's *Martereau*. Michel Butor's *Passage de Milan* followed in 1954 and Robbe-Grillet's *Le Voyeur* the next year. Robert Pinget's first fiction dates from the beginning of the 1950s and *Mahu ou le matériau* [*Mahu or the Material*] appeared in 1952. By the middle of the decade, everything was set for a major explosion. In the forefront of the onslaught was the small publishing house, Les Editions de Minuit, headed by Jérôme Lindon. Minuit had already proven its willingness to take risks by publishing Beckett's *Molloy* in 1950 after this epoch-making work was rejected by countless other publishers. Now Lindon plunged courageously into the maelstrom of experimental fiction and gave unstinting support to a new esthetic. Minuit brought out Pinget's *Graal Filibuste* in 1956; in 1957, Lindon added Robbe-Grillet's *La Jalousie* [*Jealousy*], two novels by Butor—*L'Emploi du temps* [*Passing Time*] and *La Modification* [*A Change of Heart*]—as well as Claude Simon's *Le Vent* [*The Wind*].

By the time the decade was over, Minuit had added Simon's *L'Herbe* [*The Grass*] and *La Route des Flandres* [*The Flanders Road*], Robbe-Grillet's *Dans le labyrinthe* [*In the Labyrinth*], Pinget's *Baga* [*Bega*] and *Le Fiston* [*Monsieur Levert*], and Claude Ollier's *La Mise en scène*. Meanwhile, Nathalie Sarraute was being published by Gallimard: *Portrait d'un inconnu* [*Portrait of a Man Unknown*], that had first appeared in a small press in 1948, was reissued (by the prestigious Gallimard imprint) in 1956, *Le Planétarium* [*The Planetarium*] in 1959, and the essays *L'Ere du soupçon* [*The Age of Suspicion*] in 1956. In 1960, with *Degrés* [*Degrees*], Butor turned to Gallimard for publication of his fiction.

Within the span of some half-dozen years, new concepts of reality, new conventions of fiction had surfaced on the French literary horizon. Of course, no artistic revolution arises *ex nihilo*: the immediate precursors of the Nouveau Roman include Joyce, Beckett, Kafka, Roussel, and the lineage that, inclusive of Proust and Woolf, goes back as far as Flaubert and forward to include Sartre's *La Nausée* [*Nausea*] and Camus' *L'Etranger* [*The Stranger*].

Still, however respectable its antecedents may have been, the Nouveau Roman was a radical departure from traditional forms of the novel. The familiar trappings of the nineteenth-century-type novel were deliberately downgraded and tended to disappear: chronology, cause and effect, linear plot, characters in the usual sense of the word, and often direct dialogue. Readers were confronted with fictions that drew them into their vortex and required their active collaboration in reconstituting the fictional world in order to make it accessible. The narrative techniques were multiple, as were the voices speaking to us. Whether the narration took the first-, second-, or even, at times, third-person singular (but a deceptive, unreliable third person, not the omniscient, Balzacian one), whether addressed by a single or multiple narrator, the reader of the Nouveau Roman faced major demands imposed by the author, demands that eventually yielded new esthetic rewards.

With its early insistence on objective description (giving rise to the labels "reism," "Objective Novel," and "l'école du regard"), with its deliberate restriction to a limited field of narrative vision, with its refusal to probe beneath the surface for supposed psychological depths, the New Novel fashioned a startling new (or rather, newly perceived) reality. To be sure, Sarraute, Robbe-Grillet, Simon, Butor, Pinget, Ollier each wrote in his/her very distinctive manner, and the differences among them are as numerous as their similarities; yet, the common thrust, the shared need to react against the traditional novel, binds them and justifies the group heading "New Novel," despite the clear absence of a school or a coterie. Robbe-Grillet may not have been selected as spokesman by the others, but his essays laid the theoretical foundation for the new concept of realism that more or less applied also to the universe of the other New Novelists. After recognizing that "All writers believe they are realists.... It is the real world which interests them; each one attempts as best as can [*sic*] to create 'the real,' " Robbe-Grillet pointed out that realism has always been the ambition of innovators: "out of a concern for realism each new literary school has sought to destroy the one which preceded it."[1]

As for his own worldview that informs not only the world in which he lives but also, by necessity, the world he creates, Robbe-Grillet observes that "the world is neither significant nor absurd. It *is,* quite simply. That, in any case, is the most remarkable thing about it.... Around us, defying the noisy pack of our animistic or protective adjectives, things *are there.*"[2] Rejecting essentialist views of man and a verisimilitudinous function for art, Robbe-Grillet enlists the novel in a radical adventure, the phenomenological concern with the here and now, with *Dasein,* the description of the visible and the refusal of all speculation, metaphysical or otherwise. "The revolution which has occurred is in kind," he writes, "not only do we no longer consider the world as our own, our private property, designed according to our needs and readily domesticated, but we no longer even believe in 'depth.' "[3] Fiction, then, will no longer be referential to a preexisting reality; it will create its own reality, will be self-referential. As Vivian Mercier has noted, "The greatest realism may consist in constantly reminding the reader that he is reading a 'made-up' story, not observing life."[4]

Despite its experimental nature, there is no denying the success of the Nouveau Roman in France during the first dozen years—success in terms of critical reception, influence, literary prizes, and even, in a few cases, sales as a result of the prizes. Robbe-Grillet's *Les Gommes* was awarded the Prix Fénéon in 1954 and *Le Voyeur* the Prix des Critiques the following year. In 1957, Butor received both the Prix Fénéon for *L'Emploi du temps* and the Renaudot for *La Modification*. Within the next decade, Ollier won the Médicis Prize for *La Mise en scène;* Simon, the Prix de l'Express for *La Route des Flandres* and the Médicis for *Histoire;* Pinget, the Prix des Critiques for *L'Inquisitoire* [*The Inquisitory*] and the Fémina for *Quelqu'un;* Jean Ricardou, the Fénéon for *La Prise de Constantinople,* while the "doyenne" of the New Novelists, Nathalie Sarraute, was awarded the Prix International de Littérature for *Les Fruits d'or* [*The Golden Fruits*]. If nothing else, this array of prizes attests to the celebrity and even notoriety of the New Novel by the mid-1960s. Since then, most of the writers in question have become solid fixtures in the French literary landscape and some have become contemporary classics, studied in French schools and universities (a rare occurrence for living authors), solicited for interviews, articles, and colloquia.

Thanks to the greater attention paid to contemporary writing in American universities, the New Novel quickly found a sizable public on this side of the Atlantic. Simon and Schuster began publishing Butor in 1959, Grove Press published its first Robbe-Grillet in 1958 and Pinget in 1961 (in recent years Pinget has been published by Red Dust), George Braziller has been publishing Sarraute since 1958 and brought out its first Simon in 1959. Simon's recent books, as well as reeditions of some other New Novelists, have been distributed in the United States by the English publisher of the New Novel, John Calder, through Riverrun Press. The transition of often difficult texts to English has been immensely aided by the excellent translators selected for the task; these have included Richard Howard, Barbara Wright, and Maria Jolas. Not only have practically all French titles been presented in the United States, but also American scholars have produced a significant number of critical studies. Courses on the New Novel exist everywhere. Since 1960, the leading French New Novelists have come ever more frequently to the United States to lecture, take part in conferences, and teach in universities.

Opening Remarks

New York University has been particularly fortunate in having the various writers in question as frequent visitors and colleagues.

Much has been written on the Nouveau Roman (not only in France and in the United States, but in many other parts of the world), largely—and since early on—to theorize, to announce the *death* of the New Novel, or to question its existence. For some reason, people have been eager to bury it for a long time, and yet, lo and behold, the Nouveau Roman is still very much alive three decades later. The survival of the Nouveau Roman was a major focal point in organizing this conference. Even the famous 1971 colloquium at Cerisy-la-Salle, "Nouveau Roman: hier, aujourd'hui," that brought together the major writers and critics of the New Novel (many of whom gathered at New York University for its colloquium) and that provided the critical apparatus that has enabled us to deal with the phenomenon ever since—even at Cerisy, in what one might call the heyday of the movement, Jean Ricardou began the proceedings by wondering whether the New Novel existed at all. And after having decided, to no one's surprise, that it did, Ricardou kept right on wondering whether it was already dead. That was in 1971. Whatever else can be said about the famous ten days at Cerisy, one thing is certain: Cerisy proved how very much the Nouveau Roman was alive then, even if it did give rise to the unhappy (though probably temporarily necessary) phrase "le nouveau 'Nouveau Roman'" ["the new 'New Novel'"].

But if in 1971 the redundant "nouveau nouveau" served to separate a first flowering movement from the directions taken in the second half of the 1960s, by now, with a deeper perspective, the "new new" phrase can be abolished with the realization that the New Novel was never monolithic in the first place but has, in fact, been in constant evolution—the very proof of its viability. For some of the novelists present in New York for the colloquium and for some of those not present (and I refer specifically to Butor and Ollier), the span of thirty years has been a straight line; for others, the line undulates, goes off in various directions. But no one has stood still. Thus, there is no need to add yet one more "new" and invent a grotesque label "new, new 'New Novel.'" In fact, that outworn term "new 'New Novel'" can be discarded to concentrate on the three decades as a living unit of literary production. The wisdom of the 1980s suggests that it simply be referred to as "Nouveau Roman." Period.

In 1981, I realized that in the year or so preceding, extraordinary proof had been given that the New Novel was alive and kicking. The four French novelists present at New York University for its colloquium each published a new work of fiction during that year; each of these novels was extremely well received critically and all ran up impressive sales figures—in most cases, the best ever for each author immediately on publication. I refer to *Les Géorgiques* of Claude Simon, *Apocryphe* of Robert Pinget, *L'Usage de la Parole* [*The Use of Speech*] of Nathalie Sarraute, and *Djinn* of Alain Robbe-Grillet. For a literary tendency supposedly dead or at least moribund, here was an amazing sign of life. One could not doubt that the New Novel remained vital, although one might well wonder whether it had ceased being an avant-garde and had instead become the new classicism. A general reevaluation seemed in order, an examination of these and other questions at a time when there is enough distance to take a true retrospective glance.

Because the recent writings of the visiting authors are somewhat less well known in the United States than their earlier ones, they themselves, in comments during the colloquium, will stress their recent production. In this manner, they will both fill in lacunae for many American readers and be in a position to talk about where they are today, rather than be obliged to cast retrospective glances at their own work. That is the work of the critics, and it will be done by them at this conference.

We shall also look ahead to see whether there is a new generation of the Nouveau Roman visible anywhere. We see echoes of the Nouveau Roman in many areas of literary and artistic expression, beyond the single domain of the French novel: in the cinema, the theater, the plastic arts, in the fiction of other countries, in South America, for instance, and in this country. With specific reference to the United States, a special session with John Barth, Jonathan Baumbach, Robert Coover, and John Hawkes examines links to American fiction. Since our aesthetic sensibility in the waning years of the twentieth century has been influenced by the French New Novel, this seems to be a good time to take stock.

Finally, why hold a colloquium at New York University? As mentioned earlier, the New Novel has elicited great interest in this country over the years—and in this city as well—and there is a significant public for it in the United States. The presence of so many persons for this colloquium bears witness to this fact. At New York University's Center for French Civilization and Culture, there has been a positive, ongoing relationship with the New Novel, not only through the major interest of the faculty and students but also because Robbe-Grillet, Sarraute, Simon, and Pinget, as well as Butor, Ollier, and Ricardou, have come regularly or fairly regularly for the past twenty or so years to teach, lecture, and even participate in colloquia. Another reason is that a discussion of the Nouveau Roman can perhaps better take place here, in an atmosphere less ideologically charged than in France. This greater detachment and objectivity are desirable now that the Nouveau Roman is no longer in the front lines of the first vanguard and now that the distinguished novelists are eminent literary figures rather than young turks. The acrimony of Cerisy seems far away now—far away theoretically and far away geographically and chronologically. Above and beyond past battles, in an atmosphere of open-mindedness, the New York colloquium offers a chance to assess the phenomenon of the Nouveau Roman, to weigh its contributions, to take its pulse as a measure of its vitality in the 1980s.

Notes

1. Alain Robbe-Grillet, *For a New Novel,* trans. Richard Howard (New York: Grove Press, 1965), 157-158.
2. *Ibid.*, 19.
3. *Ibid.*, 24.
4. Vivian Mercier, *The New Novel* (New York: Farrar, Straus & Giroux, 1971), 6.

Alain Robbe-Grillet

I am going to try to say why I write and to specify, perhaps with some difficulty, what my present concerns are and how they may be situated in relation to those of the 1950s. It is true that the Nouveau Roman is already a quarter-of-a-century old and this word "nouveau" [new] is therefore somewhat comical. It is comical, however, in a way which, all in all, suits me rather well and, aside from the fact that the New Novel has continually renewed itself, as Tom Bishop pointed out, it may be said that its novelty remains intact since the revolution which it started in the 1950s never really materialized. Contrary to what I naively hoped as a young man, all of literature was not really turned upside down by the Nouveau Roman and, here again, I am interested in knowing why.

First, why did I start writing? At the end of the 1940s and the beginning of the 1950s I was already thirty years old. I was not at all a novelist by profession; I was not even trained in literature. I was a scientist and suddenly I wanted to write novels, not then knowing that they would be the Nouveau Roman. I wanted, in other words, to write a certain kind of novel, but it was the way the critics received it that made me understand that what I was writing was not what was expected of a *true good* novelist. This, of course, surprised me, as I was under the impression that the criteria by which I was being judged had not been applicable to literature for a very long time and that after Proust, Kafka, Faulkner, Joyce, and so on, literature no longer bore any resemblance to the model which French academic criticism continued to impose on it. It was in reading the reviews which my first books received, reviews which opposed what I was doing with what was expected of me, that little by little I had a clearer idea of what I wanted to do. These reviews, as you know, were unfavorable at the beginning. I have in no way built my career on public acclaim, but rather on its rejection, and on an almost universal critical condemnation, at least by the academic critics in authority: those who rule in the papers and magazines. Among those who supported me at the beginning were Roland Barthes, Georges Bataille, and Maurice Blanchot, but at that time they were not as renowned as they were to be later. Barthes, in particular, who was about my age, was no more famous than I. The major critics, on the other hand, seemed to continually expect of us novelists that we copy those models which had made the nineteenth century so glorious, but which I naively believed to have been old-fashioned for a long time.

How shall I characterize this literature which I was reproached for not writing? All the novels of the nineteenth century, and later those of the twentieth century which followed in their footsteps, manifested a kind of hiatus between the narrator's speech and the characters' consciousness. This was apparent to both French and American critics. It was as if in Balzac or in Zola, as well as in a lot of others, the novelist had to render an account of something that was a change in the world. This change in the world was a splitting apart, a fragmentation: there were cracks in the world, there were rifts, and the fragmentation of the world went so deep as to touch the characters' very consciousness. Fragmentation, scattering, dissemination, these were the evils of which the characters suffered, so to speak, while it was the calm voice of the novelist which recounted these difficulties, these sufferings, and the characters' ultimate expulsion from society—for almost all the great nineteenth-century novels are ceremonies of expulsion. Fabrice del Dongo, Madame Bovary, and even Nana are people whom society expels because they do not conform to the established order.

Thus what is curious is precisely the opposition which exists between these characters, those consciousnesses which are aware of being fragmented, cracked, full of holes and contradictions, and the narration itself which is a completely reconciled story, continuous, causal, univocal. This is to say that the narrator seems not to suffer from the same troubled awareness, as he himself is perfectly coherent and competent. The coherence and competency of the narrator are fundamental in the nineteenth-century novel. That is why, as Leo Bersani has pointed out in one of his most remarkable essays, this novel, in claiming to criticize a society which fragments, scatters, and separates, seems, all in all, to denounce an evil while, in fact, it does the very opposite. As the language of the novelist is completely coherent and reassuring, the established order of society is, in a sense, reinforced by the novel. All of Zola's work, like that of Balzac, is more or less built on this model of a story whose functioning is completely vulnerable to its meaning. From beginning to end, everything has a meaning, the same meaning, while the character dies because the world lacks meaning or because its meaning is too fragmented and contradictory.

This divorce between the character's situation in the world and the writer's account of this situation is quite remarkable, for the novel is a game which both disturbs, for a considerable number of pages, and reassures, particularly at the end since, in the last analysis, if the novelist can be a coherent voice, it is precisely that the world itself is just, that God exists, and so on. And thus there is no problem of consciousness: those characters suffering from a clash either with themselves or with society are only maladjusted people whom we would do well to cure.

Every reading of a nineteenth-century and later of a twentieth-century novel—which is to say for the French novel, Mauriac, Montherlant, Maurois, and others—is based on this opposition between two possible routes. Either one tries to be in the character's consciousness and thereby feel this fragmentation of the world, this fragmentation of the self, this fragmentation of work, and this fragmentation of society or, on the other hand, one sides with the text, with the reading, and in this case one is perfectly calm and reassured. Constantly ambivalent in this sense, the novel, though seeming to criticize the established order of society, is ultimately reinforcing it.

It was in the twentieth century that, little by little, novels appeared where the narrative rules were progressively diluted. I will not recount its entire history, but well before the appearance of the New Novel as a so-called school, there were the novels of Faulkner, for example, where, as in *As I Lay Dying*, the fragmentation of the world and the fragmentation of consciousness were enacted within the very text. The famous Benjy of *The Sound and the Fury* is also to be mentioned, for he is the typical incompetent narrator, the narrator, in other words, who does not understand anything of his own story. In the context of "knowing one's own story," there is a progression to be followed in the evolution of the novel. In the medieval novel, an author who knows a story tells it to a public who already knows it as well. During the nineteenth century, an author who knows a story relates it to a public who does not yet know it. Finally, in the twentieth century, the situation has developed that gave rise to the Nouveau Roman: that of an author who does not know a story recounting it to a public who does not know it either.

When I started writing and was thus criticized, I suddenly felt that I was not being accused of having characters who suffered from this fragmentation and from this severing or separation from the world—after all, Roquentin in *La Nausée* [*Nausea*] or Mersault in *L'Etranger* [*The Stranger*] were in the same situation—but rather, that I myself was being accused of being deficient and full of contradictions. I was reproached, in short, for not being comprehensible, which meant that I, as an author, was supposed to have made clearly understandable that which the character did not understand. And I realized that it was precisely there that a characteristic of newness in modern times occurred, a characteristic which might even be one of the fundamental elements of modernity: things must take place within the text itself. It is impossible to write a text which, as a narration, is based on the old established order when its purpose is to show that this order is wavering. On the contrary. Everything must happen within the text so that severances, faults, ambiguities, mobilities, fragmentation, contradictions, holes must be enacted. It is the text which must display them.

I began at that time to find equivalent preoccupations among the novelists whose works were to be classified as "Nouveau Roman," those novelists who had in many cases been writing for a long time when I began publishing my own work. I found these preoccupations in *Tropismes* by Nathalie Sarraute, for instance, of which Tom Bishop spoke, and in the essays on literature by Nathalie Sarraute that were published in *Les Temps modernes* (and later in *L'Ere du soupçon*) and which, in effect, rendered account of the same experience of the novelist grappling with a substance—the text—which itself had to be the arena for these fights between order and disorder. I found them as well when I read *Mahu ou le matériau* by Robert Pinget. *Mahu* was published in 1952, before my first published novel, *Les Gommes*, which appeared in 1953. *Mahu* is for me a kind of premonitory text where already—though Pinget claims not to have a strong theoretical awareness—there is in the text itself a kind of theoretical formalization of these

Alain Robbe-Grillet

problems through the character's difficulty with words. (Mahu is a character whose adventures I really advise you to read. I would not dare to try to evoke them here in a mere few minutes.) Somewhat later, I had in my possession the manuscript of Claude Simon's *Le Vent,* a manuscript whose title was then much longer and which is now a subtitle: *Tentative de restitution d'un retable baroque d'après les restes trouvés dans une chapelle en ruines* [*The attempt to restore a baroque altarpiece according to the remains found in the ruins of a chapel*], which is quite a program! A narrator of questionable competence, grappling with scattered fragments! And there again, it was the text itself which staged this attempt, one which was like that of trying to exist today, to have an awareness today, to be a free consciousness today.

Nevertheless, as far as my first novels are concerned, *Les Gommes, Le Voyeur,* and *La Jalousie,* I noticed that in spite of an extremely hostile reception at the beginning, they were recouped rather quickly. The efforts of Bruce Morrissette, for example, who was supposed to be at this colloquium but who was unable to come, were very interesting for he showed that, in a way, even *La Jalousie* worked as a readable novel. This book had been considered unreadable by all the French critics. I believe that there was not even one favorable review when the book was published. And then, shortly thereafter, an American professor, unknown in France at the time, explained that this book was perfectly readable. He explained it very clearly, but he explained it according to the standards of a psychological coherence which, in fact, the book challenged. It must have also existed within the book, but Morrissette reconstituted, as it were, this coherent speech which the narrator had not been able to adopt.

I remember, apropos of this, that on the back of the book there was a blurb which began: "Le narrateur de ce récit: un mari qui surveille sa femme" [The narrator of this story: a husband keeping watch on his wife]. Though it is never said in the book that it is a husband keeping watch on his wife, I was the one who had written this introductory notice, and thus it would seem that at that moment I myself was starting to overstep the text by furnishing more or less fake keys which would allow the reader to enter the book. They would not allow it immediately, unfortunately, but Morrissette helped people to enter the story with this false key and the book again became the story of jealousy, the story, in other words, of a crisis, of a passion, with birth, development, and downfall. At the same time, we received a letter from Maurice Blanchot complaining about the jacket blurb. As it was signed "The Editors," Maurice Blanchot had sent a vehement letter to the editor saying that it was shameful to limit the scope of the book so stupidly with "The narrator: a husband keeping watch on his wife." "It is not a husband speaking in *La Jalousie*," claimed Blanchot, "but a pure anonymous presence." And, of course, Blanchot was right. I wrote to him that he was right, but that it was I who had written this blurb and that, in fact, it was not intended for him, but for those hurried critics who do not have time to read the books they have to write about in the papers. The blurb was, of course, not addressed to Maurice Blanchot who, in the cell of his tower, actually reads the books.

But what was disturbing in this affair? It was that I myself had written that blurb and thus, to a degree, I myself was a nineteenth-century novelist who had made clear and coherent a world of uncertainties, of struggles, and of contradictions. Though coherence was no longer in the book, it was now beside it. And I think that this was a very important discovery for me, a very productive discovery, as it made me understand that there is no pure revolutionary consciousness. No one can be a free consciousness: The ideology of the society in which I live is not in front of me, as though I were a kind of archangel who had escaped this ideology and who would write New Novels fallen from heaven into a world refusing of them. No, not at all! The ideology is in me, too, and consequently this longing for order and coherence, this struggle against incoherence, exists in me as well and probably, therefore, in my text, too.

Starting with *La Jalousie,* something became clear to me: this experience had to be generalized, books had to become the fighting ground. Blanchot said, "Le livre est le lieu où le monde a lieu" [Books are where the world takes place]. I would say, even more precisely, that books are where the fight of the world takes place because it is in the text that the world creates itself in the form of a fight between irreconcilable forces—forces, let us say, like the prevailing ideology and revolution, to simplify and to use stereotypes, and more generally, order and disorder. Or, to relate to the topic as I considered it at the beginning, since it is inadmissible to speak of the fragmentation without trying to remedy it, books must be, on the one hand, the site of this fragmentation and, on the other, the site of the incessant struggle to try to put these fragments in order.

For me, the turning point in my work is *Dans le labyrinthe* where, for the first time in my books, there appears a kind of rupture within the narrative word. *Le Voyeur* and *La Jalousie* are, in fact, strongly centered novels which, in the case of *La Jalousie,* means that whether called "husband" or "pure anonymous presence," there is something which is an organizing center of the whole text. This is true of *Le Voyeur* as well. Starting with *Dans le labyrinthe,* however, we have the impression of being in the presence of two distinct voices; without ever knowing which voice we are penetrating, we nevertheless feel, from time to time, their antagonism. On the one hand, there is the doctor, the one who says "me" at the end and "I" at the beginning. Yes, it is probably the doctor. I say probably the doctor because I do not have any clearer ideas about my books than those any good reader might have. And, on the other hand, there is the soldier, the central character in *Dans le labyrinthe,* who is also completely fragmented and incessantly in search of his self.

Starting with *Dans le labyrinthe,* books like *La Maison de rendez-vous, Projet pour une révolution à New York, Topologie d'une cité fantôme,* and *Souvenirs du triangle d'or* (the only one not yet translated into English) represent a clearer and clearer tendency to refuse that someone take over in the text: The text is a fight for power between irreconcilable forces. In *La Maison de rendez-vous,* one might already have the impression—and I think that this would be a good reading of the text—that there are numerous narrative forces, one of which is called Johnson, another Lady Ava, a third Edouard Manneret, and there are a lot of others. It is not only characters but also *places* (the theater of the Blue Villa, the park of the villa with its statues) which tell a story, as if each element of the narration tended at each moment to seize the narrative power. And it is this fight between the different powers which, in fact, is the subject of the book.

As I must not take up the whole session with my lecture, I will tell you very quickly how far I have come. I will say something, in other words, about my last book, *Djinn,* which was published in France in 1982 and here, in the United States, by Grove Press three or four months ago [also in 1982].

Djinn was a very old project of mine which, specifically, consisted of using as the prescribed order of the story the fundamental order which every writer faces: his language. The French language—French vocabulary and grammar—constitutes a kind of established order. Even if, in *La Jalousie,* I turned the narration upside down—let us say chronology, for example—or even a bit later, space, as in *Projet pour une révolution à New York,* there is one thing which I have always rigorously and even maniacally respected, and that is French grammar. I refer constantly to a grammar book and dictionaries when I write. I take great care to use words in their true meaning. This grammar, this vocabulary, this French language are for me, in a way, law. And this law is extremely important for the writer, for every novel is more or less generated by the language in which it was written, that which makes the difficulty, the unsolvable problems, of translation. One does not write the same novels if one writes in Japanese or in Hebrew. These are two languages which function differently, and it is the functioning of a language which produces the narrative standards and, consequently, the discrepancies in relation to the ruling discourse.

Thus I had the idea of using grammar, the French language, and of even writing a text for teaching French to foreign students. I had on hand Yvonne Lenard's books, in particular *Parole et Pensée,* where a certain number of texts were written to demonstrate the increasing difficulties of language and vocabulary. And here is what appeared to me to be a very interesting generative outline: the first chapter would consist of verbs in the present indicative, ending in -er, and this would be followed by other conjugations, other tenses, other moods, and so on, from chapter to chapter, with pronominal verbs, reflexive pronouns, complex relative clauses. It was this order that was to generate the text of the novel which was simultaneously an exercise in learning the language. It was, in fact, published by Holt, Rinehart and Winston as a textbook to study French at the intermediate college level. At the same time, however, the book is an experience in human freedom: How can a free consciousness live within a language already representing a law which cannot be circumvented?

Of course, I had a good time reproducing a few stereotypes of this kind of book: a young American woman arrives in Paris to learn French, she meets a young Frenchman. There is the shock of two civilizations and whatever else you wish. At the same time, however, this convention of the shock of two foreign consciousnesses, a man and a woman, was of particular interest to me by virtue of the very notion of strangeness.

What do I call strangeness? Almost the same thing as Freud called strangeness, or Heidegger called strangeness: *Unheimlichkeit,* the fact that the individual feels his nature to be different from that of the things and people which are before him. In the familiar world, our relations with things seem happy, without problems, and consequently coherence between the world and us is constantly preserved until, suddenly, in everyday life, in the life of every moment, we abruptly feel something else which is the strangeness of the world. All at once, we no longer understand. And it is precisely at that moment that things start to be fascinating. It is at that moment, says Heidegger, that one begins to experience freedom, for as long as a thing is understandable, it belongs to meaning and therefore to the established order. It is precisely at that moment when a thing becomes incomprehensible that the liberating shock is born within the awareness and body of man. And, indeed, this strangeness is to be found in *Djinn*: in the dual form of what may be called, on the one hand, simply a love story, and, on the other, a science-fiction novel.

In the shock of being in love, as described by the Romantics, there is something very remarkable, something which I have felt, which everybody has felt, and that is that the other is extraordinary. A young man meets a young woman, and this young woman is not the same as others. When Fabrice del Dongo suffers from never having been in love and he suddenly encounters Clélia, he has a revelation: she is different from the others. This is to say that there is the rest of the world, which is the familiar world, and then, suddenly, there is a strange being who is precisely the other. This young woman is an extraordinary being, a being who seems to have fallen from another planet. It is something that we have all experienced and that we still experience very often. The inexplicable is fascinating. And this is probably also what is found in what we today call science-fiction novels, which I pronounce the French way, of course, as in *Djinn*.

What is science fiction? It is two worlds that should not communicate one with the other, but which suddenly start communicating, which means that there is a fault in the quotidian world and through it, another world is suddenly visible. This other world functions differently and thus we are thrown into a functioning (both of consciousness and of the world) which is not the one with which we were familiar. *Djinn* has a subtitle in French: "Un trou rouge entre les pavés disjoints" [A red hole between loose cobblestones]. This subtitle was deleted in the American edition, though I do not know why. It probably is a mistake to be corrected in the next printing. It really was quite important to me: in an ordinary, familiar city, we suddenly enter a street we do not know, the cobblestones of this street are loose, and between them we can see another world. There is another world there. This is also one of the great revolutionary myths, isn't it? The revolution in May, 1968, in Paris, found a nice slogan: "sous les pavés, la plage" [under the cobblestones, the beach]. This meant that under the established order, grey and made of concrete, there is freedom which insists on emerging.

I think I have spoken longer than I was supposed to. We will have the opportunity to speak of these things again, particularly at the roundtable, so for the moment I will stop here.

Alain Robbe-Grillet:
At Play With Criticism

Michel Rybalka

In attempting to take an overall look at the work of Alain Robbe-Grillet, one cannot avoid being struck by both the attention which he has always paid to criticism and theory and by the distinct difference which exists between his creative work (both novels and film) and his critical work. Considering the complexity of the task, I wish to limit myself to two principal goals: on the one hand, a retrospective consideration of the different critical evaluations which have been associated with Robbe-Grillet's work for these last thirty years and, on the other hand, a determination of how much Robbe-Grillet has internalized these critical judgments and constituted for himself an ideological double of unquestionable originality. There is a third aspect which I will only indirectly consider but which must be evident for those who attend his classes here at New York University. It is that Robbe-Grillet is one of our best critics and lecturers and that his critical work is among that which demands our serious consideration. As Olivier Veillon rightly noticed, Robbe-Grillet has played and continues to play two simultaneous roles: "celui d'un incitateur permanent à la recherche théorique" [that of a permanent initiator of theoretical research] and "celui d'un prophète de la déception théorique qui annonce 'la faillite de tout ordre présenté comme *vrai*' " [that of a prophet of the theoretical disillusionment which announces "the failure of any order presented as *true*"].[1]

To situate more clearly the remarks that follow, I must point out that I am writing a documentary work on Robbe-Grillet, one that is similar in scope to the *Ecrits de Sartre*. My aim, therefore, is to list and analyze systematically everything related to him, with a distinct preference for his first writings and the unpublished works. I will save for another occasion, however, a detailed lecture on the twenty-odd critical reviews which Robbe-Grillet published even before *Les Gommes* came out and on his very early writings which include many poems (of which one, "Le Jugement des juges," still unpublished, would be particularly appropriate here), a short story on a thwarted love affair, and an account of a journey, "Quatre jours en Bulgarie," published in 1947 in an industrial journal.

In his 1963 preface to Bruce Morrissette's book,[2] Roland Barthes already distinguished between a first "thingist" Robbe-Grillet and a second "humanist" Robbe-Grillet. Later, at the Cerisy colloquium on the Nouveau Roman in 1971, Morrissette, in a lecture entitled "Robbe-Grillet n° 1,2, . . . X",[3] showed this kind of distinction to be arbitrary and simplifying. It would no doubt be risky to compare Robbe-Grillet's first published text, "Application de la méthode de la pyramide des âges à l'évolution du cheptel bovin français à la Libération" (1945), to his last novel, *Djinn*, or his last film, *La Belle Captive*.[4] Nevertheless, in retrospect, Robbe-Grillet's work appears to be of an extraordinary continuity. In his preface to the videographic edition of the films, Dominique Château rightly speaks of the "persistence d'une oeuvre mobile" [persistence of a moving work].[5] My own methodological prejudices, stemming from Sartre and his notion of totality as well as from my knowledge of the work, lead me to see in all that Robbe-Grillet has done an extreme coherence rather than a discontinuity, though we should perhaps say with Raymond Queneau: "Au fil des ans au fil des ans/Il est pareil et non le même" [Throughout the years throughout the years/ He is alike and not the same].[6]

This continuity, which is visible in the novels and in the films, is not found in the criticism which has accompanied Robbe-Grillet's work since 1953. As thirty years of Robbe-Grillet are being evaluated here, thirty years of Nouveau Roman, I think it useful, providing limits of this enterprise are marked, to adopt and update the periodization delineated by Roland Barthes. Another reason impels such an Aristotelian exercise, one that is provided by Tom Bishop when he characterizes, as follows, the classes given by Alain Robbe-Grillet at New York University: "Il est professeur de Robbe-Grillet, mais il professe aussi autre chose. D'ailleurs, s'il parle de lui-même, il parle simultanément de tout un entourage culturel, philosophique, romanesque, etc." [He teaches Robbe-Grillet, but he also teaches something else. If he speaks of himself, he simultaneously speaks of an entire cultural, philosophical, and novelistic background].[7]

Sartre would appeal here, as he did with regard to Flaubert in *L'Idiot de la famille,* to the notion of *programming.* To review the different critical moments which have marked Robbe-Grillet's work is, up to a certain point, to review our own history and to redefine the routes of modernity.

I intend, therefore, in evoking memories and generally accepted ideas rather than a rigorous archeology of criticism, to distinguish five periods in Robbe-Grillet's work and in its reception. The first period, that which Barthes qualifies as "thingist" and apropos of which he speaks of objective and even objectal literature, includes the first three novels (*Les Gommes, La Jalousie, Le Voyeur*), in part *Dans le labyrinthe* (published in 1959), and the texts of *Instantanés* [*Snapshots*]. The first interview with Robbe-Grillet, which was conducted by Jacques Brenner in March, 1953, was entitled "Alain Robbe-Grillet, géomètre du temps."[8] The scientific training of the writer and his taste for long and precise geometric descriptions were strongly emphasized then, as was later the case with Boris Vian. The Nouveau Roman was then defined as "le roman policier pris au sérieux" [the detective story taken seriously] and as "l'école du regard" [the school of the gaze]. Robbe-Grillet claimed to be very influenced by Raymond Roussel, and many critics appealed to phenomenology to explain his books.

Robbe-Grillet was then appreciated and backed by the best of the French intelligentsia: Bataille, Blanchot, Goldmann, Sartre. It was also at that time, however, that he was most attacked by the traditional critics, to whom he responded with several polemical texts (such as "Nature, humanisme, tragédie"), later collected in *Pour un Nouveau Roman* [*For a New Novel*]. It might be noted that this book, which as a manuscript was entitled "Pro Domo: Plaidoyer pour la littérature de demain," begins with the sentence "Je ne suis pas un théoricien du roman" [I am not a theoretician of the novel]. Interviewed in 1970, Robbe-Grillet confirmed:

> Je n'ai pas de théorie. Historiquement j'ai commencé par écrire des romans. Les critiques que m'ont adressées les spécialistes de la littérature m'ont montré qu'eux avaient une théorie sur ce que devait être le roman. Moi, je ne savais pas ce qu'il devait être. J'avais seulement l'idée qu'il fallait l'inventer. J'ai voulu répondre à ces critiques. J'essayais de détruire la conception théorique périmée qu'ils se faisaient du roman. A ce moment-là, on m'a accusé d'être un théoricien. . . .[Je suis] très opposé à toute idée de théoriser la littérature avant de l'écrire.

[I have no theory. Historically, I started by writing novels. The reviews addressed to me by specialists in literature showed me that they were the ones who had a theory of what the novel should be. I only had the idea that it was to be invented. I wanted to respond to those critics. I tried to destroy the old-fashioned theoretical conception they had of the novel. At that time, I was accused of being a theoretician. . . .[I am] very opposed to any idea of theorizing literature before writing it.]⁹

In retrospect, this period appears similar to that of the Epiphanies, to use Renato Barillo's phrase. The Nouveau Roman did not have a large following—only 500 copies of *La Jalousie* were sold the year it was published—but it had the wind in its sails: Robbe-Grillet believed in its future, though later he did not hesitate to speak of a dead end, a dead end not only endured but also sought. This period when the Nouveau Roman was on the rise may be considered the classical period, the period when, in spite of the emphasis placed on novelty and avant-garde, the most assimilated works were produced. I think that the forthcoming school editions of *La Jalousie, Le Voyeur,* and *Les Gommes* are proof of this.

In 1959, *Dans le labyrinthe* was published. This was a turning point constituting a transition toward the second period, that which Barthes called "humanist" but which I consider to be that of the fantastic, of mental realism, and of symbolism. Through works such as *Dans le labyrinthe,* the film-story *L'Année dernière à Marienbad* [*Last Year at Marienbad*], and above all, Robbe-Grillet's first movie, *L'Immortelle* [*The Immortal One*], the objectivism of the preceding period was entirely reevaluated. It was discovered that "la précision conduit en définitive au fantastique" [precision leads in fact to the fantastic]. The roundtable dedicated to the film *L'Immortelle* in *Cahiers internationaux du symbolisme*[10] may be cited as a mark of this reversal which, as Barthes noticed, was due at once to the author, the critics, and the public.

This was the time of greatest public acclaim, although some, like Roland Barthes, no longer took part in it, preferring to follow what I would consider a purist route. For them, there was a return to meaning, and Robbe-Grillet was too open to the comeback of humanism. Bruce Morrissette's book, published in 1963, toward the end of this period, seemed to confirm this presence of meaning in proposing what are essentially rather traditional keys to Robbe-Grillet's different works. It is noted that this book, the first one devoted to Robbe-Grillet, was written by an American: the Nouveau

Roman was very quickly becoming famous in the United States and, ultimately, it would become more appreciated and analyzed there than in France.

Bruce Morrissette is absent from this colloquium for reasons of health, so I wish to emphasize the essential role played by him in Robbe-Grilletian criticism. It is he who, internationally, followed most closely the work of Robbe-Grillet, and it is he who constituted from it a critical corpus which, by its perspicacity and its unclasssifiability, goes well beyond the "humanist" qualification of 1963, thereby revealing itself to be of an unmatched, and undoubtedly unmatchable, richness.

The third period began after 1963, when the Nouveau Roman became the Nouveau Nouveau Roman, although this was not really perceived before the Cerisy colloquium in 1971. It includes *La Maison de rendez-vous, Projet pour une révolution à New York* [*Project for a Revolution in New York*], and the films *Trans-Europ-Express* and *L'Homme qui ment,* though in the case of the films it is less clear than in that of the novels. This was the period of Jean Ricardou, which corresponds to the structuralist wave. In an approach paradoxically smacking of narcissism, the notion of author was then almost entirely eliminated in favor of the concepts of generator, sequence, and play. Exploiting, serially, erotic clichés, Robbe-Grillet wanted to shed light on the phantasms, on the dull and decadent mythology of the society in which we live. He described *Projet pour une révolution à New York* as "une tentative de construction formelle mobile à partir de matériaux populaires" [an attempt to make a mobile formal construction out of popular materials]. He advocated a society of play where he wanted us to learn "à jouer avec les oeuvres" [how to play with the works].

In a recent interview, Robbe-Grillet defined his position as follows: "La liberté humaine est faite de morceaux. La société sans cesse me parle et me fournit des stéréotypes que ma liberté se limite à réarranger de façon personnelle. La liberté de la parole ne consiste pas du tout en une liberté essentielle des contenus, mais dans une combinatoire" [Human freedom is made of pieces. Society always speaks to me and provides me with stereotypes which my freedom confines itself to rearranging in a personal way. Freedom of speech is not at all composed of an essential freedom of content; rather, it consists of a combinational freedom]. And Robbe-Grillet even qualified this freedom as a "liberté de réarrangement" [freedom of rearranging].¹¹ This position, on the whole, is not so far removed from that adopted by Sartre in *La Nausée,* which, as I have demonstrated elsewhere, was conceived as a "roquentin," a speech made of parts of other speeches, quotations, fragments of songs, rearranged in a structure which allows a certain discontinuity. This freedom of rearranging may be understood in terms of the distinction made by Sartre, in *L'Idiot de la famille,* between constitution and personalization.

Textualism, formalism, and eroticization of speech characterize the works produced at that time. The Nouveau Nouveau Roman provoked theoretical texts of the highest order but, considered too abstruse, it could not manage to attract a wide enough public. Works by Robbe-Grillet were no longer of use in school and, for many, they appeared condemned to repetition and a dead end.

The fourth period, beginning around 1971, retained many characteristics of the previous one, but its originality came from Robbe-Grillet's growing interest in the avant-garde of the visual arts, painting and photography. Robbe-Grillet was then writing on Magritte (to give us the splendid book *La Belle captive*), and he was working with David Hamilton, Delvaux, and Rauschenberg to produce *picto-novels,* like *Topologie d'une cité phantôme* [*Topology of a Phantom City*], and films, such as *L'Eden et après, Glissements progressifs du plaisir,* and *Le Jeu avec le feu.* The intertextual assemblages, the polyfictions created by Robbe-Grillet, who was then combining the most important elements of his previous works with circumstantial texts generated by the painting and photography of others, defined a new writing technique and impressed us with startling beauty. This transformation was remarkably perceived and analyzed by Bruce Morrissette in his latest book.¹²

As early as the beginning of the 1970s, another change occurred in Robbe-Grillet's image: having already accumulated an abundant corpus of works which were both original and linked to his time, he was from then on to be considered a historical figure. He was led, in particular in his lectures and in the courses he has given since 1971, to teach Robbe-Grillet and to respond to the biographical curiosity which has begun to emerge about him.

On a deeper level, he felt the need to recover without any pathos or sentimentality what had marked his childhood and determined his vocation as a writer. Thus he entered his fifth period, which can be called, without hesitation, autobiographical.

Michel Rybalka

By 1960, Robbe-Grillet had already planned an autobiography, and he had even promised a text to the journal *Tel Quel*. This project, however, was constantly postponed for ideological reasons: Robbe-Grillet was so strongly opposed to the notion of author, the times were so unfavorable to the notion of subject, that he did not dare to be drawn to a genre which his intellectual peers disparaged. It was only around 1976 that he decided to undertake a *Robbe-Grillet par lui-même*, probably inspired by Roland Barthes, who was then publishing a similar book at the Editions du Seuil. The entire book has not yet been completed, resistance to autobiography still being very strong, but some fascinating excerpts were published in *Minuit* in 1978[13] and in *Nota Bene* in 1981.[14] Moreover, a novel such as *Djinn* owes, it seems to me, a large part of its value to the fact that it is a return to the source of Robbe-Grillet's imagining and, specifically, to the fact that, under the guise of grammar, Robbe-Grillet yields the fragments of a phantasmic autobiography. He himself confirms this in the text published in *Minuit:*

Je n'ai jamais parlé d'autre chose que de moi. Comme c'était de l'intérieur, on ne s'en est guère aperçu. Heureusement. Car je viens là, en deux lignes, de prononcer trois termes suspects, honteux, déplorables, sur lesquels j'ai largement concouru à jeter le discrédit et qui suffiront, demain encore, à me faire condamner par plusieurs de mes pairs et la plupart de mes descendants: "moi," "intérieur," "parler de."[15]

[I have never spoken of anything other than myself. As it was from within, it was not really noticed. Fortunately, because I have just pronounced, in two lines, three suspicious, shameful, deplorable terms to whose disrepute I myself have largely contributed and which will be sufficient, tomorrow still, to have me condemned by many of my peers and most of my descendants: "myself," "within," "speak of."]

Referring then to the notion of author, he added:

J'ai moi-même beaucoup encouragé ces rassurantes niaiseries.... Elles me paraissent avoir fait leur temps: elles ont perdu en quelques années ce qu'elles pouvaient avoir de scandaleux, de corrosif, donc de révolutionnaire, pour se ranger dorénavant parmi les idées reçues.[16]

[I myself have greatly encouraged these reassuring foolishnesses.... They appear to me to have seen their better days: they have lost in a few years what was scandalous, corrosive, and therefore revolutionary about them to be classified now among generally accepted ideas.]

One may wonder of what Robbe-Grillet's autobiographic project, his current work, consists.[17] It will no doubt be very different from the autofiction which Serge Doubrovsky gave us in *Fils* and the remarkable *Un Amour de soi,* very different from books such as *Amer Eldorado* by Raymond Federman or *Le Testament amoureux* by Rezvani. Robbe-Grillet is discreet: he has never described in his books people making love. His aims above all at a phantasmic autobiography which would allow him to rewrite his own story and to return to his origins. It is in this context, I think, that he finally agreed, in 1978, to publishing his first novel, *Un Régicide*. Autobiography, and it has never been emphasized enough, is a text made out of other texts and it implies a textualization of that which has been lived by the writer. In a recent essay, Dominique Château clearly characterizes this process. For him, there is "dialectisation de l'auteur par ses personnages" [dialectization of the author by his characters] while the intrusion of the imaginary in autobiography transforms "l'habituelle reconstitution pseudo-réaliste en une poétique du souvenir" [the habitual pseudorealistic reconstitution in a poetics of memory]. Château concludes: "Robbe-Grillet entreprend aujourd'hui avec lui-même cette lutte pour la reconnaissance qu'il menait amoureusement avec Violette dans *L'Eden* ou avec Alice dans *Glissements*. Non seulement il persiste, mais il signe."[18] [Robbe-Grillet undertakes with himself this battle for recognition which he lovingly fought with Violette in *L'Eden* or Alice in *Glissement*. He not only persists in this, but also adds his personal signature to it.]

This autobiographical period is marked by numerous interviews where Robbe-Grillet abundantly disseminates biographemes and where he provides us with information on his childhood and his literary start. It is beginning to be possible to write Robbe-Grillet's biography; ten years ago it would have been absolutely out of the question.

I also notice in this period a marked comeback to the Sartrian issues. Sartre as a writer, that of *La Nausée* and *Situations I,* but not of *Les Chemins de la liberté* [*The Roads to Freedom*], considerably interests Robbe-Grillet. He took part in the colloquia on Sartre in Los Angeles and Cerisy and he even gave a lecture on *Situations I* in Brussels. There is more and more use of a Sartrian vocabulary in his critical writings. He has come back to the notion of person and project, the work as a calling, and so on. Almost as much as Sartre, he thinks against himself[19] and advocates change against prevailing ideology. In fact, Sartre, Barthes, Robbe-Grillet,

Michel Rybalka

these are three figures of modernity who, in the future, will have to be considered together.

Finally, the autobiographical period is interesting because it is both a return to past history and a new direction for writing. It is without a doubt in this perspective that Robbe-Grillet's last novel, *Djinn,* is to be situated. As Jacqueline Piatier (who, incidentally, is probably the best literary journalist there is) has rightly noticed, *Djinn* offers us an "excellente synthèse de l'univers romanesque de Robbe-Grillet" [excellent synthesis of Robbe-Grillet's novelistic universe] and furthermore, Robbe-Grillet has "jamais allé aussi loin dans ses angoisses" [never gone so far in his anguish][20].) This period has not yet found its theoretician but, in a more general context, Philippe Lejeune's excellent works may, of course, be cited.[21]

The summary periodization which I have outlined here leaves numerous unresolved difficulties. Robbe-Grillet's works are similar to the banana plantation which he describes in *La Jalousie:* "Tous les éléments du cycle ont lieu en même temps chaque jour, et les menus incidents périodiques se répètent aussi, tous à la fois, ici ou là, quotidiennement" [All the elements of the cycle occur at the same time every day, and the periodical trivial incidents also repeat themselves simultaneously, here and there, daily].[22] Overlappings, cross-checkings, opaque or blind points can all be observed. And the phenomenon of hysteresis, by which I mean the phenomenon of delay in the conception or reception of a work, comes into play as well. Criticism has always discovered after the fact what there was in a fiction. When first published, Robbe-Grillet's books generally have a rather limited success, but thereafter they are read regularly and constantly. Robbe-Grillet himself is convinced that there is a deferred appreciation of him. The main difficulty is that of programming Robbe-Grillet's works on the sociohistorical level. I leave this problem posed.

In conclusion, I would like to propose three or four topics for reflection concerning the status of critical discourse in relation to fiction. In the first place, it seems to me that Robbe-Grillet is a unique case in recent literature. With the possible exception of Butor, I do not know of any other writer of such notoriety who has had so close a link with criticism and theory. As Olivier Veillon wrote:

L'écrivain se doit d'être son premier théoricien, sans que le rapport de la théorie à la pratique soit réglé extérieurement mais toujours de "l'intérieur," dans une contamination réciproque et permanente de la théorie et de la fiction qui, bien que constitutivement différentes, voire contradictoires, sont deux éléments d'une même stratégie.

[The writer owes it to himself to be his own first theoretician, with the link between theory and pratice being governed not from the outside, but always from "within," in a reciprocal and permanent contamination of theory and fiction which, though being of two different, even contradictory, constitutions, are two elements of a single strategy.][23]

In spite of his protests, Robbe-Grillet appears a true critic. It is even more to his credit that he does not "pratiquer la théorie par théoriciens interposés" [practice theory through intermediary theoreticians].[24] The accusation made by Ricardou at the Cerisy colloquium in 1971—that Robbe-Grillet was still at a pretheoretical point—can be justified only insofar as one can say, with Barthes, that precriticism is always being written.

Moreover, the extreme continuity which characterizes Robbe-Grillet's creative works has already been stressed. These works constantly play on the same elements. They remain secure and without compromise, while Robbe-Grillet as a critic is amazingly malleable. With him, the critic is like Proteus: he makes the most of everything, he promises marriage to every theory enamored of him (though without ever fulfilling this promise), he does not hesitate to contradict himself, and he even exults in his contradictions. The creative works, however, are inherently linked to a project, to a truth whose presence is so strong from beginning to end that it resists the theories of others, and even those of Robbe-Grillet himself. To speak in Sartrian terms, it seems that in this respect there is a total commitment to literature, one that is comparable to that of Flaubert or Joyce. This commitment, however, is significantly tempered by criticism: Robbe-Grillet internalizes criticism while keeping it at a distance—a distance which, though close to empathy, can also be qualified as pathaphysical.[25]

At the Cerisy colloquium, I questioned Robbe-Grillet about the part played by criticism in the elaboration of his works and he answered:

C'est pour moi un apport extrêmement enrichissant, dans la mesure où le critique qui a mis en lumière une signification, dans mes oeuvres, ne m'indique pas une voie à suivre mais une voie à abandonner. . . . A chaque fois qu'à propos d'un de mes films ou d'un de mes romans j'ai développé moi-même un fragment théorique (quoique je n'aie pas, en général, la tête délibérément théorique, comme peut l'avoir Ricardou), à chaque fois, ce que j'ai eu envie de faire (contre moi, comme j'ai envie de le faire contre les critiques), c'est précisément *autre* chose.

[It is for me an extremely enriching contribution to the extent that the critic who sheds light on meaning in my work does not show me a path to follow, but a path to leave. Each time that I developed for myself a theoretical fragment concerning one of my films or one of my novels (though, in general, I do not have a resolutely theoretical mind, such as Ricardou may have), each time, what I wanted to do (against myself, as I want to do it against the critics) was precisely something *else*.][26]

An essential difference between Sartre and Robbe-Grillet is noticed here. Sartre practically disregarded what the critics could offer him, which is a paradox for a philosopher who placed such importance on relations with others. When he thought against himself,[27] it was from an internal point of view, distinctly his own. Robbe-Grillet, on the other hand, weighs more heavily the image people have of him: a clearly more narcissistic writer than Sartre, he internalizes in a different way, but also in a deeper way, the opinions of others. This functioning, as has been seen, does not implicate the coherence and continuity of his creative works. It affects, above all, his critical attitude and implies a kind of splitting in two.

Sartre used to say that there was the true Sartre, the one who was living and writing and whom nobody really knew, and the Other one, the one who had been created by public opinion and over whom he had no control, for he defined himself on a purely social level.[28] The same distinction, with different investments, may undoubtedly be applied to Robbe-Grillet. On the level of interest here is the notion of *ideological double* which Olivier Veillon evoked in speaking of Robbe-Grillet as a critic, a notion which may be supplemented by another, once again Sartrian, that of *ideological interest*.

The Robbe-Grillet heard here is not the true one; he was his double, his ideological mutant. Truth and its double, this merits stopping here.

Notes

1. Olivier Veillon, *Obliques*, no. 16-17 (October 1978), 51. The quotation

within the quotation is from Robbe-Grillet, *Nouveau Roman: hier, aujourd'hui*, Vol. 2 (Paris: Collection 10/18, 1972), 161.

2. Roland Barthes, preface, *Les Romans de Robbe-Grillet* (Paris: Ed. de Minuit, 1963).

3. Cf. *Nouveau Roman: hier, aujourd'hui*, Vol. 2, 119-155.

4. This film has just been presented at the Avoriaz Festival and it was released in Paris on Feb. 19, 1983.

5. Volume accompanying the videographic edition of Alain Robbe-Grillet, *Oeuvres cinématographiques* (Ministère des relations extérieures, Cellule d'animation culturelle, 1982), 8.

6. Raymond Queneau, *Fendre les flots* (Paris: Gallimard, 1969), 104. Incidentally, this book is among the best of all Queneau's work.

7. Tom Bishop, *Edition cinématographique*, 16.

8. Jacques Brenner, "Alain Robbe-Grillet, géomètre du temps," *Arts* (March 20-26, 1953).

9. Interview by O. H. [Otto Hahn] in a special issue on theory, *VH 101*, 2 (Summer 1970), 93.

10. Roundtable on *L'Immortelle* in *Cahiers internationaux du symbolisme*, 9-10 (1965-66), 97-125.

11. Alain Robbe-Grillet, *Edition vidéographique*, p. 30.

12. Bruce Morrissette, *Intertextual Assemblage in Robbe-Grillet: From "Topology" to "The Golden Triangle"* (Fredericton, N.B.: York Press, 1979). The reader is referred as well to the various studies published by François Jost.

13. Robbe-Grillet, "Fragment autobiographique imaginaire," *Minuit*, 31 (November 1978), 2-8.

14. Robbe-Grillet, "Fragments pour une autobiographie imaginaire," *Nota Bene*, 2-3 (Spring-Summer 1981), 7-20.

15. Robbe-Grillet, "Fragment autobiographique imaginaire," 2.

16. *Ibid.*, 3.

17. Editor's note: Since the writing of this essay, Robbe-Grillet's "autobiographic project" to which Rybalka refers has been published: Alain Robbe-Grillet, *Le Miroir qui revient* (Paris: Ed. de Minuit, 1984).

18. Dominique Château, *Edition vidéographique*, 9.

19. Translators' note: "Penser contre soi" is a typical Sartrianism requiring a literal translation.

20. Jacqueline Piatier, "Robbe-Grillet ensorcelle la grammaire," *Le Monde* (des livres), March 20, 1981.

21. On other levels, the perspectives indicated by Jean Baudrillard (see in particular *Simulacres et simulation*, Ed. Galilée) and by Michel Thévoz (cf. *L'Académisme et ses fantasmes*, Ed. de Minuit) should today allow for a better comprehension of Robbe-Grillet's works.

22. Alain Robbe-Grillet, *Jealousy*, trans. Richard Howard (New York: Grove Press, 1959), 98.

23. Veillon, *Obliques*, 16-17 (October 1978), 51.

24. This is an expression used by Veillon, *ibid.*, 56.

25. Concerning this, the reader is referred to the excellent essay by Jacques

Bersani, "Robbe-Grillet pour lui-même," published first in *La Nouvelle Revue Française* in 1977 and then in *Obliques,* 16-17 (October 1978), 273-276.

26. Robbe-Grillet, *Nouveau Roman: hier, aujourd'hui,* Vol. 2, 139-140.

27. Translators' note: Here again, Rybalka uses the expression "penser contre soi."

28. In a text published first in *Charlie-Hebdo* and then in *On peut cogner, chef?,* Delfeil de Ton brilliantly and logically demonstrated how it is possible to fantasize about a figure such as Sartre without any concern for the reality of facts.

From the "New Novel" to the "New Novelists"

François Jost

One specific characteristic of the debates on the Nouveau Roman is that they have almost constantly taken place between those writers grouped together under this heading and their critics. The result of this "contact" has been the mixing in a single discourse of two originally very different attitudes: while some were speaking of their activities as novelists, others were striving to theorize and codify this production through reading. It goes without saying that this duality of points of view has been (and is still, more or less) diversely appreciated by those very people who together were contributing to the constitution of a "poetics" of the Nouveau Roman (as shown by the discussions at the Cerisy colloquium, the importance of which Tom Bishop reminded us a short while ago). While adhering to theories is very important to Ricardou, it is without a doubt less so to Simon, and still less important to he who declared some twenty years ago, "Je ne suis pas un théoricien du roman" [I am not a theoretician of the novel].[1] When Robbe-Grillet added, in 1975, "Je continue volontairement à formuler des interdits que je considère moi-même comme inacceptables" [I willingly continue to formulate prohibitions which I myself consider to be unacceptable][2] or, in 1982, "Je n'attache pas une très grande importance à mes ouvrages théoriques, ce sont des ouvrages de combat" [I do not deem very significant my theoretical works; they are works of combat],[3] he confirmed that his assertions are less scientific deductions than strategic positions or alibis which the writer needs to invent in order to progress in the practice of his work.

For Robbe-Grillet, as for the other New Novelists, discourse has always served a double purpose: that of both *proscribing* a certain practice of literature—in short, the nineteenth century—and *describing* the paths of its creation. In the 1970s, during that

François Jost

third period of criticism described by Rybalka, theory was invested with a new mission: that of *prescribing*. With Ricardou, the description of the functioning of novels acquires the virtue of a prescription, of a scriptural "edict" which the budding writer is to follow to construct a fiction:

> Cette esquisse d'une théorie des générateurs, en démystifiant quelque peu la production, espère donc également ceci: inciter chacun à écrire. Il n'y a pas une aristocratie d'écrivains-nés, un clergé de professeurs et un tiers-état de consommateurs passifs. Tout homme est apte au travail du texte.
>
> [This outline of a theory of generators, while it somewhat demystifies production, equally hopes to incite everybody to write. There is no aristocracy of born writers, no clergy of professors, and no third estate of passive consumers. Everyone is capable of working a text.]⁴

The *How I wrote some of my books,* which every writer used to recount in his own way, becomes secondary and Ricardou substitutes for it a *How to write some of your books*. A strange reversal: whereas Robbe-Grillet and Sarraute were siding with the reader in order to convince—as shown by their numerous articles on novels in which they justified their interest or their impressions as readers—Ricardou sides with the writer in order to explain the determinism of his productions. In a sense, Robbe-Grillet and Sarraute taught us how to read and Ricardou teaches us how to write!

In this perspective, it may be understood how any reflection on the specificity of the writing of one or another novelist was eliminated. Indeed, what could be the importance of the relation between the writer and the world which he attempts to elaborate if the procedures which he uses can be universalized! In this concern for generalization, moreover, the label "Nouveau Roman" played its part: testifying to a community of preoccupations, it seemed to authorize the theoretician to practice a conceptual extension. Little by little, one mechanism observed in the work of one or another of the New Novelists spread and could easily be found in the work of another. And thus an outline of the production of fiction, perfectly detailed, was elaborated under the name of a "theory of generators" and, like a protocol of experience, it could be infinitely repeated, with few modifications.

For example, after having shown that the word "jaune" [yellow] generated *La Bataille de Pharsale,* Ricardou found exactly the same rules to be operative in *Projet pour une révolution à New York,* this time, however, beginning with the word "rouge" [red]. In 1975, some readers could have had the impression that choosing a word and subjecting it to numerous operations and determinations was enough for a novel to be written almost in spite of themselves. It is certainly undeniable that, at the time, there existed in Robbe-Grillet and in Simon the will to construct a fiction around a limited material; nevertheless, the fact that the text had a "generative base" never implied that, from it, "ce qui choisit le texte, c'est le texte lui-même" [what chooses the text is the text itself].⁵ If that were the case, the writing of a novel would have to be imagined no longer in accordance with the models of Judeo-Christian creation, but in accordance with that of the *causa sui* which Spinoza defined as "ce qui est en soi et pour soi" [what is in itself and by itself]. Does not that determination of the text by itself remind us, in effect, of that freedom distinctive of God: "La liberté n'est pas absolue détermination, mais détermination interne, opposée, non à la nécessité, mais à la contrainte ou à la violence, c'est-à-dire à la détermination par une autre ou détermination externe" [Freedom is not absolute determination, but internal determination, opposed not to necessity, but to constraint and violence, that is, determination by another or external determination].⁶ Such a definition of freedom, according to Spinoza, sums up rather well the mechanistic period of the theory of the Nouveau Roman: after having eliminated any explanation external to writing, including the idea of a referential stimulus, the problem of the arbitrary nature of creation could be erased by a simple transfer of the subjectivity of the demiurge to the text itself, that "inhumaine fabrique" [inhuman factory], to quote Ricardou.

It is now clear that giving the initiative to the text alone was to succumb to an essentialist illusion which produced more difficulties than solutions. Why does the writer choose one point of departure over another? How, on the basis of a few terms, does he develop an anecdote? These were two questions which remained unanswered, as they were seemingly pointless. Indeed, to that degree that it was deemed possible to produce a novel starting from a single word, from "rien" [nothing], any characteristic imaginary (this faculty which Roussel, though inclined to play on words, considered as the origin of his work: "Chez moi, l'imagination est tout" [For me, imagination is everything])⁷ was denied the novelist.

François Jost

Defining the vocabulary necessary to the engendering of a fiction in no way leads to an understanding of its organization, its functioning, and even less to its specificity. One needs only to remember the famous *Exercices de style:* in uniting under the heading "Parts of speech" all the articles, nouns, adjectives, verbs, and so on, which he uses to write a story of a few lines, Queneau presents, strictly speaking, the material from which he starts. Nevertheless, in working this vocabulary in ninety-eight different ways, he also shows that a simple list of terms does not at all reduce the immense freedom of any writer to organize as he wishes the world of which he has laid the foundations. Without reopening the old debate on the arbitrary nature of creation, one cannot ignore today that a fiction is not only a construction of neutral elements, but also a semantic universe which stimulates, in its way, numerous "sceneggiature," as Eco says.[8] Now, while "fables préfabriquées" [prefabricated tales], like the standard detective story, make use of a limited number of "ingredients" in a defined order of sequence, what characterizes the Nouveau Roman is precisely that it is not constrained by *rules of a genre*. In Robbe-Grillet and in Simon, there of course exist certain common procedures, but is it also not absolutely clear that the "sceneggiature" which they effect, as well as their organization, are very different?

In a sense, the question is simple (and I formulated it as early as 1971, at Cerisy): What is the reason why, as soon as I open a novel by Simon, Robbe-Grillet, or Pinget, I recognize its author? I imagine myself an archeologist pursuing excavations among the ruins of a bookstore. Around me, novels without covers. And I see myself, without hesitation, affixing a surname to the various New Novels which I discover. Why is this act of nomination so easy? Is it not because, beyond the similarities, there can be recognized in each fiction a necessity distinctive to the individual writer?

Why does a writer begin to write? No one is in a better position to answer this question, one which Robbe-Grillet poses often, than the writer himself. The critic, on the other hand, might wonder: What does the novelist try to solve when he writes? What is this fixed point around which he tries to have his world revolve?

It is, of course, possible to give different answers to these questions according to whether one practices a sociological, anthropological, or psychoanalytic reading; but I think that it is also time to reintroduce this issue within the very interior of the text itself. Consider it no longer as a machine with internal laws, but as the result of symbolic activities which tend basically toward a single goal—even if this was at one time shocking—which is to build an imaginary universe, even if it be a contradictory one.

A little scandal was provoked by Pinget in 1971 at Cerisy when he related that, through the writing of his fiction, he was searching for a "rythme intérieur" [inner rhythm], a "ton" [tone]. At a time when the idea of a textual "inhuman factory" was strongly upheld, it is not surprising that Pinget's remarks could hardly be taken seriously. Yet, a decade later, it is obvious that such an approach is no more reductive than that which consists of reducing the text to a self-generating mechanism. The novels published these last ten years by Robbe-Grillet or Simon convince me that the will to sever scriptural activity from any phantasmic or obsessional universe, from any "subjectivity," as Ricardou says, was very illusory. Between *Projet pour une révolution à New York* and *Djinn*, for instance, there are very few common narrative processes left. And between *Djinn* and *Les Géorgiques*, there are no doubt even less. In spite of the deep disparity between the narratives, however, I feel that there is something which links *Djinn* and *Projet* and that what separates them is not at all comparable to what separates a novel by Robbe-Grillet from a novel by Simon. This "something" is, of course, not easy to define and nobody has really cared, up to now, to pay attention to it; people have been too preoccupied with forging a unique and homogeneous poetics of the Nouveau Roman. It is, if you will, this specific obstacle which the writing of each author attempts to erode.

Like the waves which break on the beach, each novel of an author seems at every moment to replay a lost story, a whole contradictory world. And like the sea, which draws, by the slow labors of erosion, a more precise outline of the coasts, the writing of each author turns back unceasingly on its own tracks to define what escapes him. The New Novel has often been called "l'Ecole du regard" [the School of the gaze] and what is striking today, beyond the precision of the descriptions to which this literary tendency has often been reduced, is this kind of semantic "fuzziness" that each book, like a slowly focusing lens, tries to reduce.

The case of Robbe-Grillet is quite clear in this regard. His films, of course, differ profoundly from his novels insofar as he works very much within the specificity of the material which he uses in any of his artistic activities, but has not a common universe, distinctive of Robbe-Grillet, become visible these last few years? After the 1971 Cerisy colloquium, it was in bad taste to dare to make such observations: as soon as a likeness between any given novels by the same author was noticed, it was discreetly baptized "quotation." For instance, after he had listed the various points in common between *Projet* and *Les Gommes* or *La Maison de rendez-vous,* one lecturer concluded: "On devine bien qu'un semblable réseau de similitude puisse se penser comme la marque manifeste d'une permanence, et ce ne serait pas sans présupposé idéaliste d'un fond thématique de l'auteur." [It is easily guessed that such a network of similarities might be understood as the obvious mark of a permanence, and it would not be without an idealistic presupposition of a thematic content of the author].[9] This negation of continuity in the fictional imaginary, the logical outcome of the impersonal mechanization of the text, had become the "souci du texte de se citer comme tel" [text's preoccupation with quoting itself as such].[10] It is easily understandable that this naive regression from text to text is *ad infinitum,* and that it only evades the problem. Whoever analyzes closely Robbe-Grillet's novels or films clearly realizes that, beyond the quotations, the reminiscences, and the common themes, the whole world of the fiction is organized around semantic cores that constitute its very logic.

From *Glissements* to *Topologie,* from *Le Jeu avec le feu* to *Souvenirs,* from *Djinn* to the movie *La Belle captive,* there exists a constant principle which, despite the variations, forms a link between these works. To simplify, it could be said that two antagonistic forces tear at each of them.

The first one, centripetal, tends to *tighten* all the constitutive elements of the diegesis and the narrative. "Impression, déjà, que les choses se rétrécissent" [Impression, already, that things shrink]: this inaugural sentence of *Souvenirs du triangle d'or* might well sum up the constitution of Robbe-Grillet's novelistic world. On the anecdotes, the characters, the narrators, the (generally circular) narrative itself, there constantly presses a crushing power, and the whole narrative effort is to find openings, paths that lead to something. This struggle against being closed in is, of course, particularly clear in a novel like *Dans le labyrinthe,* which begins with a "shelter," almost a cell, to end with the opening onto the city (the famous "et toute la ville derriére moi" [and the whole city behind me]),[11] but it is no less characteristic of all Robbe-Grillet's literary works since *Projet*: in each of them, the fiction is inaugurated by the delimitation of two spaces, the inside and outside, often materialized by a door:

Je suis en train de refermer *la porte* derriére moi, lourde porte de bois plein percée d'une petite fenêtre rectangulaire, étroite, toute en hauteur, dont la vitre est protégée par une grille de fonte au dessin compliqué (imitant le fer forgé de façon grossière) qui la masque presque entière.

[I am closing *the door* behind me, a heavy wooden door with a tiny narrow oblong window near the top, its pane protected by a cast-iron grille (clumsily imitating wrought iron) which almost entirely covers it.][12]

Voici. *Je suis seul.* Il est tard. Je veille. Dernière sentinelle après la pluie, après le feu, après la guerre, j'écoute encore à travers des épaisseurs sans fin de glace blanche les imperceptibles bruits absents.... Dehors par les vitres poussiéreuses.

[Right. *I am alone.* It is late. I am keeping watch. The last watchman after the rain, after the fire, after the war, I listen still through endless thicknesses of white ice for the imperceptible, absent sounds.... Outside, through the dusty panes.][13]

Impression, déjà, que les choses se rétrécissent.... L'entrée de l'immeuble, sur la rue, n'a rien d'exceptionnel: une *porte* laquée noire, d'une taille moyenne.... On ne peut pas deviner si le battant s'ouvre à droite ou à gauche. A la limite cela pourrait même ne pas être une porte. Eviter cette voie qui ne mène à rien.

[Impression already that things shrink.... The entrance of the building, on the street, is nothing exceptional: a black lacquered *door,* of average size.... One cannot guess whether it opens to the left or right. It could, in fact, not even be a door. Avoid this way which leads to nothing.][14]

J'arrive exactement à l'heure fixée: il est six heures et demie. Il fait presque nuit déjà. Le hangar n'est pas fermé. J'entre en poussant *la porte,* qui n'a plus de serrure.

[I arrive exactly at the prescribed hour: it is six-thirty. It is almost dark. The warehouse is not closed. I walk in, pushing *the door,* which has no more locks.][15]

Whatever the novel, the crossing of the boundary between outside and inside is always the germ, the origin or the cause of the adventure. And indeed the "shelter" of *Dans le labyrinthe* appears really as a fantasized place where the narrator is, in one way or another, a prisoner. How can I escape? How can I get out? These

François Jost

are questions which not only torment the characters, but also which the narration asks itself with acuity. In the space of the diegetics, as in the space of the narration, the difficulty is to find "une voie qui mène à quelque chose" [a way which leads to something]. Every fiction is then pervaded by this centrifugal search for an exit to rush toward. Generally, it is the sea which offers the largest opening. The cell of *Glissements* opens onto the sea (suggested by the sound track) and the heroine phantasmatically projects herself into it. The narrator of *Souvenirs,* lost in a labyrinthian course, from room to room, is "à la recherche de celle dont la fenêtre grande ouverte donnerait sur les rochers, le sable et la mer" [searching for the one whose open window looks out on the rocks, the sand and the sea].[16] The hero of the movie *La Belle captive* escapes from his nocturnal prison by imaginatively projecting himself toward dunes and waves, sites of liberty and death.

Within the scope of this short study, it is not possible to enumerate the examples, but it could easily be shown that this struggle against a progressive enclosure is one of the things which Robbe-Grillet's fiction delineates, each time a little more precisely. (It may also be noted in passing that Robbe-Grillet's first two poems, from 1946, dealt with prison and the sea.)[17]

Our purpose is not to indicate a single direction which would be characteristic of all the books and all the films of an author. Between a paradigmatic analysis which records all the semantic items, without making more explicit their narratological articulation, and a pure scriptural determinism, which does not take into account the specificity of the writer's imaginary world, however, a new critical route, endeavoring to show how the constitution of a semantic universe around a few nodal points produces various narrative solutions which echo them, must be traced. We will limit ourselves to mapping out a few trails.

On the level of the structure of the diegetic world, the opening/enclosing conflict which we have described, is this freedom for the narrator to invent a complete world and to find himself, little by little, imprisoned within it. Remember Boris Varissa in *L'Homme qui ment,* who believes that he is building the world by his own speech, for example, when he asserts the problematic existence of a Doctor Müller who saved, he claims, Jean Robin:

Sylvia: Et après? Vous avez trouvé un médecin?

Boris: Oui, bien sûr.
Sylvia: Qui était-ce?
Boris: Le docteur Müller.
Sylvia: Il n'y a pas de village entre ici et la frontière.
Boris: Non, j'ai dû revenir jusqu'ici.
Sylvia: Il n'y a pas chez nous de Docteur Müller.
Boris: Müller, bien sûr, c'était un surnom. On avait tous des noms de code. Müller, c'était le docteur. Oui, on avait tous des surnoms à l'époque. Moi, c'était l'Ukranien; le vrai nom du docteur, c'était . . . non j'ai oublié.[18]

[*Sylvia:* And then? Did you find a doctor?
Boris: Yes, of course.
Sylvia: Who was he?
Boris: Doctor Müller.
Sylvia: There is no village between here and the border.
Boris: No, I had to come here.
Sylvia: There is no Doctor Müller here.
Boris: Müller, of course, was an assumed name. All of us had code names. Müller was the doctor. Yes, we all had assumed names at the time. I myself was the Ukranian; the doctor's real name was . . . no I have forgotten.]

This universe which he built by his imagination alone wavers when, at the end of the film, he faces the doctor who has come to sign the dead father's burial certificate:

Boris: Permettez-moi de me présenter. C'est moi, hélas, qui suis arrivé près du corps sans vie de notre père. Boris Varissa!
Le médecin: Docteur Müller!

(*Boris vacille*)

Vous êtes souffrant?
Boris: Non, non merci, ça va très bien. Nous nous sommes déjà rencontré, n'est-ce pas?
Le médecin: Non, c'est impossible, je ne suis installé ici que depuis hier.[19]

[*Boris:* Let me introduce myself. It was I, alas, who arrived near the lifeless body of our poor father. Boris Varissa!
The Doctor: Doctor Müller!

(*Boris staggers*)

Are you ill?
Boris: No, no thank you. I am okay. We have already met, have we not?

The Doctor: No, that is impossible. I settled here only yesterday.]

This kind of scene, where what happens to the character is closely akin to what he invented, dreamed, or imagined, is found very often in Robbe-Grillet's work: it is also the structure of *Djinn* or of *Glissements* or of the film *La Belle captive*. From the point of view of the constitution of the semantic universe, it could be said that the Robbe-Grilletian character's drama—and I am aware of the implications of this word "drama"—resides in a modal transformation which leads from a present unreality, or mood of potentiality, to the actuality of the present indicative. The progression of the narrative *verifies* the most fantastic suppositions elaborated by the character or the narrator—the dreamed world is nightmarish, not because it is inhabited by ghosts, but because it is already real, as the "hero" of *Djinn* perceives:

Mais Simon Lecoeur sentait, de façon confuse, que toute cette histoire de gare, de train de voyageur qu'il ne fallait pas manquer était périmée, révolue: ce futur appartenait déjà au passé, quelque chose brouillait le temps.

[But Simon Lecoeur felt, in a confused way, that this whole story of a station, of a passenger train not to be missed, was outdated, bygone: this future already belonged to the past, something muddled time.][20]

Conversely, it happens that the character's most familiar world topples over into obvious impossibility: for example, when the same Simon Lecoeur no longer recognizes the café which he had just visited the day before.[21]

Here, too, examples abound: Whether the characters discover that what they consider to have invented is true or, on the contrary, that what seems to them unquestionable and of everyday life topples over into the nonexistent, the impossible, throughout Robbe-Grillet's works, an inevitable conflict can be found: that of the potential and the indicative, the actualized. This incessant shifting which provokes anxiousness in familiarity is, in its own way, another kind of enclosure: the reality encloses the characters in their fiction and the fiction always contaminates what they think to be reality. The opening of the imaginary is a trap which, sooner or later, shuts again.

From the point of view of the narration, in the technical sense given by Genette,[22] the same semantic structure can be witnessed. More and more often, a first-person narrator is found in Robbe-

Grillet's novels: a character tells his story. Generally, in classical literature, this kind of narration is accompanied either by a zero focalization or an inner focalization: either the narrator knows everything or, at the very least, he knows what he lives or what he sees. Robbe-Grillet, however, presents the paradoxical situation of a homodiegetic narrator[23] in external focalization. When the "voice" of *Souvenirs* formulates the following hypothesis: "*Ce serait donc moi* le mystérieux criminel de seconde main, venu ensuite sur les lieux pour parachever le supplice?" [*It would be me then,* the mysterious second-hand criminal, who came to the scene of the crime to complete the ordeal?],[24] it seems that the narrative situation is rather new. Readers are confronted by a character who does not know exactly who he is and what he does. His only power, his only freedom, is to recount, but he is the prisoner of events which happen without his having a very clear, or even any, awareness of them. And, once more, this combination homodiegetic narration/ external focalization, very distinctive from a narratological point of view, leads to enclosure:

> C'est sans doute par mégarde, ou par une faute imperceptible de calcul, que je me retrouve aussi enfermé moi-même dans la prison aux poupées de porcelaine martyrisées.... J'aurais pourtant dû me méfier dès le début et flairer le piège.... Je vais en tout cas pouvoir, tout à loisir, réfléchir aux aléas de ma situation ainsi qu'au seul moyen raisonnable de m'en sortir: la constitution d'un objet sans bavures qui, aux yeux de mes juges, équivaudrait sinon à mon innocence, du moins à ma non-culpabilité.
>
> J'avais d'abord cru que la simple description de ma cellule constituerait une trame narrative suffisante. Je pense à présent que c'était une erreur.[25]
>
> [It must be by mistake, or by an imperceptible miscalculation, that I, too, find myself imprisoned in the jail of the martyrized porcelain dolls.... I should really have been careful from the beginning and sensed the trap.... In any case, I will have plenty of time to reflect on the hazards of my situation and on the only reasonable means to get out of it: the constitution of an impeccable object which, in the eyes of my judges, would amount, if not to my innocence, at least to my nonculpability.
>
> I first believed that the simple description of my cell would constitute a sufficient narrative pattern. I think now that I was wrong.]

To break away, to escape this noose which tightens more and more, "an impeccable object" must be constituted, a book which holds up only as a function of its own inner coherence, and all the writing is pervaded by the struggle to find an opening.

There is no doubt that the use of the same method in an analysis of the novels of Pinget, Simon, or Sarraute would allow definition of this necessity confronted by the scriptural act. The world of fiction is neither a self-sufficient machine nor the copy of a world which preexists it. It is this problematic totality which both touches the reader because he finds familiarity within it and troubles him because it is, nevertheless, still a little foreign to him. It is in delimiting this totality that the particular poetics appropriate to an analysis of the differences inherent within the Nouveau Roman and to the characterization of its writers are to be found.

Notes

1. Alain Robbe-Grillet, *Pour un Nouveau Roman* (Paris: Ed. de Minuit, 1963), 7.
2. Alain Robbe-Grillet, *Robbe-Grillet, Colloque de Cerisy,* vol. 1 (Paris: U.G.E., collection 10/18, 1976), 35.
3. Alain Robbe-Grillet, "Entretien d'Alain Robbe-Grillet avec François Jost" in *Alain Robbe-Grillet, Edition vidéographique critique* (Paris: Ministère des relations extérieures, 1982), 25.
4. Jean Ricardou, "Eléments pour une théorie des générateurs" in *De la créativité* (Paris: U.G.E., collection 10/18, 1972), 113.
5. Jean Ricardou, *Nouveaux problèmes du roman* (Paris: Ed. du Seuil, 1978), 245.
6. M. Gueroult, *Spinoza, Dieu (Ethique,1)* (Paris: Aubier, 1968), 97.
7. Roussel, *Comment j'ai écrit certains de mes livres* (Paris: J. J. Pauvert, 1963), 271.
8. Umberto Eco, *Lector in fabula* (Milan: Bompiani, 1979), 79, 80. By "sceneggiature," Eco translates more or less the term "frames" used by theoreticians of artificial intelligence. I employ the Italian word which has the advantage of including the idea of a "virtual text or of a condensed story" and that of a "motif" in Tomachevsky's sense.
9. J. C. Raillon, "Je fais mon rapport, un point c'est tout" in *Robbe-Grillet, Cerisy,* vol. 1, p. 344.
10. *Ibid.*
11. Alain Robbe-Grillet, *Dans le labyrinthe* (Paris: Ed. de Minuit, 1959), 221.
12. Alain Robbe-Grillet, *Projet pour une révolution à New York,* trans. Richard Howard (New York: Grove Press, 1972), 1. (Emphasis added.)
13. Alain Robbe-Grillet, *Topologie d'une cité fântome* (Paris: Ed. de Minuit,

1976), 10, 13); *Topology of a Phantom City,* trans. J. A. Underwood (London: John Calder, 1978), 9-11. (Emphasis added.)

14. Alain Robbe-Grillet, *Souvenirs du triangle d'or* (Paris: Ed. de Minuit, 1978), 7-8. (Emphasis added.)

15. Alain Robbe-Grillet, *Djinn* (Paris: Ed. de Minuit, 1981), 11. (Emphasis added.)

16. Robbe-Grillet, *Souvenirs,* 85.

17. *Obliques,* 16-17 (October 1978), *Numero spécial Robbe-Grillet,* François Jost, ed.

18. Alain Robbe-Grillet, *L'Homme qui ment,* n.d., n.p., n. pag.

19. *Ibid.*

20. Robbe-Grillet, *Djinn,* 83-84.

21. *Ibid.,* 91.

22. Genette uses this term to indicate the "productive narrative act" as opposed to the account (narrative text itself) and the story (narrative content). Cf. *Figures III* (Paris: Ed. du Seuil, 1972), 72.

23. Let it be remembered that by "homodiegetic narrator" Genette characterizes a present narrator as a character in the story he tells.

24. Robbe-Grillet, *Souvenirs,* 21.

25. *Ibid.,* 115-116.

Publishing the New Novel

Barney Rosset

Recently I read "Robots in Love," a review of Alain Robbe-Grillet's *Djinn* by John Perreault that appeared in the *Village Voice*. Perreault commenced by saying "Alain Robbe-Grillet is still associated with the so-called New Novel: cold, boring, intellectual, plotless, and in French."[1] If this opening were true, then certainly Grove Press had been a co-villain in having worked assiduously to make Robbe-Grillet known to American readers.

It started with Samuel Beckett. Through him I encountered Alain Robbe-Grillet. Prior to 1953 or 1952, I had somehow stumbled upon Samuel Beckett's work — bits and pieces of it — at The New School, and had spoken to such people as Wallace Fowlie, who had impressed me tremendously not only with his knowledge, but also with his taste and sensibility. When he assured me that I was correct in thinking that *Waiting for Godot* was a great play and that I should publish it, Grove decided to do so. Then I set off to France to meet the author.

Around that time there were several things that were particularly exciting: what Beckett was doing — and quite soon that meant also what Robbe-Grillet was doing — and earlier, what came to be known as abstract expressionist painting. It was not the kind of painting that Alain had written of in "The Erasers" (*Les Gommes*) — it was Franz Kline, Jackson Pollock, and Joan Mitchell. I saw the breaking up of form, a changing concept of content, of structure, and of the emotional reactions, in order to get down to seeing only what was on the canvas — having its own internal movement. I began to sense a new kind of objectivity which came across in Alain's writing and in Beckett's, as well as in motion pictures. In the latter, I refer to such devices as instant replays from multiple angles which have still not been exploited enough in film (although Alain has explored it in his writing techniques and flashbacks). Instant replay is something that, today, the TV sports people still do the best. But the "creative" people will get to that; we will get over our snobbism and eventually get around to using it under another name. When *Waiting for Godot* was put on and Beckett was asked if it could be made into a film, he said no, he had written the work for the stage. Many people took this response to mean that Beckett did not like film as a medium. But that was not the point at all. He had written *Waiting for Godot* to be seen from the middle of a theater audience—let's say from the eighth row—and he thought close-ups and other film techniques would make it a different work.

Alain, however, had gone a different way in making a "montage," giving a marvelous sense of visual imagery in his writing. He had objectified the emotional impact of viewing events in the same way instant replay does on television. If, when a baseball player runs from first base to second, the umpire calls him out, you might think it is because the umpire is black and the player white—or vice versa—or that it is because the umpire is from New Orleans and the team from New York. But if you see it from five different camera angles, each of them really trying to be quite objective, the same play will still look different each time and you will begin to get a completely different perception of what has happened. In 1964, we commissioned Alain to write a script for a film which unfortunately has not been produced. It was a series of flash-forwards of someone who was out to accomplish three or four goals. Each time he gets closer to achieving what he wants to do, he rethinks his position. We, as viewers, are shown the coming events, which always shift, just as we believe them to be credible. The protagonist achieves his goals ultimately, but in a totally different way from that in which he had first envisaged them. The goals were technically the same, but were they really?

Our first publication of Robbe-Grillet, in 1957, was an article called "A Fresh Start for Fiction." Despite the fact that Alain is French and that he writes in French, he has always seemed a kind of Midwesterner to me, a non–Eastern Establishment person, more like me, from Chicago. It was very important because to certain others he did seem as though he belonged to the French establishment. After all, Jackson Pollack and Franz Kline never got to France in their lifetimes. I also had the feeling that we shared inferiority-superiority feelings. It is not for nothing that Chicago is called "the second city," insulted yet bragging, and it is not for nothing that

Alain was not first a writer fresh from the Sorbonne, but a botanical engineer from L'Ecole, like coming from MIT rather than Princeton.

In that first article we published, Alain said: "The traditional role of the writer consisted in excavating Nature, in burrowing deeper and deeper to reach some ever more intimate strata, in finally bringing to light some fragment of a disconcerting secret. Having descended into the abyss of human passions, he would send to the seemingly tranquil world (the one on the surface) triumphant messages describing the mysteries he had actually touched with his own hands."

He stated that "This profundity is functional like a trap in which the writer had captured the universe in order to hand it over to society.... The revolution which has taken place is in proportion to the power of the old order. Not only do we no longer consider the world as our very own, our private property, designed according to our needs and readily domesticated, but we no longer believe in its depth."

Juxtapose the above to Willem de Kooning's great painting *Excavation*. Perhaps coincidentally—but only perhaps—the issue of *Evergreen* in which this article appeared also had Jackson Pollock on the cover.

Alain went on to say, "It is therefore the whole literary language that has to change, that is changing already. We witness from day to day the growing repugnance that people of greater awareness feel for words of a visceral, analogical, incantatory character. On the other hand, the visual or descriptive adjective—the word that contents itself with measuring, locating, limiting, defining—indicates a difficult but most likely direction for a novel of the future."[2]

After publishing that article, we then published a novel of Alain's, *The Voyeur*, translated from the Les Editions de Minuit edition. And here Alain adds his own history: he says that we passed over his first book, *Les Gommes*, and published *Le Voyeur* because the title was sexier. It was true—partially. Who could translate *Les Gommes* into English anyway? "The Erasers" is a very unsatisfactory title and "Bum Shoes" would have been equally so. With *La Jalousie* we had the same problem. In fact, the only novel whose title easily translated into English was *Le Voyeur* [*The Voyeur*]. The second reason I can give for our not publishing *The Erasers* first was that I resented the way Alain spoke about painting in the book. His intense visualness is in his words, somehow written as if by a blind person feeling his way by touch.

Eventually, we did get back to *The Erasers*. After that, in 1958, we published—again in *Evergreen Review*—an article by Roland Barthes which started with a quotation from the *Oxford English Dictionary*: "Objective: Noun. In optics, the lens situated nearest to the object to be observed and receiving the rays of light directly from it." Barthes went on to say about Robbe-Grillet:

> His writing has no alibis, no resonance, no depth, keeping to the surface of things, examining without emphasis, favoring no one quality at the expense of another—it is as far as possible from poetry or poetic prose. It does not explode, this language, or explore, nor is it obliged to charge upon the object and pluck from the very heart of its substance the one ambiguous name that will sum it up forever. For Robbe-Grillet, the function of langauge is not a raid on the absolute, a violation of the abyss, but a progression of names over a surface, a patient unfolding that will gradually "paint" the object, caress it, and along its whole extent deposit a patina of tentative identifications, no single term of which could stand by itself for the presented object.[3]

Again, think of de Kooning's *Excavation*.

Roland Barthes understood Alain's relationship to painting much better than Alain did himself. Beginning another point with a quotation from Heidegger, Barthes continued:

> "The human condition is to be THERE." Robbe-Grillet himself has quoted this remark apropos of *Waiting for Godot,* and it applies no less to his own objects, of which the chief condition, too, is to be THERE. The whole purpose of this author's work, in fact, is to confer upon an object its "being THERE," to keep it from being "something." ... To find a comparable strictness of procedure, one must turn to modern painting, where, the rational destruction of the classical object may readily be discerned in all its anguish. Robbe-Grillet is important because he has attacked the last bastion of the traditional art of writing: the organization of literary space. His stuggles parallel in significance those of surrealism with rationalism, of the avant-garde theater (Beckett, Ionesco, Adamov) with the conventions of the middle-class stage.[4]

However, beyond the above, we at Grove Press were basically publishing something that we simply liked. It not only was there, it also was new. We are still publishing his work twenty-five years later, just as we are still publishing Beckett, Ionesco, and Pinter— four writers who came to us during the same era.

In a later article Alain said, "Tragedy is but a means of accepting human misfortune, of subsuming human misery, and therefore of justifying it as necessary, as a kind of wisdom or purification. To reject this salvage operation and to seek out technical means not to yield treasonably to it (for nothing is more insidious than tragedy) is in our time a necessary undertaking." I believe that very strongly! As Alain said a little while ago, he is an optimist. I am one, too. He has found a very new and important way to be an optimist.

At the same time, which I believe was in 1959, Alain said that he had:

> made an effort to define the direction which might be taken by a new and as yet hesitant spirit of research in fiction. One point which I took for granted was the complete rejection of the old myths of "profondeur," or depth of meaning in objects. The almost unanimously violent reactions of critics, the objections raised by many apparently sincere readers, and the criticisms expressed by esteemed friends proved, however, that I had proceeded much too hastily. Aside from a few persons who were themselves engaged in similar artistic, literary, or philosophic endeavors, no one was willing to concede that such a position did not lead necessarily to a denial of man himself. It became apparent, in fact, that there existed a quite tenacious fidelity of those old "myths."[5]

Correlate this to the first production here of *Godot* which appeared around the same time. It was as thoroughly denounced as anything I can ever remember. After a while it was thought of as being rather funny, just as Schoenberg was thought of as an insane person, someone who wrote music without following any rules, and Pollock and his group were thought to be painters who just "smeared" paint. Of this new ferment in artistic freedom and its implicit hopefulness, Alain wrote:

> Today the rule of tragedy encompasses all my feelings and thoughts, it conditions me utterly. My body may be satisfied, my heart happy, but my conscience remains anxious. I claim that this anxiety, this misery, is SITUATED in space and time, like all unhappiness, like everything in the world. I claim that man, some day, will free himself of it. But I have no proof of the future. For me, also, it is a bet. "Man is a sick animal," wrote Unamuno in *The Tragic Sense of Life*. The bet consists in holding that he can be cured, and that if this is true it would be folly to shut him up forever in his present sickness and unhappiness. I have nothing to lose. The bet, all things considered, is the only reasonable one.

And I think that is a bet that Beckett has also taken.

Three Decades of the French New Novel

In 1959, Grove published *Jealousy*, a book whose brilliant French title—"Jalousie"—also did not translate into English. The book was based in large part on the marvelous idea of looking through a window blind: having one's vision circumscribed, restricted to the space between the slats. But if you called it "The Venetian Blinds," it became ludicrous and wrong, although, fascinatingly, it brings to mind jokes about blind Venetians. In this book they were French. And if you called it "Jealousy," which we did, you got rid of half of its meaning, and two halves do not necessarily make a whole.

Despite its opening paragraph, I was most pleased to read the Perreault review of *Djinn* in *The Village Voice*. The first part of it was already quoted, and now, its ending: "We are living through a time when the novel has been reduced to an entertainment property, not an exploratory text, a work of art. One may not approve of Robbe-Grillet's professed apolitical stance, yet in the long run one must admire his commitment to the novel as literature. His novels continue to be, like most good art, formally innovative and truly subversive."[6]

Notes

1. John Perreault, *The Village Voice*, October 5, 1982.
2. Alain Robbe-Grillet, "A Fresh Start for Fiction," trans. Richard Howard, in *Evergreen Review*, 1, 3 (1957), 97-104.
3. Roland Barthes, "Alain Robbe-Grillet," trans. Richard Howard, *Evergreen Review*, 2, 5 (1958), 113-126.
4. *Ibid.*
5. Alain Robbe-Grillet, "Old 'Values' and the New Novel," trans. Bruce Morrissette, *Evergreen Review*, 1, 3 (1957).
6. *The Village Voice*, October 5, 1982.

Discussion

Question: I find a possible paradox in your writing, Alain Robbe-Grillet, and in that of the other New Novelists. In presenting the fragmentation of the world and of the characters in order to make sense, and it does make sense, the writing is so skillfully done that in a way it presents a new pattern rather than a fragmentation. It calls attention to itself as being very carefully structured. I wonder if you would agree that this is so.

Alain Robbe-Grillet: If I had had a little more time, my lecture would have continued along this line. In the last analysis, the writer's project cannot be limited to fragments as such. This is out of the question. The writer remains a builder. The problem is how to build *me* and, consequently, how to build a world given that any attempt to have the fragmentation disappear is going to, in fact, be a negation of the world itself. The question really becomes: How can one proceed to build a work with fragmented materials? And the answer that I offer is precisely mobility.

You notice that there is a pattern, a very solid structure in my books. This structure, however, cannot be assimilated to *one* meaning, to one single meaning, because this structure is mobile. The mobility of structures may be one of the most important things in modern art as a whole. There is never one good reading of a book, for instance, since that good reading would reduce the book to a single structure, to a single meaning. All my work, all my effort, is to constitute extremely solid structures which would not impose themselves as essential truths, which would be strong structures but which would appear for a while and then leave room for other alternatives. I may be wrong. Perhaps in reality I take refuge, more than I admit, behind this mobility which I forge within the material arrangements of the texts. And perhaps this is why some other writers, often younger than I, have reproached me for writing, like my predecessors, works for the museum. You know, this is something that greatly worried Robert Rauschenberg: If we find in the museum works which should have escaped being there and we find in the Pantheon writers who fought against the established order, it is that they are representative of the established order and I myself am, similarly, no more than a nineteenth-century writer, only a little more advanced. This remains to be seen. And, as I have often said, one is never completely revolutionary. While I claim that my works can be read as revolutionary, I know that they can probably also be read as something else.

Mary Folliet: Who is the last living American author who intrigued you?

Alain Robbe-Grillet: The last American writer who really intrigued me, fascinated me as much as Faulkner or Kafka, is Nabokov, and he is not living, as you know.

Mary Folliet: Neither is he American!

Alain Robbe-Grillet: But he is! Looking for the nationality of his birth, seeking an identity by birth.... He wrote in English, he lived at Cornell, and consequently he is an American author! He is also a Russian author since he wrote in Russian.... For me, a book like *Pale Fire* is an absolutely remarkable book. There are American writers currently alive who are very interesting, but about whom I am less enthusiastic. This is to say that I don't feel in such direct communication with them. They are those generally listed together with Pynchon, Barth, Barthelme, Coover, and Hawkes, the list that everybody knows and that one would expect to find among the readings of any modern writer. As for poets, I don't know them very well because this is not at all my field.

Mary Folliet: I say living, because I think that at present the American list is very poor. They are all dead: Delmore Schwartz, John Berryman, Robert Lowell, and the others.

Alain Robbe-Grillet: Yes, we are feeling something, but not only in America—in Paris, in Tokyo, throughout the world—and that is that we are not living in a great period of creative euphoria. It is obvious that the 1950s and 1960s were marked in Europe, as in America, by a kind of explosion of new efforts. In the 1960s there were articles in *L'Express* about Maurice Blanchot. This would be unimaginable today! In France, there was the New Novel in literature, and in the field of music, music existed which made reputations for composers who had already died: Schoenberg, Berg, and Webern. And then there were the painters in France of the new reality. Here, in the United States, there was what was called Pop Art—Lichtenstein, Rauschenberg, Jasper Johns, and Warhol. They made this period, throughout the entire world, really astonishing.

What is happening today? Perhaps something is happening and we do not yet know it. But what must also be said is that that period was a time of great hope. People believed, for example, in socialism. People knew that Stalin was an assassin, but they thought it was by accident, because he was crazy. But socialism, Marxism, they existed! Then Marxism turned out badly everywhere, not only in Soviet Russia. And so, at a certain moment, people took refuge in saying that, nevertheless, there were Poland, Cuba, Vietnam. Then, little by little, all these territories had to be abandoned, and now, it is true, there is in the revolutionary political consciousness a kind of defeatism. As for myself, I am deeply optimistic by nature and, consequently, I regret that people think that all these things are impossible. I believe that once again there are flames, ferments, which are stirring and which are going to become manifest. Maybe we'll know it even by tomorrow. Perhaps it is going on even today and we are just not yet aware of it. Maybe there are great poets and we don't yet know of them.

Question: I would like to ask you, Alain Robbe-Grillet, if you see yourself in a literary tradition or if you think that the Nouveau Roman, and therefore your own awareness as a writer, is more or less a starting point.

Alain Robbe-Grillet: I have very often tried to show that the Nouveau Roman did not appear just like that, out of a magician's hat, but that, on the contrary, it has an entire past. Flaubert was already a kind of New Novelist, as was Laurence Sterne, and, indeed, *Tristram Shandy* is to be cited as one of these predecessors. Nevertheless, there probably were revolutionary periods and periods of freezing, of a concentration of meaning. It is obvious that the end of the eighteenth century—let us say with Sterne in England and Diderot in France—was marked by a great revolutionary fermentation, a calling into question of meaning.

The end of the eighteenth century was much more revolutionary. No nineteenth-century novel is comparable to *Jacques le Fataliste* in its modernity. When reading the beginning of *Jacques le Fataliste,* we think of the first sentence in Beckett's *L'Innomable* [*The Unnamable*]: "Where now? Who now? When now?" I claim that there are periods of invention, but this is only my personal opinion. The early nineteenth century was marked by a kind of ossification. It was a period when truth was taken en masse. But of course it is a simplification to speak of "*the* nineteenth century." It is even a simplification to speak of Balzac, since when I speak of the Balzac of *Eugenie Grandet* or *Le Père Goriot,* I am setting aside that of *Seraphita.*

In any case, in speaking of literature, we are more or less obliged to create syntagmas and paradigms. The New Novel is a paradigm. This is to say that there are some writers who, in the same period of time, have certain concerns in common. Obviously, as soon as we try to specify them, this idea no longer works, as it contradicts itself. As you will see, each of us maintains different opinions and I have spoken only on my own behalf. By syntagmas, on the other hand, I mean historical chains which go, for example, from Flaubert to Beckett, by way of Proust and others. This is also a means of simplifying my discourse, for it is obvious that the Robbe-Grillet, professor of literature, is forcibly siding with the established order. I cannot give courses on literature which would be forever mobile, contradictory, and rejecting of meaning. I would be expelled from the university. Nevertheless, if I accept this function, it is that there is an established order within me, as I have already said, and the established order is simplifying. To accommodate the needs of speech, I organize historical chains in time and groupings in space in order to speak.

Question: I would like to ask Alain Robbe-Grillet what he thinks of the future of the New Novel as a form of photo-novel, and if he himself thinks about writing photo-novels.

Alain Robbe-Grillet: I had a project for a photo-novel which never materialized. Here is what I imagined: There is a Japanese novelist, whom you may know, by the name of Abe Kobo. He writes plays and novels, and he also loves to photograph. The last time I met Abe Kobo, in Japan, he told me that he suffered greatly from not being at all recognized as a photographer. He was famous as a novelist, famous as a playwright, but as a photographer, people considered him to be playing with the camera. When I looked at his pictures, I found them very strange. They were of rather deserted places in Tokyo, and of wastelands and delapidated areas, and it seemed that there was in his pictures a kind of latent crime. I proposed to Abe Kobo, who agreed immediately, that he give me some pictures without telling me what they were of and without classifying them. I would be like a detective having evidence in his hands. I would have to write a story somewhat as I wrote *La Belle captive,* by classifying seventy-five paintings by Magritte. This project never came about as I had many other things to do and because Abe Kobo delayed in sending me the complete series. But this was a possible project for a photo-novel. We would have published the pictures and the texts.

There are other projects in which I have been somewhat involved. There is the American project of Edward Lachman, for instance, which is called *Chausse-Trappes* in French, for which I wrote the preface. I must say that there is one problem which one immediately encounters with respect to the publication of such projects: There is really no public at all for this kind of book and these books are expensive. If there is only a small public, the price has to be tremendously high. Practically speaking, there would be virtually no public at all because for these books to be interesting, the pictures must be of the highest quality. They really have to be very beautiful photographs. So I think that the current problem with the photo-novel, and that of its future, is an economic one.

At this time, problems of distribution are very significant in the world of artistic creation. The book, in particular, is a product which is not expensive, or relatively inexpensive, and consequently it has some chance. Film, on the other hand, is more and more dominated by money. It is because movies are expensive to make that they need a tremendous public. The economic problems posed by the photo-novel are close to those of cinema.

You may know that while few copies of my novels are sold when they first come out, they sell for a long time. Books have the advantage of staying in the bookstore. In France or in America, there is no need to buy my books immediately. They are in the bookstore. They can wait. The movie cannot. This means that the movie must be an immediate success. This is one of the reasons why it is absolutely impossible that cinema ever take the place of literature.

Anna Otten: Thinking of your Magritte and the explanations of Rauschenberg, I wonder if the same question applies. Is it very difficult to find a public for these books?

Alain Robbe-Grillet: The book I did with Robert Rauschenberg is a particularly striking example of a book with no public. There are in all thirty-five copies. These thirty-five copies are signed, by hand, on each page, by Rauschenberg and by me. (Of course a writer's signature is not as valuable as that of a painter.) The current sale price of the few remaining copies is $10,000. This is a typical example of a book which appeals to a very limited public, which is something that I deeply regret as it is really an astonishing book.

Here is how the book was done: A woman named Tatiana Grossman (who recently died and left a very important name in the history of lithography in the United States), attended, by chance, one of my lectures some twelve or fifteen years ago in which I spoke of Rauschenberg. I had considered Rauschenberg an example of a painter of a fragmented world which seeks a unity in order to be hung on the wall. Tatiana Grossman came to see me at the end of the meeting to tell me that she had intended for many years to write me a letter offering me the opportunity to work with Rauschenberg. We immediately concluded that Rauschenberg and I would collaborate. I determined that what would interest me was not at all a book written by me and illustrated by Robert Rauschenberg, but rather a kind of common book, a dialogue, a story, a fiction. It was done over four years. I exchanged elements with Rauschenberg: I had returned to Paris, he was in Florida, and we were exchanging things. I sent him three handwritten pages of text and he sent me back three pages of lithography. I sent him back three pages of text, as if it were a simple story that we were both writing which had chapters in images and chapters in words. Then when all was done, after twelve exchanges, we met on Long Island, New York, in Tatiana Grossman's studio, and we agonized over the layout. We mixed up everything in order to decide on the colors and this produced a very exciting book. The Museum of Modern Art in New York bought one and there are copies in several universities: UCLA, Buffalo, and elsewhere.

Helen Bishop: Who started?

Alain Robbe-Grillet: The text did. What was very good about working with Rauschenberg was that instead of having the tendency to extend what I had writen, he sometimes sent images which related and sometimes images which did not relate and which I integrated into the text afterward. For someone who might like to make a careful study of the work, it really is a surprising ensemble.

Claude Simon

Before I begin, I would like to ask that you excuse me if the lecture which I am going to give lacks a certain rigor and takes in a bit of everything. For reasons beyond my control (as they say), I learned that I would be allowed to come here only twelve days before my departure. This left me very little time to try to set in some order the notes I had taken while thinking about this colloquium and to compose in haste a text which would have profited from being more concentrated. But this was not my fault.

And, as a preamble, I must warn those who have come to listen to me that they are facing a simple, self-taught writer whose knowledge of literature does not surpass the level of amateurism. The majority of you, whether professors, essayists, or students, certainly know much more than I about the novel, theater, or poetry, as well as literary theory, semiology, or linguistics, with regard to which I often wonder, moreover, whether, contrary to what Barthes believed, this was not a poisoned gift that Roman Jakobson granted to literature, as were, in other respects, sociology and psychoanalysis by others.

But, after all, perhaps art is doomed to sail periodically among the dreadful reefs of scientism. For example, at the end of the last century, a painter whose name would otherwise have been long forgotten, Paul Sérusier, elaborated a "théorie des complémentaires," as seductive as it was inoperative in practice. And, over these last few years, we have seen writers wear themselves out building, carefully, so as not to be outdone, texts which rest completely on some dreary series of anagrammatical acrobatics more or less inspired either by Saussure or a famous guru of psychoanalysis.

It is not that I want to throw out the baby with the bath water but that, just as Lenin revealed a "maladie infantile" [an infantile disease] of communism (which still seems to perpetuate itself), there exists a chronic disease of art and literature—and I do not know whether it is infantile or senile—which scientists of all persuasions devote themselves with constancy not to curing, but to aggravating.

As far as I am concerned, my cultural experience (if I may use this expression) is that of a dilettante. When I was young, I was made to study mathematics (which, alas, I have long forgotten!) and I do not even have my degree in philosophy. The little that I know was acquired by reading, traveling, visiting museums, and attending concerts, always in a rather disconnected way, without ever determining to study a subject in depth and obeying only the rules of pleasure. For example, it took my being a prisoner (and I think that one of the more fortunate aspects of my existence is that I lived the first part of it in a rather troubled Europe which enabled me—as, by force of circumstances, I was involved in certain events—to learn, I believe, something other than can be found in books). It took being a prisoner for me to read Kant and Spinoza, not because I chose to, but because that was what fell into my hands. The experience I had at that time, moreoever, was instructive in two ways: first, I discovered that, in a space surrounded by barbed wire where it was strictly prohibited to own whatever was not absolutely necessary for the most primitive survival, it was possible to find almost everything, from women's garters to *The Capital*, including obscene postcards and the *Acts of the Apostles*. Second, that if Kant and Spinoza were not at all practically or morally useful to a starving man (they did not in any way help me to accept my misery), those books offered, nevertheless, even to the layman in philosophy that I am, this possibility for a gratuitous—and by this very gratuitousness, irreplaceable—excitement which is provided, as by music or painting, by reading.

So this was my education or, if you prefer, my cultural "baggage," constituted mainly of deficits and contained in this kind of sieve which is my mind, a mind retaining here and there only scraps of knowledge, at least consciously, for, after all, it is possible that Kant and Spinoza, swallowed, like mathematics, almost forcibly (and I do not have a very clear remembrance of them either), did contribute without my awareness to shaping it, as did (at least negatively) all the books which I have never wanted to reopen: for example, *La Princesse de Clèves, Les Liaisons dangereuses, Lucien Leuwen,* as well as those I could never finish because they were too boring,

Claude Simon

whether *La Cousine Bette* or *L'Education sentimentale*. I must confess, most nineteenth-century French novels and their twentieth-century epigones, with their characters of a too foreseeable, too rational fate (as opposed, for example, to those of Dostoevski), remind me of those bulls so appreciated by matadors called, in the slang of the corridas, "ferrocarils," which means "set on rails" because they rush straight, and without warning, for the lure. (By the way, and since I have just mentioned Dostoevski, I must say how surprised I am that each time I hear people speaking of the so-called traditional novel, they refer inevitably to Balzac, Stendhal, or Zola, forgetting, as though he had not existed, one of the three or four greatest writers in the history of literature and to whom, precisely, we owe fiction which is the contrary of those univocal novels so abundantly produced by the French nineteenth century and which give of the world this far from reassuring—and even eminently frightening—image mentioned yesterday by Robbe-Grillet.)

To come back to myself, if I am asked the famous question "Why do you write?," I must confess to my great shame that I have never had, like some others, even the least ambitious motivations: it has never occurred to me (and I have never wondered about it) that I should write to fight against the established order or to criticize it. If I have written (and still write), it is very prosaically, and maybe very selfishly, because I was impelled (as everyone is in his field, I think) by a certain need of "doing." If I am asked why I "have done" in literature rather than anywhere else, and if I want to be sincere, I will answer "because I wasn't capable of anything else."

When I was young, I was rather lazy and, at the same time, like all young people, rather romantic (which, after careful thought, may be a form of laziness). I was led by these two shortcomings to throwing myself into various experiences like painting or, for a while, revolutionary action which my incurable dilettantish mind rather quickly caused me to abandon and which, nevertheless, still causes me all kinds of problems each time I want to come to this country.

There remained the possibility of writing, which I thought to be easier than painting or revolution and, naturally, of writing what I believe required the least specialization or discipline: this kind of carry-all which is the novel, a genre whose rules (if there are any!)

are not well defined and in which one thinks, at the beginning, that one can do and put down just about anything.

Unfortunately, I was not aware that here, too, I lacked the gift of seriousness which enables one to produce books likely to be of interest. Naively, I thought that in once again choosing (as I had for my readings) mere pleasure as a rule, this pleasure would be communicative and that I would be able to pass on a part of it to those reading my books. In spite of my various experiences as a revolutionary and as an amateur warrior (for war as I practiced it—in open country, on horseback, and armed with a saber, complete with musketoon, against planes and armored cars—though awfully deadly, it bordered on caricature), I did not yet know that the general public (of which every writer dreams) is tremendously "self-interested" (as we say of those game of cards or dice where money is involved). This is to say that the kind of pleasure, or rather of "profit," that it expects from a novel is either that of an escape—where one forgets oneself for a few hours to identify with an exemplary hero or heroine comparable to some archetype (either good or evil)—or that of a teaching, of a bearing of knowledge which would propose a solution to the problems with which it is preoccupied—whether problems of social or love relations, the meaning of life or that of History, even without a capital letter—or, as, for example, in a detective story when the name of the murderer is revealed.

Given this, I soon had to resign myself to admitting that in this field, as well, I would never be a true professional. To tell the truth, as indicative of the profits my books have brought me over thirty years, I think that they must be more or less equal to those of an unemployed worker. Once more lacking the erudition and the skills which would have allowed me to earn my living by publishing articles or teaching in universities (but teaching what?), I am wondering how, if I had not been lucky enough to inherit a small fortune, I would have managed to provide myself with clothes, a place to live, or even very simply food, and to maintain myself in this marginal situation thanks to which I can, without conceding to any considerations of profit or opportunity, write and say whatever I think good.

By some miracle (or maybe by some misunderstanding), I was lucky, in spite of the limited circulation of my books, to find in my life a first, then a second, and finally a third publisher, one who happened to also be that of other writers whose books, except Samuel Beckett's, I had never read and among whom, some, however, assured me (maybe once more by misunderstanding) that my work was moving in the same direction as theirs. That was extremely kind of them and flattering to me. Though, I must confess, not very clear to me when I became familiar with their works, except that for them, as for me, the time of a certain form, an even unbearable form, of novel seemed outdated and that, like me, they were trying to do "something else."

Unlike my new friends, however (and as it could be detected in the very contradictory statements made by each of us at a meeting about ten years ago which united us all under the firm rule of a severe schoolmaster), I had never theoretically thought either about the problems which were posed, or about the way to solve them. I was proceeding by trial and error and, as a consequence, I had the impression that I was like a kind of M. Jourdain to whom his grammar teacher explains that he is speaking prose without knowing it. For instance, I read in the papers[1] that in the course of another, more recent colloquium, our friend Robbe-Grillet had drawn the conclusion that he and Nathalie Sarraute were the spiritual inheritors of Jean-Paul Sartre, that which he confirmed yesterday evening to the approval, moreover, of Michel Rybalka. Of course, I do not know the laws of genetics, but I must again confess that, despite careful self-examination, I discern nothing in myself which would allow me to claim this strange paternity—unless, in this matter as well, I am still like M. Jourdain.

Because as far as I am concerned, whether it be thirty years ago or now, I was working, and am still working, in a completely empirical way, taking from the start what suited me and rejecting what did not suit me in one or another of the writers whom I liked to read, like Dostoevski, Conrad (and, by the way, I am surprised that his amazing preface to *Nigger of the Narcissus* seems to have been forgotten), Joyce, Proust, and Faulkner. I was moving (and am still moving) forward rather gropingly, without ever knowing when I start a text what it will turn out to be (in the last analysis, it is always very different from the original project which is so deeply modified in the process that generally very little remains of it), and I know even less what the text "should be" in order to obey certain canons.

Finally, I must add that I am somewhat afraid that it is once more because of a misunderstanding that I am here today, somewhat embarrassed and disturbed at having crossed the entire Atlantic Ocean to, ultimately, perhaps disappoint those who have invited me, for I have little more to formulate than a few amateurish reflections made after the fact about my works, accompanied by a few very unimaginative remarks.

What this means is that I feel at ease to request of those listening to me that they do not in any way consider the remainder of my talk as a magisterial lesson on the novel, and that I will gratefully welcome objections and perhaps even observations revealing my errors. That would be for me an opportunity to learn and enrich myself. In advance, therefore, I thank you.

And as I have just spoken of misunderstandings, perhaps it would be best to start with those revealed by certain questions asked of me either during interviews or privately a little more than a year ago when my last novel, *Les Géorgiques,* was published. These show rather well how most readers continue, still today, to conceive of and receive the novel, fiction, and, more generally, literary texts.

Two things in particular struck me: First, that many of my interlocutors insisted on the fact that the characters of that novel had, they claimed, "existed," that they were "real" characters (some critics even believed that they could identify them). Second (and this was said with no malevolent intention), that there were (still in that novel) phenomena of "fragmentation" and "discontinuity," phenomena which, according to some, would be characteristic of "modernity" in the sense that (to quote word for word one of my interviewers) "l'écriture y contrecarre sans cesse la poussée narrative" [The writing unceasingly works against the narrative thrust]. This thinking is typical, I believe, of a kind of uncertainty, and even bewilderment, the result of the conflict between, on the one hand, old reading habits and, on the other, certain maximalist theories which, more or less harebrained and smelling of terrorism, were made fashionable over these last few years.

To this kind of observation, I am instinctively tempted to reply: "narration" *of what?* "Fragmentation and discontinuity" *of what?*

I will not launch into a critical analysis here of the "realistic" novel such as it was throughout the nineteenth century in France and such as it continues to be today in serving for many as a model.

But, in a few words, what strikes me in this kind of novel (and probably what bores me so) is less that "nonconformist" hero's expulsion from the established order that Robbe-Grillet spoke about yesterday than its pedagogical and documentary pretentions. And what strikes me as well is that, following in the wake of the fable, the parable, the philosophical tale, and conceived as a demonstration of some moralizing thesis, whether in the social or psychic domain ("un enseignement social" [a social teaching], Balzac used to say), this kind of novel displays precisely all the characteristics of fragmentation and discontinuity.

Contrary to its pretention of describing the "real," it is obvious that, unable materially to say *everything*, the realistic novel is limited to showing the successive fragments of the story whose discontinuity is masked from the reader's eyes only by the author's assurance that he is relating only the "essential." Others have maliciously stressed all that was arbitrary and questionable in this notion of "essential." Others, as well, indicating on two parallel ordinates so-called referential time (that of the clock) and so-called literal time (that of the text), have easily shown how, in the latter, the former is subjugated to constant processes of dilation (when the text lingers over one event or one description), alternating with overwhelming compressions (when the text skims over, merely mentioning them, events considered "minor"). The text is even sometimes nullified (when the author decides, as he sometimes writes, that for one hour, one day, or several, nothing "important" has happened) or even inverted, through the process of looking back, of flashbacks recounting what, to use the expression, happened elsewhere "in the meanwhile."

The principle which governs the composition of this sort of novel, where the author hides behind a false objectivity (hence the most biting condemnation of realism which is this phrase of Baudelaire: "La nature comme si je n'étais pas là pour la dire" [Nature as if I were not there to tell it]), the principle which governs the succession of events recounted in the text is that of *causality*, a linking of causes and effects leading the characters and the reader to that famous dénouement considered by Emile Faguet as the "couronnement logique" [logical coronation] of the novel, with the characters, therefore, being narrowly *determined*. Thus another critic, Henri Martineau, could claim that when he started writing *Le Rouge et le noir* [*The Red and the Black*], Stendhal already knew how Julien

Sorel was "to end up," which, by the way, is true since we know that Stendhal wrote this novel (as Flaubert did *Madame Bovary*) from a news item read in a local paper. This also demonstrates that this kind of novel has the status of a fable: it is not because a wolf devours a lamb that "la raison du plus fort est toujours la meilleure" [the reason of the strongest is always the best] but, on the contrary, it is to demonstrate this axiom that the fabulist shaped a little fiction ending with an allegorical wolf devouring a no less allegorical lamb. In the same way, to justify the revolver shot fired by Julien Sorel at Madame de Rênal or Emma's arsenic suicide, Stendhal and Flaubert had first to fill hundreds of pages with psychosociological explanations of what led their hero and heroine to these acts.

Fortunately (and we must hasten to say it), between these intentions more or less flaunted by these authors and what they really gave us to read, there exists, for the salvation of literature, something more which in no way competes with these laborious "teachings" and in which resides, precisely, their respective geniuses, even if they would have perhaps considered this something to be "inessential." (And I say "perhaps," for when reading the numerous "scenarios" written by Flaubert in planning for *Madame Bovary*, it appears that they are precisely and *essentially* composed of notations of fragrances, colors, sounds, and sensations of any kind. So much so that one is led to wonder if, eighty years prior to a claim put forth by Tynianov, and despite the famous caricature showing him brandishing at the tip of a scalpel Emma's bleeding heart, Flaubert did not consider his *fable* to be mainly the *pretext* for an accumulation of descriptions.)

To come to "modernity" (or rather to our modernity, for each period has its own, and there is no great writer, no great painter, no great musician who is not an innovator), which unquestionably marks an important break (undoubtedly one of the most spectacular since Giotto's break with Byzantine hieratism), it dates, in my opinion, from the end of the last century and the beginning of the one in which we live.

I know that it is always perilous to venture comparisons and parallels between different arts, and I am no more a specialist in the history of painting than in literature, but it appears to me, though I may be wrong, that the decisive break was initiated not by writers but by painters who overtly (and I say "overtly" because the "subject" in painting had long been no more than an alibi) called into question the principle (or rather the dogma) of realism and proclaimed that their work aimed at rendering images no longer of the "real" world, but only (that which is entirely different) of the *impressions* they received from it. In other words, from then on, the concern was no longer with "la nature comme si je n'étais pas là pour la dire" [nature as though I were not there to relate it], but with the world as seen through me, this partial, distorted, and personal vision that I have of it.

It was on this horizon that Cézanne appeared. It was he who challenged the word "impression," preferring that of "sensation." "We *know*," Jakobson said, "but we do not *see*." And it was in seeking to rid himself of this ready-made knowledge that comes between our true sensation and our mind that Cézanne managed, at the very least, to completely modify painting.

To explain myself, I will say that in Cézanne's contribution, I am particularly struck by two things. On the one hand, he left behind apparently unfinished paintings (I say "apparently" because the question of the "finish" of a work, whether it be painted or written, is, in itself, an entire problem deserving reflection). Cézanne left us apparently unfinished paintings where only the "strong points" of the motif are accounted for, which is to say that here and there, on the virgin and neutral surface of the canvas, there exist only a few lines and a few spots between which the spectator's eye is invited to grasp "connections" by confronting them without passing through any intermediary filler.

On the other hand, always careful to grasp his feelings with precision, he noticed that "les plans se chevauchent" [the planes overlap] and even, as he was to say to Jochim Gasquet, that "les objets se pénètrent entre eux" [objects penetrate each other], that which is characteristic, if we think about it, of our way of perceiving the visible world, with a kind of imprecision or indistinction, and our perception of the entire world (shapes, colors, smells, sounds, and so on) as well—as much in the present as in our memory where, unceasingly, memories, images, and emotions veer into one another, superimpose on, associate with, and interpenetrate one another.

And it is from there (which is to say where we really apprehend things only by discontinuous fragments that overlap and combine *to form, on the other hand, an emotive or sensorial continuity in our minds*) that the Cubists were led, in a first step, to practice what was called "analytic Cubism." This, following Cézanne's example, arranged *on a neutral background* a few lines (horizontal or oblique) and a few spots—or rather a few modulations. In a second step, in 1913, came "synthetic Cubism," which, *without any solution then of continuity,* and with no other principle than their qualitative affinities (shapes, colors, rhythms), had fragments of objects, imagined or even sometimes "real," like sheets of newspaper, pieces of tapestry, of "faux-bois," and so on, agglutinate, interfere, and intermingle with each other *in the way that we really perceive them.* Then later, after the collages and sculptures of Picasso, artists like Kurt Schwitters, Louise Nevelson, or Robert Rauschenberg conceived vast compositions or assemblages executed with the help of various materials: boards, tarred paper, debris from pieces of furniture or machines, the pouring of raw paint, and so on. To the extent that, if the word were not so devaluated today, one could call it a true realism in the dual sense that from a meditation on the at once both chaotic and very coherent nature of our perception and our memory, objects are thereby effected which seek their reality only within themselves.

If I had to sum up with an incisive and necessarily simplifying formula the change which thus occurred, I would venture that over the principle of the establishment of relations justified by *causality* and necessitating a kind of totalizing (and illusory as well) inventory, the principle of the establishment of above all *qualitative* relations took precedence.

If I have insisted on this date 1913 in a way which some might find a bit pedantic, it is that, at the same moment, Proust and (though to a lesser extent) Joyce (for *Ulysses* was still considered to be full of more or less esoteric significations) undertook to construct texts in which considerations of quality would have priority over the succession or, if you prefer, the confrontation of the elements.

That the streams of cause and effect linking the different episodes of a story intended to show the excellence of some moral or of some thesis could seem as arbitrary and questionable as that which, in this new perspective, associates two events of a text with no demonstrative pretention seems to be to me irrefutable. I may still think, despite what Balzac wanted to have me believe, that César Birrotteau could just as well, despite his honesty, have never again risen from his ruin. I may still think that it is because of a series of very strange coincidences that Fabrice del Dongo commits the murder which causes him so many troubles and reveals to us the mechanisms and intrigues of power. I may remain skeptical (if not amazed) when I read in Faulkner's plan for a preface to *The Sound and the Fury* that

> Si on avait envoyé les enfants passer l'après-midi dans le pré pour qu'ils ne restent pas à la maison . . . c'était *afin que* les trois frères et les petits noirs *puissent* lever les yeux vers le fond souillé de la coulotte de Caddy grimpée dans l'arbre.
>
> [If the children were sent off to spend the afternoon in the meadow so that they would not remain at home . . . it was *in order that* the three brothers and the little blacks *could* have a look at the soiled panties of Caddy perched in the tree.][2]

On the other hand, however, I cannot question the fact that the unevenness of a cobblestone associates the courtyard of the Guermantes Hotel with two paving-stones of Saint Marc's Baptistry. I cannot question, so obvious it seems to me, that the juicy flavor of the fruit which she plans to buy at the market leads Molly Bloom to an erotic daydream. Neither can I question that the word "Caddy" shouted by the golf players makes Benjy shriek with pain. It appears to me that, on this basis, on this principle, Proust, Joyce, and Faulkner built constructions of which the solidity, the reliability, and the *continuity* seem much more determinative, if we want to use this word, than the chance meeting of two characters or of two animals in a fable. These other meetings, while they are dictated by associations of impressions or images, are also (like the strokes of the Impressionists) inseparable from the material (which is to say the language that, as has rightly been said, "parle avant nous" [speaks before us]), speaks by what is called its "figures," its tropes (metaphors, metonyms), and by its very dynamics (sometimes only phonetic effects), which itself provokes rapprochements, associations, and *transports*. (Must we be reminded that the word $\mu\epsilon\tau\alpha\zeta o\rho\grave{\alpha}$ is, in Greece, written on trucks?)

It seems that there exist two excesses (or, if you prefer, two maximalisms, two terrorisms) whose effects are equally negative. In the same way that Valéry used to say that the world was threatened by two dangers, order and disorder, language could be said to be threatened by two dangers as well: on the one hand, that of being considered only as a vehicle of meaning and, on the other hand, that of being considered only as a structure, for it is always *simultaneously* both. It is really in these two potentialities and their perpetual interference that there appears to dwell this wonderful ambiguity provides language with so many tremendous powers.

To those, therefore, who claim to bend it only to the requirements of expression and representation, we can answer with Lacan (and also already with Proust: let us not forget that the last part of *Du Côté de chez Swann* [*Swann's Way*] is entitled *Noms de pays: le nom* [*Place-Names: The Name*]) that the word is not only a "sign," but "a network of significations." As I wrote in my preface to *Orions Aveugle,* a "carrefour de sens" [a crossroad of meanings], which is to say that, like the elements of the Cubist painting or "assemblages," the word is, *in itself,* a reality. While the word, of course, evokes the image or the concept of the object which it designates, it simultaneously calls up numerous other concepts, other images—those of objects sometimes very far away in the time of clocks and the measurable space of the "real" object and with which it is soon linked—to the extent that, *at the moment of writing,* a multitude of propositions are provided. Taken into consideration, these propositions will considerably distort the author's first intention to the point where we can say that he who works language is at the same time worked by it, that which naturally implies a deflection in the meaning which is therefore not "expressed" but, in accordance with the accepted terminology, *produced.*

As for the hard and fast terrorists of the other side who fearfully resist any notion of meaning or of "referent," their declarations always remind me of this little apologue of an art critic who remarked that when the Impressionists were first starting, when they were not yet established and when the public was seeing in their painting only "barbouillages informes" [shapeless daubs], their, at that time, rare defenders would say to people (in front of Monet's *Nymphéas* [*Water Lilies*], for example): "Stand back, stand back, and you will see that it depicts something!" A few years ago, at the time when the Tachists were fashionable, their defenders, seeking to justify them by finding respectable ancestors for them, would bring people before these same *Nymphéas* saying, "Come closer, come closer, and you will see that it does not depict anything!"

I was asked to speak specifically here of my last novel, *Les Géorgiques,* and I have but a little time left, though in fact I have really done nothing else for more than a half an hour now. It is naive to believe that, as I heard an essayist say, one whom I nevertheless esteem (this took place at a colloquium on Proust organized by New York University at the Ecole Normale Supérieure in Paris), by who knows what perversity, a novelist fragments a totality to reassemble its pieces according to his fancy. As I have already said, this kind of suspicion would be accurately based only on an examining of the methods used by the so-called realistic novelists.

As with each plan I have had for a novel, that of *Les Géorgiques* was, at the beginning, very vague. I am, as I have also already said, neither a philosopher ("Heureusement pour vous!" [Fortunately for you!], Merleau-Ponty once said to me, "Si vous l'étiez, vous seriez bien incapable d'écrire vos romans!" [If you were, you would certainly be incapable of writing your novels!]), a moralist, or a believer. That is why I have nothing special to reveal about the great questions which are posed by mankind, like sex, the meaning of History, of life, evil or good. Naturally, like everyone else, and because I have in my life been involved in some rather tumultuous events, I have, of course, a few ideas concerning these things, but, in fact, they are too vague and sometimes too contradictory for me to consider them worth publishing.

The question which I had to answer was not "What have I to say," but rather "What could I *do*" with a slew of old papers left by one of my ancestors who had been a member of the Convention, and then a general during the French Revolution and during the First Empire. And here we come to the question of the "referent" which, apropos of me, seemed so disturbing to my friend Robbe-Grillet at the Cerisy colloquium. As I am no more a historian than a philosopher, I have no ambition to write the life of this character by going to various ministries and searching through official archives for documents which would have allowed me to complete my information. Despite the abundance of papers which had come into my possession (letters, mémoires, travel accounts, drafts of speeches, and numerous military orders), huge gaps or, if you prefer, huge "black holes" were left in the history of that life.

Moreover, in spite of these holes, the mass of images which was conjured up in me by these documents was sufficient enough to constitute a stimulant. This made me want, without searching further, to do "something" with them, and with others, other images of war, other images of revolution, which I was preserving from my personal experience.

For, while there was actually a *discontinuity* in the fragments of information which I possessed, as there is in all those which we receive from the world surrounding us at every moment, I also perceived an extraordinary thematic *continuity*. (Thematics is nowadays condemned by a certain university fashion, but this does not matter....) Thus I found a disturbing relationship, one so close that at moments time seemed abolished, between events which had taken place some hundred years earlier and those which I had witnessed in Barcelona in 1936 or in Belgium in 1940, or even the account which George Orwell rendered of his experience in Spain, an account which is in itself a perfect model, from its very first page, of an account by more or less voluntary omissions, and thus itself an account full of holes.

What I tried to do, therefore, was gather all this scattered material into a composition which would owe its coherence to those principles of quality which I mentioned earlier, by interweaving themes like those of a fugue, developing variations, and so on. I have related elsewhere how my work reminds me of the title of the first lesson of the study of Advanced Mathematics which is called "Arrangements, Permutations, Combinations," and I cannot explain why I have the feeling that, just as there exist syntactic laws governing the organization and the coherence of a sentence into main, relative, and subordinate clauses, there exists as well, though not codified, an internal logic of language which requires a syntax of the text in its entirety, from the first to the last line, and from which, if one manages to follow those hidden laws, "something" will tell *itself* for, were this not so, all discourse would be nothing but conventional chatter. "Il en va du langage comme des formules mathématiques" [Language is comparable to mathematic formulas], Novalis wrote almost two centuries ago: "(membres de la nature) elles constituent un monde en soi, pour elles seules; elles jouent entre elles exclusivement, n'expriment rien, si ce n'est leur propre nature merveilleuse, ce qui justement fait qu'elles sont si expressives, que justement en elles se reflète le jeu étrange des rapports entre les choses" [(members of nature) they constitute a world in itself, for them alone; they play among themselves exclusively, express nothing but their own wonderful nature, which is precisely the reason why they are so expressive, why precisely the strange interplay of the relations between things is reflected in them].

And actually, from these discontinuous fragments of history, thus organized and interrelated in a way which I thought proper to forming a continuity, from this *composition* there emerges for me no "message," no "moral," no "fatality" which, as has pompously been said, "introduirait la tragédie grecque dans le roman" [would introduce Greek tragedy into the novel]. Neither does there emerge any mockery: in a word, there is no kind of "teaching" beyond the single acknowledgment of these thematic or simply emotive "correspondences."

Nothing, moreover, allowed me to arrange these events in a progression leading to a dénouement which would have constituted what Faguet called a "couronnement logique" [logical coronation]. After having confronted all the dangers which a man can face during his lifetime, General L.S.M. dies very prosaically by his hearth, "O," for his part, escapes only by chance from the agents of the Guépéou who have pitilessly hunted him down in Barcelona like his companions of the P.O.U.M., and the General's great-grandson gets away without a scratch from the slaughter to which the French generals had sent the calvary in 1940.

Need I point out that in speaking of these various characters I have just used the *present tense*? Must I emphasize after all that I have just said that they existed (that they were actually alive) only to the extent that the text was writing itself, and that they were continually modified by the addition, the suppression, or the moving of a paragraph or of a sentence? That, made of words and of the images which these words provoke (and of the referential gaps as well), L.S.M. is not, nor can he be, a portrait of General Lacombe Saint-Michel, just as "O" is not George Orwell (who, moreover, was himself not George Orwell since, in reality, he was named Eric Arthur Blair . . .). That the old lady is not my grandmother and that the General's great-grandson, *a character of the novel just as the others are,* also bears but a distant and limited connection with me?

These characters, of course, borrow many of their features from people who "really" existed and in this way they may be differentiated from those characters, one may call them allegorical, usually found in works of fiction either in France or elsewhere, characters shaped out of nothing to suit the needs of the cause and intended, through their behavior and their adventures, to show what happens to the avaricious, the liar, the extravagant, the ambitious, or other such conventional "personalities."

Neither L.S.M.'s life nor his death prove anything at all and neither any kind of "moral" nor any kind of teaching is to be drawn from them—no more than from "O's" adventures or from the acts of the other characters who appear in this novel. Moreover, too many unknowns remain, too many contradictions, too many doubts.

And it is perhaps this uncertainty which, beyond our differences and at times even our divergences, unites me with my friends in this movement of the "Nouveau Roman," a movement which has given rise to a lot of misunderstandings, a lot of exaggerations, a lot of superficial commentaries, but in which, I believe, we are gathered by a common feeling that one can never be entirely sure of anything and that we are constantly treading on quicksand.

Thank you for your patience.

Notes

1. *Le Monde,* January 22, 1982.
2. William Faulkner, *Oeuvre romanesque,* vol. 1, trans. Michel Grenet (Paris: La Pleiade), n.d., n.p. Translators' note: this quotation was retranslated into English by us.

Toward a Simonian Mimetics

Ralph Sarkonak

S'annonce ainsi une division intérieure de la *mimesis,* une auto-duplication de la répétition même; à l'infini, puisque ce mouvement entretient sa propre prolifération. Peut-être y a-t-il donc toujours plus qu'une seule *mimesis;* et peut-être est-ce dans l'étrange miroir qui réfléchit, mais aussi se déplace et déforme une *mimesis* dans l'autre, comme si elle avait pour destin de se mimer, de se masquer elle-même, que se loge l'histoire—de la littérature—comme la totalité de son interprétation.

[An inner division of *mimesis* is thus announced, a self-duplication of the repetition itself; to infinity, as this movement generates its own proliferation. Perhaps there is always more than a single *mimesis* and perhaps it is in this strange mirror which reflects, but also moves and distorts one *mimesis* in the other, as though its fate were to mimic itself, to mask itself, that the history—of literature—dwells as the totality of its interpretation.]

Jacques Derrida

I would like to begin with a brief digression in order to situate the title of my contribution to this colloquium to which Tom Bishop was kind enough to invite me. The "toward" in my title is to be read with two different meanings. The first is "in pursuance of," for the few remarks that I am going to make today constitute only the rough outline of an attempt to approach a very vast problem. This effort will be continued, prolonged by others, or so I hope, for it seems to me that the notion of *mimesis* is not irrelevant to the way we read Claude Simon's fiction. This leads me to the second meaning of the word "toward" in my title. This "toward" bears witness to a certain uneasiness, as well as a certain wish on my part, which is to say that it challenges an "antimimetic" tendency, bias, or prejudice, if one may refer to it as such, which, however implicit, nonetheless marks a good number of studies written on Simon's work.

Since the great colloquium *Nouveau Roman: hier, aujourd'hui,*[1] many pages have been written about the status of a possible referent in Simon's novels. This has raised not only the thorny issue of actual pictorial models (whether postcards or paintings), but also the much more interesting question of built-in textual ambiguities, autorepresentation, as well as textual analogies of all sorts. From these analogies emerges a referential effect which unceasingly stages itself as such and, in so doing, duplicates itself over and over again in texts which overtly demonstrate themselves to be autoreflexive artifacts.

Also raised by the consideration of the status of a possible referent in Simon is the question, already studied by many, of captures [*mises en images*] and animations, in short, of all sorts of textual *mutations*.[2] If I sometimes feel a vague but very real uneasiness when reading certain essays on Simon's fiction, it is because I have the distinct impression that some critics would have us believe that those texts do not "represent" anything, do not "produce" anything. You may suppose correctly that I put the last two verbs in apposition on purpose. For it is time for us readers of Simon to begin to come to terms with mimesis, a mimesis which must be conceived less as the imitation of an already existing model than as the production of meaning in a textual artifact. I use the word "mimesis" for the moment since it enables us to situate the debate within a critical and theoretical context which is noticeably wider than that, for example, of the so-called ascendant vertical self-representation, though my intention is not to invalidate the pertinence of such a mimetic category.[3]

It is rather that for too long the Nouveau Roman has been considered apart from the mainstream of textual production, a marginal case, as though nothing were to come of it, while, in fact, the Nouveau Roman—and in particular Claude Simon's novels— pose the most fundamental problems of *all* literary texts. I would express my wish this way: that Simonian studies now ask the very old, but not old-fashioned, question—what is mimesis? Actually I think that by tackling the problem of mimesis in Simon, we might well learn something of what constitutes the essential literariness of Simon's writing and, ultimately, of the literary text *qua* text. End of digression.

As gratifying as the reconstruction of Simon's fictional universe may be, it is upstaged by the performance of that most celebrated actor, language, by the staging not only *by* language but also *of* language and thus of its inherent capacities and limits. Here, I intend to examine one aspect of this rather spectacular performance: a mimetic striptease. As a partial solution to the eternal problem of the inadequacy of language as a mere tool of communication and, therefore, to the inadequacy of the represented as a "copy" of an existing model, this unveiling by mimesis of her many charms is but part of the larger picture of textual productivity in Simon.

It is well known that in *The Republic* Plato identifies mimesis with tragedy and comedy, which are characterized as completely mimetic in contrast with the epic form whose mixed style combines *mimesis,* where "le poète parle en son nom sans chercher à nous faire croire que c'est un autre que lui qui parle"[4] [the poet speaks in his own name without seeking to have us believe that it is someone other than he who is speaking], and *diegesis,* where the poet attempts to give the illusion that it is the character himself who is speaking without the author's intervention (392c-395). In fact, according to Plato, mimesis is everywhere, for ultimately everything in nature is a copy of the ideal model, to the extent that a painting is but the "imitation of an imitation." Hence the condemnation of poetry as a simulacrum or copy of something which is itself only an image of the Platonic ideal.

In Aristotle, on the other hand, "mimesis" loses its negative connotation while at one and the same time the semantic field of the word is subjected to both a contraction and an expansion. The meaning of the term is noticeably restricted as it now applies to the sole domain of man's artistic endeavors. And yet the concept is extended, for in Aristotle mimesis is no longer limited to the direct discourse of theater. The epic, as well as tragedy and comedy, are subsumed by the general category of mimesis, the main difference between the narrative and the dramatic being ascribed to their respective mimetic modes.

Roughly summarizing centuries of literary criticism and theory, one can say that since the *Poetics* the traditional concept of mimesis has been founded on the idea, or perhaps it would be better to say the belief, that the relations of the work of art to extratextual reality are to be thought of in terms of a model which is already there. For our purposes, we will appropriate a very general definition of "mimesis" from Gérard Genette who defines poetic mimesis as follows: "le fait de représenter par des moyens verbaux une réalité non-verbale, et, exceptionnellement, verbale"⁵ [the fact of representing by verbal means a nonverbal and, on occasion, a verbal reality].

Here several problems of a theoretical and methodological nature are encountered. The first concerns translation of the word "mimesis" itself. In translating it by "imitation," as there is an unfortuante tendency to do, emphasis is put on the imitated, not to say copied, *model*. If it is translated by "representation," however, the result is ambiguous, as is shown by the following sentence where the direct object can refer either to the thing which is imitated or to the thing which is produced: "This painting represents an apple." Curiously, the problem dates back to the ancients, for the Greek would be no less ambiguous than the French or the English in this regard.⁶ But that is not all. Since the "revolution in poetic language" of the last century, the conception of just what constitutes poetic or literary mimesis has undergone a major shock.⁷ It is no longer possible to limit mimesis to imitation alone, if, indeed, it ever was, for mimesis does not and cannot exclude the realm of textual productivity: on the contrary, the two are inextricably linked. As Paul Ricoeur so rightly states: "Il n'y a de *mimesis* que là où il y a un 'faire' "⁸ [There is mimesis only where there is a "doing"].

As may well be suspected, this clarification risks making our task even more difficult, since to undertake an overall study of mimetic language in Simon, one would have to examine at the same time all of the lines of productive force by which the text is crossed [*travaillé*] and significance produced.⁹ Such cannot, however, be the scope of my modest proposal this afternoon. Here I am obliged to divide, however artificially, the textual material into the staging of language and language as stage-manager. At the same time, from what I have just said, it follows that it is not possible to limit mimesis to "mere" referentiality. Though the latter is, indeed, one of the avatars of a Simonian mimetics, it is far from being the sole one. Thus the term "mimesis," at once too general and too restricted, is apt to give rise to many an ambiguity. Hence the need for a more neutral term, one with fewer connotations, to describe the different forms that can be assumed by a global mimesis. At the same time, it is well to be reminded of these "mini-mimeses" of the origin of the problem. Let us call them *mimetisms*.¹⁰

Obviously, this word, too, must be clarified if it is to be of use; we can do so by qualifying it with a series of adjectives in order to refer to the various mimetic modes that are to be distinguished. Let us call *referential mimetism* the relation which is thought to join (if not unite) words and things and which is likely to lead to the so-called referential illusion when the subject overlooks the impassible gulf which, in fact, separates them. *Self-referential mimetism*, also known as "mise en abyme" [auto-reflexivity], offers a partial solution to the innumerable problems posed by "simple" representation. While leading to enigmatic aporias, it undoubtedly constitutes the most textually productive mimetic mode in Simon's later fiction. Inspired once again by Genette, I will call *cratylian mimetism* that relation of imitation, or possibly of identity, which from time to time seems to establish itself between the signifiers and the signifieds of certain "transparent" signs. Most often ascribed to an error of youth (and reading), Simon's mimologisms are the literal pretext of many a musing on langauge, reveries which enable the texts to produce meaning "sensually," that is, according to a logic that is situated in the very heart of the linguistic sign.

As for the fourth mimetic mode to be distinguished here, it recalls the original mimesis of Plato: direct representation of language. Here I am referring to the textual staging of graphic entities, the representation in question taking the form of a direct contact with the alleged referent. I call this mode *graphic mimetism*.[11] While it is true that direct discourse, dialogue, constitutes a verbal reality of the kind referred to here, I shall limit myself to the domain of written language, to those small texts (whether real or doubly fictitious) that depict a graphic reality claiming to be such and thereby apparently distinguishing itself from the rest of the text. Is this mimetic mode more "faithful," more "imitative," than, say, referential mimetism? What effect will the implementation of this mimetic mode have on the reader when he comes to the break (*brisure*) between the referential and the graphic? And finally, does graphic mimetism enable the text to throw off the yoke of mimesis once and for all? These are some of the questions that will be posed in the course of this journey to the land of Simonian mimetics.

To begin, then, let us consider the small drawings incorporated into the narrative fabric of *La Bataille de Pharsale*. These pictograms border on pictorial mimesis, but as they are integrated into the very topography of the text, I would rather consider them under the category of graphic mimetism and, more specifically, under that of a variant which can be called *iconic mimetism*.[12] Now it is true that the reader can verbalize them by substituting for the drawing the corresponding word (for example, *flèche*). However, it is also possible for the reader to receive these "signs" as images which need not be "translated" into a natural spoken/written language: "César la Guerre des Gaules la Guerre Civile → s'enfonçant dans la bouche ouverte clouant la langue de ce Latin langue morte." [Caesar the Gallic War the Civil War → thrusting into the open mouth nailing the tongue of that Latin dead language.]¹³

In other cases, the pictogram in question replaces a single letter, such as in this sign of a men's clothing store, where the A of *pants* is replaced by the drawing of a pair of legs and the V of *vest* by the drawing of a jacket lapel:

"Le V et la A remplacés par Comment dire: idéogrammes? LA MAISON DU ⱱESTON ET DU PⱭNTⱭLON." [The V and the A replaced by What do you call them: ideograms? LA MAISON DU ⱱESTON ET DU PⱭNTⱭLON.]¹⁴

Thus the text creates its own alphabet, or better still, its own *iconography*, for once the drawing of the legs which depicts the letter A is identified with the word *pants,* it can replace it in other contexts.¹⁵ Moreover, a hybrid text could be imagined which would border on the illegible, a text which would be composed of more and more such pictograms as each of the words of the text was replaced by another new image.

As far as the fiction is concerned, the icons in *La Bataille de Pharsale* are associated with the narrator's youth, or, if you prefer, that of the ubiquitous O. One remembers the discussion between Charles and his nephew during which the former suggests to the latter several ways to avoid using verbal signs, notably by resorting to gestures.

"Je voudrais une 🯄 et. S'exprimer par. Signes interrogés. Avant la bataille présages sacrifice aux dieux pour se concilier savoir."¹⁶ [I'd like a 🯄 and. To express yourself by. Interrogating signs. Omens before the battle sacrifices to the gods in order to gain their favor.]

It is significant that the text, binding itself to the most faithful of mimetic relations, represents a gesture by an icon, a nonverbal "sign," for the use of what I have called iconic mimetism is doubly warranted here. On the one hand, it depicts the gestural mind envisaged by Charles, a mime which is not only the oldest but also, undoubtedly, the *least imperfect* of the many kinds of mimesis attempted by man since early times. On the other hand, on the level of the story, these examples of iconic mimetism correspond to a certain "referential uneasiness" on the part of the narrator/scriptor, an uneasiness which is illustrated by the text's numerous "beginnings." Fiction and writing are interwoven as closely as possible, as though the adult narrator/scriptor were as troubled by referential language as he was as a child by his Latin translation exercises. Whether gestural mime or iconic mimetism, the relation between the "represented" and the "representing" here at least appears to be closer than in the case of referential mimetism. And yet, O. (character-narrator-scriptor) still writes even while he continues to question and challenge the very principle without which his writing would border on the nonsensical.

Graphic mimetism is not limited to the use of icons since written language may also be subjected to a typographical re-presentation: let us call it *verbal mimetism*. There are, of course, numerous ways for a text to indicate that it is representing another text, the simplest being the use of quotation marks. In Simon, however, it is most often italics or capital letters that are used to indicate the (pseudo-)citational status of a textual fragment. Now there is something fundamentally troubling about putting one text into another, as Michel Butor points out in his essay on the book as an object:

La reproduction d'une page, ou même d'une ligne à l'intérieur d'une autre page permet un découpage optique dont les propriétés sont toutes différentes de celles du découpage habituel des citations. Il sert à introduire dans le texte des tensions nouvelles, celles mêmes que nous éprouvons si souvent aujourd'hui, dans nos cités couvertes de slogans.[17]

[The reproduction of a page, or even of a line within another page, allows for an optical fragmentating whose properties are entirely different from those of the usual excerpting of quotations. It is used to introduce into the text new tensions, the very ones we feel so often today in our cities covered with slogans.]

Now consider the following passage taken from *Histoire*, which is typical of the sort of "mimetic shock" evoked by Butor:

... et de gros poissons écailleux lippus fouettant de leurs queues les vagues aux reflets de jade de rose l'écume frisée sous un nuage de feu de fumées se tordant se convulsant s'épanouissant en éclaboussures en tantacules en forme de pétales de fleurs bleues roses la tête du dragon hérissée d'une crinière de flammes de glaives les replis de son corps apparaissant et disparaissant en méandres l'espace tout entier rempli ciselé de volutes de tourbillons de viscères de tumulte nuées flammes écume poissons monstre sans un repos sans un vide ///CHOLON—Intérieur de Pagode.[18] (My division.)

... [and big scaly thick-lipped fish whipping with their tails waves with glints of jade of pink the curly foam under a cloud of fire of smoke convulsed writhing convulsing blooming into splashes into tentacles shaped like petals of blue pink flowers the head of the dragon bristling with a mane of flames of swords the wrinkles of its body appearing and disappearing into twists the entire space full chiseled into spirals into whirls of viscera into tumult clouds flames foam fish monster without a rest without a void /// CHOLON—Interior of a pagoda.]

One cannot help but be struck by the contrast between the first part of the passage, which makes use of referential mimetism, albeit of a rather special, innovative kind, and the second, much shorter part, where verbal mimetism ends the passage with its characteristic mark [*frappe*]. Moreover, it is only when the reader reaches the caption that he realizes that what he has just read is not the description of a supposedly "real" scene, but rather the description of *double* representation, the photographic reproduction of an artistic representation (painted and sculpted). The fundamental ambiguity of referentiality—the same words can describe both movement and arrested movement—as well as language's intrinsic productive capacity to generate language, are skillfully demonstrated here by Simon, as in some kind of textual exemplum. As is the case for most of the descriptions of representations, whether of a simple postcard or a famous painting by Uccello, that which is described matters far less than the production of a sequence, a *text* that acquires its own rhythm and dynamics based on an internal logic. Words leading to other words, present participles engendering, generating, and producing other present participles in a series without end. Moreover, the scene seems to be self-sufficient, constituting as it does a kind of "mini-drama" (of writing?), for the description here, as elsewhere in Simon, fulfills what is clearly a narrative function. Thus for the reader who enjoys the luxuriance of Simon's writing, the caption of the postcard may well seem "weak" and reductive. In fact, it seems to have very little to do with the (doubly) fictitious scene which the reader has (re)constructed in his imagination. At first sight, the function of verbal mimetism appears to be the staging of and the emphasis on the inadequacy of any attempt to attribute names to the unnameable, the folly, if not the outright impossibility, of any attempt to label the world. Does this mean that the verbal richness of the descriptive passage abolishes and nullifies the importance of the verbal mimetism?

It seems to me that to think so would be a careless evaluation. Here is why. In the first part of the passage just cited, the description follows the linear thread of the writing and extends itself through the text, while the perception that the narrator has of the picture on the card is, one can suppose, instantaneous. On the other hand, in the case of the caption, it deals with a quotation from a text made up of words, a literal representation of a certain number of graphemes, so that there is a close relation between the two captions, the one fictitious, the other literal. From this point of view, it is the use of verbal mimetism that appears to be the most mimetic, for our reading literally reproduces that of the narrator. Hence the importance of the means used to indicate the change from one mimetic mode to another, to underline the mimetic "break" that both cuts and unifies the text. When the reader reaches the caption in his reading of the text, it stands out from the rest of the page due to the use of capital letters. This emphasis upon the word, the name, is also an enhancing of mimesis as such. It is an unveiling of mimesis [*la mimeuse*] in front of the startled reader-spectator, for he is witness to the very process upon which representation is based. Before his very eyes, verbal mimetism performs what might be seen as an "unnatural" act, at least an unrealistic one, as it folds itself back into the word-by-word production of the text into which it merges. The interweaving of mimesis and language productivity leads to a true *textualization* of mimesis.[19]

At the same time, this folding back allows a kind of infinite mimesis, the reabsorption of mimesis into the textual fabric of the novel being reminiscent of the "readymades" of today or earlier *collages* in the domain of the visual arts. In view of this, it is certainly not by accident that a text in which graphic mimetism (both iconic *and* verbal) plays such an important part (*La Bataille de Pharsale*) was followed by *Orion aveugle*. In this text not only is a drawing by Simon himself reproduced, but also there are reproductions of works by Robert Rauschenberg, a painter who does not hesitate to "quote" other artists by integrating copies of their works into his own or to juxtapose the representation of objects with real objects.²⁰ In Simon's case, the confrontation of two types of mimetic relations, the referential and the graphic, cannot fail to have a disruptive effect on the reader. It is already known that Simon often makes use of a fictional technique by means of which images thought to be "real" are transformed into a written or figured representation, or vice versa. Such a process undoubtedly puts into question the traditional unity of the novelistic text. And yet, the passage from referential mimetism to graphic mimetism is no less disruptive [*troublant*]. In the first case, it is the fictitious referent that changes status, being either "captured" or "freed," whereas in the second case, there is a true change in the *mimetic mode* of the text. It is a little as though from an eighteenth-century portrait real blood suddenly started to flow.²¹

Now, as can be easily imagined, this change of mimetic mode is so fundamental to the functioning of the text that it could be wondered whether there is even reason to speak of mimesis in the case of graphic mimetism. Does the latter not reach a level of imitative perfection that should logically exclude the very notion of mimesis?

Le langage ne peut imiter parfaitement que du langage, ou plus précisément un discours ne peut imiter parfaitement qu'un discours parfaitement identique: bref, un discours ne peut imiter que lui-même ... l'imitation directe est, exactement, une tautologie.²²

[Language can perfectly imitate only language, or more precisely, speech can imitate only perfectly identical speech: in short, speech can only imitate itself ... direct imitation is, specifically, a tautology.]

And Genette concludes, "l'imitation parfaite n'est plus une imitation, c'est la chose même"²³ [perfect imitation is no longer an imitation, but the thing itself]. But therein lies the real interest of this type of mimetic relation: On the one hand, graphic mimetism appears to be pure imitation, a simple reproduction, while on the other hand, it seems to be pure production of language. These two aspects of mimesis, representation and reproduction, can probably be considered as inherent to all language activity—does nonfigurative language have any "meaning"?—but they are of crucial importance as far as this borderline case of mimesis is concerned.

Far from constituting a "perfect" imitation of a preexisting model, graphic mimetism in Simon very often serves to represent the precariousness of all mimetic relations. The absence of punctuation marks, ellipses, "mistakes" in spelling, the use of special type fonts and foreign alphabets, or of type reversed as though seen in a mirror, as well as the truncation of syllables essential to the restitution of a univocal meaning—all have to be mentioned. These procedures emphasize the precarious materiality of written language and the many ways in which it poses a barrier to the "simple" imitation of reality, even when that reality is textual by nature. At the same time, word play—so often associated with verbal mimetism in Simon—underscores the productivity of language as it is exploited by the text. Hence one can consider graphic mimetism as the perfect imitation only if one subscribes to the "dogma of Expression-Representation," as defined by Jean Ricardou.[24] Rather than speak of a copy or an imitation, therefore, would it not be better to speak of a *transmutation,* a notion which in the Simonian universe always has the connotation of loss? The loss in question is illustrated by the staging [*mise en oeuvre*] of deliberately deceitful (micro-) texts in which the loss is double, both referential *and* material.[25]

To say, then, that in the case of graphic mimetism, we are in the presence of the thing itself does not seem possible either. To be sure, language in Simon has a tendency to be reified, to become an artifact subject to the destruction wrought by time, and so on. And yet, this reification of language on the *thematic* level of the text must not lead to the referential error or illusion. As faithful as the work of verbal mimetism may be, it remains only that, namely, a representation that should not be confused with the "thing" itself, even when the language is of the most concrete or descriptive nature. Ultimately, the mimetic capacities of language are limited precisely to this sort of relation, language being able to represent only language which represents language, and so on. There will always be a problematic relation between a textual fragment that we read and the caption of a postcard supposedly deciphered by a character of the fictive universe, be he a first-person narrator/scriptor. For here the referent is and must remain fictitious: the words merely mime other words that are an integral part of the novelistic universe. Far from having before us a real postcard, we are in the presence of a *text* which stages through various processes and mimetic modes the parts of an entirely fictitious card, which exists only *in* and *by* language (aside from any question of extratextual stimuli). In other words, graphic mimetism poses a borderline case, one that forces us to extend simultaneously the notion of mimesis toward the twin poles of its semantic field: imitation-secondarity/creation-productivity. It is undoubtedly in this context that we ought to explain the important role accorded in Simon's texts to this folding back of mimesis onto itself. This interweaving of scription and mimesis is not surprising in a writer for whom the junction of world—including that of the world of language—and word remains forever so problematic.

That is not all, for there remains one more step to take with regard to the relations between graphic mimetism and textual productivity. Breaking the homogeneity of the text, graphic mimetism draws the reader's attention to the "strangeness" of the text, of any *text,* in contrast to all that is not both concrete *and* aesthetic. Pictograms which risk short-circuiting verbalization, "phonetic" transcriptions which require a great effort to decipher, not to mention letters printed in reverse—such are the means by which the Simonian text seeks to underscore the materiality and the specificity of written language. These procedures also allow the text to designate itself as such. This emphasis on the materiality of language is one way for the written word to become *perceptible,* sometimes audible, but most often *visible.* Claude Simon is obviously not the first writer to make use of this process: he follows in the tradition of Apollinaire and Mallarmé, a tradition that dates back to Rabelais and, still farther back, to the medieval scribes, not to mention even earlier scriptors of hieroglyphs, those makers of text and tomb. But perhaps a more interesting way to consider the process would be from the perspective of its theoretical implications. Here I am thinking specifically of the comparisons which can be drawn between the textual manifestations of mimetic language and other attempts to make the perception of the aesthetic object more "direct":

Considérer le mot comme un objet, ce serait donc (provisoirement) faire abstraction de sa signification et le traiter comme pure "réalité" phonique et/ou graphique, analogue (ou du moins parallèle) à ces réalités sonores ou plastiques que manient la musique ou la peinture.[26]

[To consider the word as an object would be, therefore, to abstract (temporarily) its signification and to treat it as a pure phonic and/or graphic "reality," analogous to (or at least parallel with) those sonorous or plastic realities handled by music or painting.]

From this point of view, the corollary of an effort to make writing *visible* is an attempt to make what is "written" *readable* in painting.[27] Simon's work is, in fact, part and parcel of "un des secteurs privilégiés de la sémiologie de la mimesis [qui] est . . . constitué par les objets hybrides, concrétions des interférences entre le texte comme écriture et le tableau comme figure"[28] [one of the privileged fields of the semiology of mimesis (which) is . . . constituted by hybrid objects, the concrete manifestations of interferences between the text as writing and the painting as figure]. To paint with words has become a cliché of a certain type of comparative discourse. And yet this is exactly what is evoked by the links and tensions that exist between visible (or pictorial) mimesis and readable (or language-constituted) mimesis. Due to this "vacillation de la lecture et de la vision"[29] [vascillating of reading and seeing], Simon's texts can be situated alongside the works of a Miró or a Rauschenberg, painters who willingly incorporate written texts into their compositions, for the ways in which Simon makes language visible rather than merely readable are characteristic of a specifically *pictorial* technique. Seeking to paint with "signs" (words, letters, and icons), he writes his texts so that they may be not only (just) read but also *seen*.

This distinction between readable and visible mimesis is not quite the same as that nonoppositional binary "opposition" established by Roland Barthes between the "lisible" [readerly] text and the "scriptible" [writerly] text.[30] And yet, given the link between the play of written forms made visible and word play in general, it can be said that there is a homological relation between the two pairs of terms. To make visible what is written is always already to take a step toward the text of bliss [*jouissance*], the writerly text. To join readable language (the break-up of the signifier) is to achieve, in the fullest sense of the word, the pleasure of the text. Graphic mimetism emphasizes the *poetic effect* (in Roman Jakobson's sense of the term)[31] of the Simonian text, since microtexts are made to stand out in all their material *strangeness,* a strangeness which ultimately reflects upon the totality of the larger textual question at stake.

Simon's novels invest so much in the problem (and problematization) of mimesis that it would not be an exaggeration to say that we are dealing with a true "Simonian mimetics." If this eternal return to the origins of mimesis never becomes boring, it is due to the astonishing variety of forms that can be effected by the mimetisms of language. Of course, this should not overshadow the fact that Simon pursues in his own very special and unique way an age-old endeavor, that of *homo faber*:

Et par la suite, tout ce qu'Adam a créé depuis ce jour, tout ce qu'il a écrit, peint, sculpté, bâti ou calculé, ça n'a jamais été que dessiner et redessiner la pomme. Aussi bien quand il en a véritablement posé trois sur une table ou dans une assiette *pour ne pas les copier mais établir à l'aide de pinceaux et de couleurs entre elles et le monde de mystérieux et irrécusables rapports,* que lorsqu'il a inscrit leur chute dans une formule.[32] [My italics.]

[And later, all that Adam created since that day, all that he wrote, painted, sculpted, built, and calculated, was never anything other than drawing and redrawing the apple. As much when he actually put three of them on a table or in a plate *in order not to copy them but to establish, with the use of brushes and colors, mysterious and irrecusable relations* between them and the world, as when he inscribed their fall in a formula.]

Mimesis is indeed an enormous problem for any lucid creator, probably the most fundamental problem in all art, hence the temptation, not to mention the necessity, to return to it incessantly. Although Simon does not theorize in his fiction, it can be said that, in one way or another, he keeps on staging the drama of this old friend/enemy of every writer, of every artist in the end: for there is only one solution to this unending battle with mimesis and that is to come to blows with it (again) by representing mimesis itself.[33]

Notes

1. Jean Ricardou and Françoise van Rossum-Guyon, eds., *Nouveau Roman: hier, aujoud'hui* (Paris: Collection 10/18, 1972), 2 vols.
2. See Jean Ricardou, *Le Nouveau Roman* (Paris: Seuil ["Ecrivains de Toujours"], 1973), 109-124.
3. See Jean Ricardou, *Nouveaux problèmes du roman* (Paris: Seuil ["Poétique"], 1978), 160.
4. Gérard Genette, *Figures II* (Paris: Seuil ["Tel Quel"], 1969), 184.
5. *Ibid.,* 53-54.
6. Cf. "sauf présence d'éléments discriminants dans le contexte, 'représenter un homme' offre la même ambiguïté que *mimeisthai anthrôpon,* alors que la traduction traditionnelle par 'imiter' sélectionne abusivement l'interprétation de l'accusatif comme celui du modèle." [Unless there are discriminant elements in the context, "to represent a man" has the same ambiguity as *mimeisthai anthrôpon,* while its traditional translation as "to imitate" improperly selects the interpretation of the accusative as that of the model.] Translator's note in Aristotle, *La Poétique. Le texte grec avec une traduction et des notes de lecture par Roselyne Dupont-Roc et Jean Lallot* (Paris: Seuil ["Poétique"], 1980), 145.
7. See Julia Kristeva, *La Révolution du langage poétique* (Paris: Seuil ["Tel

Quel"], 1974), and Jacques Derrida, "La double séance," *La Dissémination* (Paris: Seuil ["Tel Quel"], 1972), 199-318.

8. Paul Ricoeur, *La Métaphore vive* (Paris: Seuil ["L'Ordre philosophique"], 1975), 54. Cf. "C'est donc par un grave contresens que la *mimesis* aristotélicienne a pu être confondue avec l'imitation au sens de copie. Si la *mimesis* comporte une référence initiale au réel, cette référence ne distingue pas autre chose que le règne même de la nature sur toute production. Mais ce mouvement de référence est inséparable de la dimension créatrice. La *mimesis* est *poiesis*, et réciproquement." (*Ibid.*, 56).

[It was due to a serious mistranslation, therefore, that the Aristotelian *mimesis* was confused with imitation in the sense of copy. If *mimesis* includes an initial reference to the real, this reference does not distinguish something other than the very reign of nature over all production. And this movement of reference cannot be separated from the creative dimension. *Mimesis* is *poiesis*, and vice versa.]

9. For the word *significance*, see the very fine article by Roland Barthes, "Texte (Théorie du)," *Encyclopaedia universalis* (1973).

10. "Se dit de toutes les formes d'imitation, considérées dans leurs caractères généraux, et des rassemblances qu'elles produisent." André Lalande, *Vocabulaire technique et critique de la philosophie* (Paris: Presses Universitaires de France, 1968 [1926]), 627. [It is said of all forms of imitation, considered in their general nature, and the likenesses they produce.]

11. Among the numerous studies on the role of the referent in literature, I will mention only two: George Lavis, "Le texte littéraire, le référent, le réel, le vrai," *Cahiers d'analyse textuelle*, 13 (1971), 7-22; Maurice-Jean Lefebve, *Structure du discours de la poésie et du récit* (Neuchâtel: A la Baconnière, 1971), 23, 55, 99, 106-119. The reader is referred to the very fine study by Lucien Dällenbach on self-referentiality: *Le Recit spéculaire: Essai sur la mise en abyme* (Paris: Seuil ["Poétique"], 1977). See, in particular, his analysis of two novels by Claude Simon, pp. 171-173 and 193-200, as well as the section entitled "De la reproduction à la production," pp. 200-208. With regard to the notion of "mimologism," the reader is referred to Gérard Genette's study: *Mimologiques. Voyage en Cratylie* (Paris: Seuil ["Poétique"], 1976). For another approach to what I call *graphic mimetism*, see William Wimsatt, "In Search of Verbal Mimesis," *Yale French Studies*, 52 (1975), 229-248.

12. The term is borrowed from Charles Pierce's vocabulary: "l'*icone* est ce qui exhibe la même qualité, ou la même configuration de qualités, que l'objet dénoté, par exemple une tache noire pour la couleur noire: les onomatopées; les diagrammes qui reproduisent des relations entre propriétés" (Oswald Ducrot and Tzvetan Todorov, *Dictionnaire encyclopédique des sciences du langage* [Paris: Seuil, 1972], 115). [The *icon* is that which displays the same quality, or the same configuration of qualities, as the denoted object, for instance, a black spot for the color black: onomatopoeias, the diagrams which reproduce the relations between properties.]

13. Claude Simon, *La Bataille de Pharsale* (Paris: Minuit, 1969), 18. English translation: *The Battle of Pharsalus,* trans. Richard Howard (London: George Braziller, Inc., 1971), 9.

14. *Ibid.*, 21. English translation, 11.

15. Cf. Dard dans la bouche mort dans l'âme je ne savais pas. Sans parler de mots comme passion ou amour même écrits avec un p ou un a miniscules et au pluriel tout juste bons à faire ricaner. Je ne savais pas encore un certain nombre de nécessités pas encore eaux mortes langue morte parler par signes je voudrais une 👕 et un 👖 à pont à fermature éclair à braguette espèce de tuyau mou pendant prolongement fragile d'organes tièdes intérieurs dard rose ceinture dégrafée tombant en accordéon sur les mollets alors rouge vif dressé. *Ibid.*, 22.
[Arrow in the mouth sick at heart I didn't know. Not to mention words like passion or love even written with a capital P or L in the plural barely enough to draw a sneer. I didn't yet know a certain number of necessities not yet dead secret dead language speaking in sign language I'd like a 👕 and a 👖 with a zipper fly a kind of soft tube hanging fragile extension of the warm internal organs pink arrow belt unbuckled hanging, in accordian folds down the calves then bright red erect.] English trans., 12.

16. *Ibid.*, 44. English trans., 27.

17. Michel Butor, *Essais sur le roman* (Paris: Gallimard ["Idées"], 1969), 155.

18. Claude Simon, *Histoire* (Paris: Minuit, 1967), 258.

19. See my forthcoming study, *Claude Simon: les earrefours du texte*.

20. Cf. the reproductions of "Charlene" and "Canyon" in Claude Simon, *Orion aveugle* (Geneva: Skira ["Les Sentiers de la Création"], 1970), 49, 59.

21. Cf. "la tache qui s'étalait, verticale et déchiquetée, à partir de la tempe, descendait sur le cou délicat, presque féminin dans l'échancrure de la chemise, venait souiller la veste de chasse, n'était plus maintenant la préparation rougeâtre de la toile mise à nu par la peinture écaillée, mais quelque chose de sombre et grumeleux s'écoulant lentement, comme si, à travers un trou pratiqué dans le tableau, on avait pressé par derrière une sorte de confiture épaisse et sombre qui glissait, dégoulinait peu à peu sur la surface lisse de la peinture" (Claude Simon, *La Route des Flandres* [Paris: Minuit, 1960], 74).
[The spot which spread, vertical and jagged, from the temple, along the delicate, almost feminine neck, through the neckline of the shirt and on down to spoil the hunting jacket was now no longer the reddish sizing of the canvas uncovered by the chipped painting, but something dark and lumpy flowing slowly, as if a kind of thick and dark jam slipping and trickling gradually along the smooth surface of the painting had been squeezed behind it through a hole made in the canvas.]

22. Gérard Genette, *Figures II*, 55. In Aristotle, the pleasure of *mimesis* does not come from the represented thing as such, but from the fact that we *recognize* in the image in question the representation of a previously known natural object. The mimetic pleasure is to be found in the very difference that distinguishes the thing from the human artifact, a product of poetic *mimesis*. Descartes observed the following: " 'il faut au moins remarquer qu'il n'y a aucunes images qui doivent *en tout* ressembler aux objets qu'elles représentent: car autrement, il n'y aurait point de distinction entre l'objet et son image' " (cited by Louis Marin, *Etudes sémiologiques, Ecritures, peintures* [Paris: Klincksieck, 1971], 75). [It must at least

be noted that there are no images that look *entirely* like the objects they represent: otherwise, there would be no distinction between the object and its image.]

23. Genette, *Figures II*, 56.

24. Jean Ricardou, *Pour une théorie du Nouveau Roman* (Paris: Seuil ["Tel Quel" series], 1971), 20-22. It goes without saying that the presence in Simon's work of different kinds of mimetisms does not make them "representational" works, in Ricardou's sense of the term, any more than artistic works, moreover, which play with the effects produced by the juxtaposition of different processes of visual *mimesis* would be considered traditional figurative works.

25. I am referring to the fragmented citing of advertising slogans in *Les Corps conducteurs* (Paris: Minuit, 1971), 158; of novels in *La Bataille de Pharsale*, 178; of election posters in *Histoire*, 215.

26. Genette, *Mimologiques*, 296.

27. See Michel Butor, *Les Mots dans la peinture* (Geneva: Skira ["Les Sentiers de la Creation"], 1969).

28. Marin, *Etudes sémiologiques*, 10.

29. *Ibid.*, 72.

30. See Roland Barthes, *S/Z* (Paris: Seuil ["Tel Quel"], 1970), 9-12, as well as *Le Plaisir du texte* (Paris: Seuil ["Tel Quel"], 1973), 82-83.

31. Roman Jakobson, *Essais de linguistique générale* (Paris: Minuit, 1963), 218-219.

32. Claude Simon, *Le Sacre du printemps* (Paris: Calmann-Levy, 1954), 263.

33. Cf. "il n'y a qu'un remède, infiniment précaire, et dangereux, instable, contre la représentation: la représentation elle-même." Philippe Lacoue-Labarthe, "Typographie," *Mimesis des articulations* (Paris: Aubier-Flammarion ["La philosophie en effet" series], 1975), 247. [There is only one remedy, infinitely precarious and dangerous, shaky, against representation: representation itself.]

Discussion

Leon Roudiez: I would like to express a slight and friendly disagreement with what Claude Simon said at the beginning of his text. It concerns the worrisome problem of the relation between theory and practice. I think that if there were an error—and, as far as I know, neither Claude Simon nor Alain Robbe-Grillet, neither Robert Pinget nor Nathalie Sarraute, has committed this error—if there were an error, it was made by those writers who imagined that they had to believe and apply what the theoreticians said, while writers really do not have to be concerned with theoreticians. They have only to let the theoreticians say what they wish while they go on doing what they had to do. It is the theoreticians who have to worry about what the writers are doing. If, after having constructed a theory based on certain texts, other texts appear which contradict this theory, it is not up to the theoreticians to find fault with these texts. Rather, the theoreticians must admit that there is something wrong in this theory and modify it. In short, to repeat something of what Lacan said about Marguerite Duras—and here I quote from memory, so I paraphrase rather than quote—"Elle sait sans avoir suivi mes séminaires ce que j'enseigne" [She knows without having attended my lectures what I teach]. Lacan was only making more specific what Freud had said earlier in a more general way: that everywhere the artist precedes the psychoanalyst. It can be generated as well that the artist precedes all theoreticians.

Alain Robbe-Grillet: I would like to go a little further than Leon Roudiez's comments about Claude Simon's lecture. Claude Simon said that he is here due to a misunderstanding. Wherever a writer is, it is always due to a misunderstanding. It is obvious that the writer is someone without a place. His only place is his work, and perhaps not even that. And when he accepts an invitation to a gathering like this, it is under a heading such as that of the

"Nouveau Roman." It is obvious that this cannot be but a misunderstanding.

On the other hand, Claude Simon's entire presentation made me think that the misunderstanding in this case is very slight, as all that he said about his preoccupations may really be considered a theory of the New Novel. For me, his text is a kind of manifesto for this vague thing, moving and changing over the course of time and people, which may be called the New Novel. All that he said about "realism," his visible hatred of traditional "realism," is already a common denominator.

I would like, therefore, to add a couple of things to those upon which Claude Simon touched. Flaubert himself hated the term "realism" and Flaubert denied the idea of there having been a model for *Madame Bovary,* a piece of news read in the papers. All Flaubert specialists know that there were numerous models for *Madame Bovary.* For Flaubert, as for Claude Simon and myself, information did come from the outside world, various facts or experiences like that of Claude Simon in Barcelona or in Flanders. But it is obvious that for Flaubert, as for Claude Simon and myself, what matters is the actual construction of something. So the New Novel does not date back merely to the end of the nineteenth century, as Simon said, but perhaps even to the middle, when Flaubert was first published.

As for Dostoevski, if he is rarely mentioned in this context, it is precisely because, for us, he already belongs, more or less, to the twentieth century. And it is obvious that a novel such as *The Possessed* could already be considered a magnificent example of what the lack, the hole, or the absence represents in a work. The central character of *The Possessed,* Stavroguine, is absent from the story. He is almost never seen. He is always somewhere else. He is in Switzerland. He is in Germany. We know of him only by what others say of him. At times he appears center stage where he does things that no one understands. The other characters wonder why he did whatever it was that he did and, at the end of the novel, what is magnificent is that, having decided at last to explain himself, he makes his confession to the Bishop Tikhone. It is not even at the end of the novel, for when the novel was published, the editor eliminated a chapter—now called "Stavroguine's Confession"—and when this chapter was added back, it was put at the end of the book. Therefore it is in the wrong place in the story: there is a chapter at the end which is "Stavroguine's Confession" and yet, in the book, he is already dead. The editor did not know where to put it since the chapters had been numbered successively, so he just put it at the end.

This chapter is very strange because when Stavroguine makes his confession to the Bishop Tikhone, he tears out a page. The Bishop asks him if he wants to make a confession, if he wants to say why he tore out a page, and Stavroguine says that it is because he does not yet know whether the other deserves to read it. Thus the text gives what the Bishop reads without the page in question, and the novel ends with this extremely curious paragraph where the narrator says that it is not very important whether or not he tore out a page because, as he has continually lied during his entire life, he probably lied in his confession as well, including in the torn-out page. There is an early example of a phenomenon typical of the New Novel: the character who is a hole in the text. When the nineteenth century is spoken of facilely and in generalities, as I have already pointed out, it does not even include all of Balzac's work.

The name Ricardou hardly appeared in Claude Simon's presentation, but it was nevertheless present. It was the absent name. Simon did pronounce it at least once, at the end, but for a very long time only the initiated could know that it was Ricardou who was to be read between the lines. Ricardou has an extremely interesting personality, a fascinating one. Roughly speaking, Ricardou, Claude Simon, and I can be said to have been urged to say things which we ourselves did not want to say. By this I mean that in all that is of theoretical interest for literature, some things immediately appear to us as wrong and at the same time as interesting. And I almost think that it is more important that they be interesting than true. Ricardou was the one who accepted to theorize very explicitly about totally outrageous things having to do with the author disappearing from his work and the construction of the text. Yet Ricardou must not be reproached for that. These things had to be said. The only thing for which Ricardou can be criticized is that he believed that it was all true and that he had again founded as a kind of established order this "Nouveau Roman" which did not want to be an established order, but rather an order unceasingly moving, searching, remaking, and contradicting itself.

If, after some time, Claude Simon and I rejected Ricardou, it was actually because he said that he had become our leader. Obviously this is not a reason to think that Ricardou's works and theories are useless. In fact they are very useful—for knowing which excesses are to be avoided! But excesses are necessary. They are the landmarks that continually blaze our trails. We invariably move forward between excesses, between two rows of excesses. We come from one excess and we go on to another.

At the present time, we are obviously further along. By this I mean that other excesses are now necessary and that those are historically outdated. But Claude Simon insisted on the fact that he had not had any moral plan in writing his book and particularly not that of fighting the established order. The mere fact that he noisily broke with Ricardou shows, however, that he does fight the established order since he did not like people to establish an order of the Nouveau Roman. And, generally speaking, his fighting of the established order appeared continully throughout his lecture, particularly when he opposed to this established order the pleasure principle. (The criticism of the 1960s and 1970s speaks more readily of this "pleasure.") This is also very clearly demonstrated in the article by Leo Bersani called "Le Réalisme et la peur du désir," where Bersani precisely shows that realism rejects desire, afraid that it might endanger this established order supported by realism. I believe that to present pleasure or desire as the single force able to move the writer already sets him up as an opponent, as a subversive, as someone who does not want to remain in line.

I would also, and this will be my last point, like to speak in defense of Sartre (having done so for Ricardou). I understand very well that what I said about Sartre may have shocked some of you. *Le Monde* had asked me to write an article on Sartre since I had often said that I owed so much to him. I had given this article a title that was a reference to a famous article which you all know, in *Situations I,* called "Monsieur François Mauriac et la liberté," where Sartre specifically opposes the character of Stavroguine to that of Thérèse Desqueyroux. I had entitled my article "Monsieur Jean-Paul Sartre et la liberté," saying how François Mauriac's ghost must have been laughing when he read Jean-Paul Sartre's last novels. *Le Monde* changed my title and put in its place "Les Héritiers de *La Nausée,* c'est nous." Now obviously Nathalie Sarraute could protest, since she had started writing long before *La Nausée* was published and also since Sartre's later opinions were entirely unacceptable, and particularly to us. All that he wrote in *Qu'est-ce que la littérature?* and his novels after *La Nausée* evolved in a way that could not at all be that of the New Novel. I pointed out in this article that in spite of everything there was a reason why Sartre, at this colloquium in Leningrad to which I had gone with Nathalie Sarraute, had introduced us as, all in all, the true existentialist novelists. Sartre recognized in writers such as Butor, Simon, Sarraute, and myself people who put in their texts the existential freedom of which he had spoken—the theory of existential freedom such as it appeared in his theoretical works of the 1930s and 1940s and which started to emerge in the world of the novel with *La Nausée*—and on whose aspirations he had reproached the post-nineteenth-century novel for trampling.

It is evident that Sartre's work is extremely polymorphous and polysemous and that we can always do whatever we want with it, given that he so readily contradicted himself. But he was for us, at least for me, the introducer in France of German philosophy, not only that of Husserl and Heidegger, but of Hegel as well, who very few people (among the amateurs) knew before having read Sartre. People started to read Husserl and Heidegger, but Sartre was this ferment. And here, too, I think that if I am so interested in Sartre's ideas, it is because I do not feel at all compelled to consider them true. Sartre was really the one who was always wrong about everything and yet, in always being wrong about everything, he was, in my opinion, one of the ferments of the literary and intellectual—though fortunately not political—life of France in those years.

Lucien Dällenbach: I was fascinated by Claude Simon's presentation, and I think that one of the key points of the colloquium might well be that of fragmentation, since Alain Robbe-Grillet also spoke of that yesterday. What I found very interesting is that fragmentation in Claude Simon's work was seen in a perspective of continuity, that which sounds, in fact, very surprising to those who are at all familiar with theories of fragmentation in a modernist perspective. In this regard, therefore, I confess that, despite Robbe-Grillet's obviously very enlightening explanations, I find it difficult to understand this Sartrian paternity, as it seems to me that Sartre is *the* man of totalization par excellence. Alain Robbe-Grillet spoke of the dangers of Ricardou's theory, and it seems to me that there is an enormous one in linking oneself to the Sartrean tradition. It also seems to me that if fiction exercises the logic of paradoxical compatibilities, perhaps we ought to at least be cautious as far as these paternities are concerned. In any case, personally, I was surprised, a little shocked, and I think that the scope of this discussion could be extended to something I believe to be essential: namely, the relation between order and disorder in the text and the relation between the text and its environment, that which was alluded to both by Claude Simon and Alain Robbe-Grillet yesterday. I think that it would be very important to examine this point more closely.

Alain Robbe-Grillet: I will respond immediately to this point because it is one which, fortunately, will bring Sartre and Claude Simon closer together. You have all read *La Nausée* and you know that the central character, Roquentin, is collecting rare and contradictory papers concerning the life of the Marquis de Rollebon. Now Claude Simon says: "It's not my fault if they are fragments. I had my grandfather's papers. Obviously, there were some missing. . . . There were holes." But this is precisely what fascinated him! There were holes and there were pieces that overlapped. There were things that perhaps could not be dated, and this is because he was dealing with a human existence, that of a character who may have existed — who probably did exist in the case of Simon's ancestor, though it is less sure for the Marquis de Rollebon — but who was certainly present, just like those appearances and disappearances of Stavroguine mentioned in regard to *The Possessed*.

Now what is *La Nausée*? It is the story of someone who, at the beginning, is in the familiar world; Roquentin is supposedly living in harmony with the world. Later we have some doubts about that harmony but, in short, one day he presumably picks up a pebble and all of a sudden he feels this phenomenon of strangeness. He supposedly then questions everything that he has been doing at the library in an effort to assemble the Marquis de Rollebon's papers, to create an existence out of them. His plan at the beginning was to be a historian, like Balzac in a sense, to write a more or less novelized life of Rollebon which would be accurate, real, and in keeping with the truth about this individual. And, little by little, the hero's entire experience in *La Nausée* becomes the experience of one who, grappling with fragments, is fascinated by the fact that these *are* fragments and that he is facing the impossibility of assembling them as a totality without being a "salaud."[1]

But actually, Sartre very early on chose to be a "salaud" and this is what I was saying in the article in question: that, contrary to *La Nausée*, he began to imagine an entire totalitarian system which is his philosophy. In Leningrad that year, I had endless discussions with him specifically about this principle of totality. I concluded from these discussions that he was, indeed, the last great philosopher of the nineteenth century, apart from the fact that, except for *La Nausée*, he never finished any of his books. (After *La Nausée*, Sartre continually undertook series of great works: First it was a series of novels, *Les Chemins de la liberté* [*The Roads to Freedom*]; he stopped in the middle. Whether *La Critique de la raison dialectique* [*Critique of Dialectical Reason*] or the *Flaubert*, all his great investigative works were experiences which led to incompletion, and it seems to me that this is really a significant phenomenon of unfulfilled totality that brings him directly to modernity itself.

François Jost: I find Ralph Sarkonak's text very interesting because, indeed, it poses a very crucial problem, a problem which, as you said, Ralph Sarkonak, literature has been facing since its beginning: namely, its relation to the world, the problem of mimesis. There is, however, something which troubled me a little in what you said and I would like to ask you a question about it. You spoke of the relation of the text to the world and you described four kinds of referential mimetisms. But I think that to try to work on an immediate relation between language and the writer's world is to economize on something else; namely, the story. It seems impossible to me to work on the mimetic relations of language to the world while avoiding this specificity of fiction which is the story. Now the story implies a certain number of laws, constructions, determinations which have nothing to do with the determinations at work only in language. The literary story is not an amplification of language, but a specific use of language (just as geography, history, or certain sciences are other uses of language). It does not seem to me to be possible to work directly on the relation which language maintains with the world.

Many theoreticians have tried to solve this problem. It is one with which they have always clashed and it is one which still persists. I think that this is what Philippe Hamon showed rather well in an article entitled "Le Discours contraint" published in *Poétique* a few years ago.[2] He said that realism is precisely never the relation between the work and the world. It is possible to speak of literary realism only in alluding to a specific period when a certain number of laws were used as codes to make people believe in the mimetism of fiction. In the same way, the New Novel inevitably speaks of the world, for it must speak of the world, but there again we cannot make this qualificative leap from fiction to the world itself. There are surely procedures in Claude Simon or in other writers of the Nouveau Roman which either give the reader a certain impression of mimetism or, on the contrary, do not give him this impression of mimetism. But these are specifically literary procedures which cannot be studied, in my opinion, by quickly leaping over to Cratylus' side in the argument which opposes Hermogenes to Cratylus in Plato's work.

It would appear that we should also reintroduce, if we wish to work on the problem of mimetism in Claude Simon or, more generally, in literature, what are called possible worlds, that which I spoke of yesterday. What holds a fiction together and gives it a consistency? It is not that language more or less imitates things—more or less, and for me rather less—but rather the fact that fiction has a certain number of laws that vary from book to book, from author to author, and which render a book coherent. This is a problem which is beginning to be somewhat clarified (and I am thinking specifically of Umberto Eco's book on the reader in the fable[3] which is extremely interesting in this respect), but which is much more able to be clarified in worlds belonging to a "genre"—fantasy, for example—than in the contradictory worlds brought into play by the New Novels.

A second minor comment on the fourth mimetism, the one you call "graphic mimetism." It seems to me that you use the phrase "graphic mimetism" in a rather different sense than Genette.[4] Gérard Genette speaks of graphic mimetism with regard to several writers, Claudel among them, and he shows that certain writers thought that words imitated things. Let us take an example: Claudel thought that the word "toît" [roof] was well formed because there were two walls, there was the o which was obviously the woman, the i which was the man, and the circumflex accent which enclosed them both.[5] He also considered the word "locomotive," in which the l expressed the smoke, the o's expressed the wheels, and the whole word was underlined to imitate the track. Various writers have done this sort of thing.

Let us note in passing that Ricardou himself, in his last book, explains that *La Prise de Constantinople* brings into play the struggle between a man and a woman, and that is why he calls it *La Prise/ La Prose,* the i being the male constituent and the o the female constituent. (I do not know whether Ricardou realized that he was returning to Claudel. This would surprise him in any case. I will tell him sometime.) It does not seem to me, therefore, that the intervention of those pictograms in Simon's texts should be linked with a "graphic mimetism." Rather, they are pictograms, as you said, signs that do not speak for something else, but which are simply signs that tend to depict the object itself. They are not graphic signs of language. In a way, when I see the pants or the jacket drawn in Simon's text, I can imagine that they are simply smaller than those that Simon is describing. In any case, they are no longer language signs. This seems to me to really be the subject of a study not of mimetism, but rather of what I specifically called, in a 1976 text, the "picto-roman" [picto-novel].[6]

Indeed, a certain number of writers, particularly over the last ten years, are seeking to work in conjunction with painting or graphic representation. This presents a problem which is not a problem of imitation, if you will, but a problem of structure: What can be done with these fragments?, as Claude Simon might ask. How can I play with them? In fact, the writer becomes a bit of a painter and the painter participates in writing. This is a problem which for me is no longer a problem of language, but one which would be much closer to the problem that a filmmaker might encounter when he works on language, since he both makes dialogues and uses images.

The filmmaker is always obliged to work simultaneously on two aspects: on the one hand, the image, and on the other, the dialogue. It so happens that in literary tradition these two systems of signs have always been clearly separate. Philippe Hamon, in "Un Discours contraint," shows precisely that one of the dogmas of literary realism is to ensure that whenever there is an illustration, there is no break with the text. In the nineteenth-century novel, illustration tries to stick as closely as possible to what is told. What specifically becomes problematic in the New Novel is the fact that while illustrations are integrated within the work, these illustrations become conflictual with it. This is a situation that comes much closer to the problems of the audiovisual arts, of film, than to purely linguistic problems.

Ralph Sarkonak: As far as the study of the story is concerned, of course the one does not preclude the other. I conceive of the situation as follows: What would constitute the residue of an analysis of the story would be those graphics I spoke of, this iconic and verbal mimetism. It is obvious that the entire question of what I called referential mimetism, which includes the story, must be studied according to narratological criteria. There I think that we completely agree. It seems to me, however, that something happens which exceeds the mere narrative dimension and which is therefore worth being considered. I am referring to textual phenomena which, on the most manifest level, the reader literally cannot miss, for they are visual processes which shape the text in its most material layers. In a way, it may be said that "pure" graphics continually sabotages, undermines the story, as achronological as it may be, for it is a deconstruction of mimesis which is much more disruptive of a linear reading and even of any reading at all. That is why I think that we can and even must look into such mimetic *and* textual phenomena once the analysis of the story is done. And although there still remains much to be said about the story—since the appearance of the remarkable works of Jean Ricardou, whose enormous contribution to the study of the New Novel I wish to stress, and of others as well—we are beginning to understand the innovative processes at work in Simon's works, at least those prior to *Les Géorgiques,* which is a very fine text and one which must be closely studied.

To return to your question, I alluded not only to Genette's study on cratylisms, *Mimologiques,* but also to *Frontières du récit,* where he tries to define the story by distinguishing it from description and from narration. Of course, cratylism would be one of the mimetic categories. In Simon, there are a certain number of mimologisms which, most often, are ascribed to an error of youth, to a kind of "poor reading" of a narrator who is still at the stage of an apprenticeship to language, if you will, and who has not yet reached the stage of scriptural production where the narration itself of those supposed "errors" bears witness precisely to this scriptural production. In *La Bataille de Pharsale,* O. deconstructs the word "libidineux" [libidinous] into *lit, bite,* and *noeud* ["the word libidinous with its odd consonance, suggesting the word lip and the word bitten, a rubbery emotion, so to speak"],[7] for instance. And in this way, all of a sudden, certain words are seemingly struck with a transparency that Genette called mimophonic and that is innate within the signs themselves. There are not an enormous number of examples, but there are some, and they are extremely significant in the context of the overall construction of these texts. Therefore, it is one of the mimetics which I outlined; it is important, but it is far from being the only one, for it takes its place alongside the referential, autoreferential, and graphic mimetisms.

Lucien Dällenbach: I confess that I was somewhat surprised to hear Ralph Sarkonak's presentation after that of Claude Simon. It seems to me that some of the things that you have just said are incompatible with what we first heard. I think that the word "mimesis" is very dangerous and that in the way you use it, as this literal mimesis, you too quickly cover a lot of ground and thereby run the risk of driving the text back toward an impasse from which the New Novel has been striving to escape since its birth. Moreover, you say that mimesis may also designate a productive activity. In that case, I think that the word "praxis" is less ambiguous than mimesis used in this sense. I personally would not use the word mimesis. Whether we like it or not, it refers to an idea of a model, and literature is distinctive in producing its own model. I do not deny that there is a mimetic activity in literature, but it is precisely the relation to the model which is problematic, as this model is created by literature itself. Thus, like François Jost, moreover, I think that if there is a Simonian mimesis or mimetics, it may not be on the order of language. I would see it in terms not of the relation of the text to the external world, but in terms of the relation of the productive subject to another subject, that which is thematicized in Simon by way of a double—a more advanced, more perfect ancestor or relative (either through marriage or adoption) whom the author tries to imitate—the relation of imitation, of emulation, to one whose life he tries to piece together from scraps. This would appear to be more interesting because we are dealing with the issue of the identity of the subject, the subject being able to be constituted only by means of another, by proxy.

Thus we have the very, very critical issue of the double in Simon where we find the explanation for several phenomena: attachment, for instance, the Simonian fascination for certain objects—paintings or others—not insofar as a referential relation would seem very important but insofar as it becomes, in this perspective, a question of transitional objects, in a sense, like the Simonian text, objects which are ferments, supports, of thinking, of dreaming. I think, therefore, that speaking of a Simonian mimetics should lead us first to conceive of Simonian writing as an imaginary activity. On that level, there would be a first transference relayed to or worked on by a second transference, if you will. I would insist on this transferential rather than mimetic activity which is the work done by Simon on language, on words, and which operates precisely within this first imaginary transference. And it is in this perspective, it seems to me, that we might renew the question of imitation and tie up this debate, which is really very close to the debate on realism.

Ralph Sarkonak: First of all, I completely disagree with your conclusion. I did not mention realism and for good reason. I refer you to the well-known article by Roman Jakobson where he demonstrates that the word realism is redefined by each generation of writers and commentators for their own purpose. It is perhaps now time to get rid of it, particularly in view of the works of Roland Barthes and Jacques Derrida that have so skillfully shown that the only reality of the text is the reality of language. Remember that the first New Novel was also said, and I think a little naively, to be "realistic." I think that the word mimesis, on the other hand, is far more useful, more functional, for it links us, as I said at the beginning of my talk, to a very old—yet very current—textual, critical, and theoretical issue. The similarities among the different New Novelists have often been discussed. In my opinion, it is now time that we study what differentiates each of them, on the one hand, and, on the other, what the resemblances are between the New Novels and other very short texts. That is why I began with this somewhat polemical opening which, I hope, did not shock you.

As far as the doublings are concerned, it is quite evident that what I called autoreferential mimetism touches on the question of textual doubling, a question that you yourself have studied from the point of view of "mise en abyme" [autoreflexivity], whether it be the doubling of fiction, of statement, or whatever. There I agree with you completely. What intrigues me about the question of mimesis is that it is specifically not to be posed in banal terms by saying that text "imitates" reality. And Simon's texts have taught us well that reality is a pretense, a lure, a construction, a production from the start. Even in Simon's first texts, there is always an element of *making*, of *producing*. What interests me, in the last analysis, is this withdrawal of mimesis into the very substance of language, this reabsorption which brings us back to the first question. I agree completely that the word mimesis may be dangerous, as you said, but I also believe that dangerous words are to be used, if only to situation the debate on a more general level. The New Novel proved itself long ago. It is now time to compare it with other texts said to be mimetic to see in what ways they differ and in what ways they are similar. What, in fact, is at stake is literality, and this is not limited, it must be said, only to the New Novel. Obviously, when it is a matter of a withdrawal of mimesis into the text, both by fictional doublings and autoreflexivities ["mises en abyme"], which do not cease to short-circuit each other, it is a far more complicated mimesis than a mimesis conceived as self-evident. But I think that it is in studying certain textual phenomena, including graphic mimetism, under this theoretical rubric, that we just might come to better understand this mimesis which claims to be self-evident, but which, of course, never is. Studying the so-called conventional novel with the New Novel as a point of departure, one can better understand how the former deconstructs, in a sense, before our very eyes, for to read is always to reread and to reread, above all, the ancients starting with the moderns. That is why I wanted to situate the debate on a more general level than is usually done at colloquia on the New Novel.

Question: I am interested in the comment made by François Jost, who tried, in a sense, to invalidate your analysis, Ralph Sarkonak, by a kind of Lévi-Straussian argument which claims that we all have separate languages inside our own intellectual discourse that we all really know to be the same intellectual discourse because we are having it right now. To say, therefore, that there is a language of geography, a language of history, and so on, is true if one wants to speak in those terms, but we also know that intellectual culture in the Western world has a common language and that we can decide what sort of culture of language we wish to utilize to exclude or include something. In so doing, Jost negated your rather Platonic analysis, irritating to anyone wanting to be modern.

This is of particular interest to me insofar as it relates to Alain Robbe-Grillet's claim that he cannot be "completely revolutionary." And the reason that I find your analysis interesting, even if it is irritating to many, is because in order to make a new word in intellectual discourse, one cannot, as Robbe-Grillet said, invent it, pull it out of the sky, just like that. Other words must be used, an alchemy must be made, to produce a new meaning which would make it revolutionary and would constitute a break with the past. The problem, therefore, is that one has to choose something that has a model, which, in other words, comes from the past, before one can try to break the model away from the past. I do not think that the New Novel can make its own model, as Lucien Dällenbach claims, for then one could be "completely revolutionary." And I think that, in a sense, both of your positions are necessary for a true appreciation of the present situation. Thus, while I found Ralph Sarkonak's talk very interesting, I also think that if we stood further back, we would see that both positions can be useful to us as we reflect on the New Novel.

Question: I would like to ask Claude Simon a question that concerns both the history of painting and of writing in our century. You spoke of the Impressionists, of the year 1913, and of "l'objet réel" [the ready-made object], and I think that there is one French painter whom you neglected to mention, Marcel Duchamp, who, in 1917, designated as art the most famous "ready-made object" in the history of twentieth-century art: this was his famous urinal that he signed R. MUTT. I would like to hear you comment on the work of Duchamp.

Claude Simon: It is amusing that you ask me specifically about Duchamp. You perhaps know that a rather old work of his was exhibited several years ago in Philadelphia, if I am not mistaken, one which had never been shown and which was seen there for the first time. It consisted of a barn door whose wall had a hole drilled in it, through which, in looking intently, one could see inside a naked woman laying on her back. Now, in *Triptyque,* published about a year before this exhibit, I had described a curiously similar scene, except that instead of a hole in the door, there was a slit between two boards. But to get back to your question about the urinal, when Duchamp, in the same way, displayed on the moquette of an art gallery an ordinary bottle dryer, such as is normally found in a wine cellar, he did nothing, it seems to me, other than to implement this definition of a "literary fact" (valid as well for any artistic fact) given by Shlovski, one which seems to me exemplary, namely: "Le transfert d'un objet de sa zone de perception habituelle dans la sphère d'une nouvelle perception" [The transference of an object from its habitual zone of perception to the realm of a new perception]. I tried elsewhere to show to what degree this definition is illustrated by Proust's description of the fish found on the dining-room table of the Grand Hôtel of Balbec where the young Marcel has lunch with his grandmother. It is a long sentence which ends with these words: "polychrome cathédrale de la mer" [polychromatic cathedral of the sea]. I will not undertake to relate it in detail here (it is, by itself, of such richness that we find in it a true "mise en abyme" [autoreflexivity] of the *Jeunes filles*), but one can follow step by step the process by which this fish is wrenched from its "zone of perception," its context in the "real world" (Proust enumerates it explicitly: table, knives, forks, and so on), to be transferred or rather transported (need we be reminded that transport, in Greek, is metaphora?) into an entirely different context where (among others) concepts of prehistory, architecture, construction, and so on emerge.

Notes

1. Translators' note: The term "salaud" has been variously translated as "bastard" or "swine." It, of course, was used by Sartre to denote the existential notion of the individual who functions according to the determination and acceptance of others.

2. Philippe Hamon, "Le Discours contraint," *Poétique,* 16 (Paris: Seuil, 1973).

3. Umberto Eco, *Lector in fabula* (Milan: Bompiani, 1979).

4. Gérard Genette, *Mimologiques* (Paris: Seuil, 1976).

5. Genette points out that Claudel stressed this mimetism "au moyen d'une graphie plus évocatrice: toît" [by using a more evocative written form: toît] *Mimologiques,* 342).

6. François Jost, "Le Picto-roman," *Revue d'esthétique,* 4 (Paris: U.G.E. collection 10/18, 1976).

7. Claude Simon, *La Bataille de Pharsale* (Paris: Minuit, 1969), 139. English translation: *The Battle of Pharsalus,* trans. Richard Howard (London: George Braziller, Inc., 1971), 95.

Nathalie Sarraute

I have not prepared a lecture for, to tell the truth, I did not think that I would be giving one at this colloquium. I can, therefore, only speak in an improvised way and I excuse myself in advance for all the deficiencies of such an improvisation.

Where shall I begin? Well, I will start by offering you a few words on the beginnings of my work. It seems to me now that this work—or rather the taste for this work—dates back to my first assignments in French, first in elementary school, then at the Lycée Fénélon, and finally at the Sorbonne.

As soon as I entered elementary school, I was seized by a true passion for "compositions." I read a lot and I very much liked to imitate as best I could the authors I was reading at that time or the texts that we wrote as dictations. I must confess that I had a certain gift for imitation that my teachers, first in elementary and then in high school, seemed to encourage.

My models were René Boylesve or André Theuriet and later Balzac. These imitations of "style," when I adapted them to the subject of the essay I had to write, filled me with a satisfaction that, unfortunately for me, I was never to know again later when writing the texts that I have published.

When, filled with contentment, I would reread one of my essays before turning it in, I could not see the difference between what I had just written and what Balzac, for instance, had written. The feeling of pride that I had when the teacher would hand back the papers and praise mine made me understand this peaceful pride, this self-confidence, which I observed later among writers who imitate the classics. They undoubtedly have the certainty of being on the right road, they have reliable guarantors, they must feel equal to the "Great Masters" whose form they have so remarkably adapted to new content. They must not be aware that those "Great Masters" drew all their strength and their qualities from the fact that they created new forms that alone could reveal an unknown "content," ...a strength and qualities that they conserved.

I liked nothing so much as these assignments in French: I thought about them incessantly, I dwelled on every sentence, I turned them in, often late, only when I thought that they had reached the required stage of perfection.

I was then completely enclosed in a language whose rules I accepted totally. I could not conceive of their being disobeyed. I tried to conform as strictly as possible to all the rules of grammar. It was not this acceptance of rules that Alain Robbe-Grillet spoke of yesterday—a deliberate, meditated acceptance that manages to invigorate the language that is compelled to submit to them.

It was a docile acceptance that enabled an imitated language to be molded on images, themselves conventional, which I adapted to the subject of my French assignment.

This taste for "French compositions" and this satisfaction were perpetuated at the Sorbonne, where I rivaled a student of the Ecole Normale Supérieure whose name, I still remember, was Boeuf. Monsieur Chamard, who corrected our work, compared us constantly with one another and I think that the worst misfortune which I could suffer was to receive a grade lower than his!

As for writing, writing for myself, it was out of the question. I could only respond to what I was asked.

After graduating, when I wanted to choose a profession, I thought that law would suit me, not because I liked law—it became clear that law bored me very much—but because I like to discuss, to debate, to speak my mind....

I did not know that the issues of civil law, commercial law, financial law would be so forbidding, so difficult for me, and as for penal law, the speeches in the court of assizes, especially at that time, seemed to me to be unbearably grandiloquent and sentimental.

But during my years of training at the Courts of Law, I registered for the training seminar where young lawyers were given legal, and also sometimes quite literary or psychological, topics to prepare. On one of these topics, I prepared and delivered a speech that was a great success. But this was only the first round. For the second and last round, I did not manage to be so inspired by a legal issue. I would never have believed then, even after this failure, that this preparation at the training seminar would in any way be of use to me. But it occurred to me later that this work had torn me away from the written form—fixed in grammatical correctness, rigorously imposed—to which I was locked in. Through it, I attained the more spontaneous, more direct, and freer spoken form.

I have to tell you that, at that time, there were several of us who thought that the nineteenth-century novel was dead. I personally thought so because I had read—it was a real shock—during the summer of 1924... *Du Côté de chez Swann* [*Swann's Way*] by Proust... and, soon afterward, *Ulysses* by Joyce and, I think it was the following year, *Mrs. Dalloway* by Virginia Woolf. I had the impression that a new world was opening up, carried by new forms, and that it was impossible, after these revolutionary works, to write as one had written before. It was also impossible to imitate them. Their strength came from the novelty of their discoveries. Certain poets, moreover, like André Breton and Max Jacob, were claiming that the novel was no longer an art.

It also seemed to me that, apart from those great revolutionaries of the first quarter of the century, those novels that were successful were not very worthwhile. I did not like *Bella* by Jean Giraudoux, or *Les Enfants terribles* by Cocteau, that were so greatly acclaimed. One needed a certain amount of courage to dare to criticize them. Thus I thought that despite the pleasures I had drawn from my "French compositions" and the boredom that legal work instilled within me, nothing could incite me to write.

And then one fine day, moved by a strong sensation, I wrote—a little like one writes a first poem. It was, if I remember well, during the winter of 1932-33, a first text that is now included in my first book, *Tropismes*.

It seems to me now... but this may be wrong, perhaps I thought about it before... it seems to me that it emerged without preparation, that it took a certain shape despite me, a certain rhythm. I wrote it almost without any erasures and I left it as it was.

I had no real idea of what I was trying to show. When I reread it, I had the impression that it was not a part of what had already been written. It was something which was there in and of itself, a kind of movement, an invisible dramatic action between two people seated facing each other. Presumably, nothing was happening, nothing definable, nothing that could be classified according to any psychological category. This interested me very much; I wanted to keep on showing movements of the same kind, unknown, undefinable, self-sufficient. . . .

It was rather difficult to find them and to make them live through language, but I was excited by the search. There I was in an area that was all my own, that belonged to me. I felt at home there.

I did not claim to have made any discovery in the field of psychology. That was not what interested me at first. What was important to me was that these movements gave rise to a form that seemed alive.

It was alive because it brought to the outside something still intact, something which had not already been taken over by language, something still vague, still hazy. In order to take shape, it had to be carried by words, to slide into words, to melt with a language from which it would be inseparable.

There was an interaction between this initial sensation and the language: without the language, it did not come into being. But thanks to it, the language was alive.

This interplay has always been indispensable to me.

It is still not possible for me today to read with interest a literary text where I do not feel that something deeply felt runs through it, makes it stand, gives it shape.

When I started looking for some of these undefinable sensations that I thought still intact, outside of any language, I encountered great difficulties.

These sensations had to be self-sufficient, had to hold the reader's entire attention. It was very difficult to isolate them and to give shape to them. They would appear, after a long time of searching and of waiting, as though fleeting, evanescent, very hazy... I had to hold on to them, to develop them, to ripen them so that they would make the language spring, give it its rhythm, its images.... This language, as I have already said, would not exist without those sensations, but alone allows them to come to life, to be perceived outside, sufficiently distinct and strong.

When I had thus gathered (and it took many years, between 1932 and 1937) several texts, I entitled them *Tropismes* [*Tropisms*]. I thought that this title would render rather well the instinctive, irrepressible aspect of these inner movements, generally provoked, like those of plants, by an exterior excitement, by the presence of someone or some object.... When I had gathered a number of these "Tropismes," I tried to publish them.

They were refused everywhere. I still have the letters of rejection sent by the publishers Gallimard, Grasset.... At last, in 1938, a young editor offered to publish them. He was Robert Denoël, who had already published Céline, who had, too, been rejected everywhere. He told me that he wanted to publish my *Tropismes* in the same series that he had published *Chêne et Chien* by Raymond Queneau, an author whom I did not know. Robert Denoël gave me *Chêne et Chien,* telling me that it was remarkable, and I found that he was right. I read and reread it, and I still know passages of it by heart. Thus I was delighted to be published in the same series.

My book came out in February, 1939, a short time before the war. I did not know anyone in the literary circles. Robert Denoël advised me to send it to Sartre, who had just achieved great success with *La Nausée,* and to Max Jacob—Denoël was sure that it would interest him—and also to Charles Mauron, who Denoël so esteemed as a critic. All three answered me very encouragingly, and for that reason I mention their names here.

But there were but a few lines in the papers. I no longer remember exactly where they appeared, and a complimentary article by Victor Moremans in *La Gazette de Liège.* Apart from that—nothing.

A short time later, the war broke out, and when I met Sartre during the Occupation, it was not to speak of literature.

Right after the Libération, however, I was with some friends at the Café de Flore and Sartre came up to me and asked what I was "up to." I told him that I was writing a novel.... "Really! a novel.... I would like to see it." (Actually, what I was writing could only be called a novel.)

For two or three years, from 1939 to around 1941, I had wanted to continue writing "tropisms," but they became more and more difficult to find.... Each time it was like starting a new work. Max Jacob had written to me that "je pêchais à la ligne dans l'immense bocal" [I was fishing in the immense fishbowl]. The image was accurate. For days, for weeks sometimes, not a single fish would bite and hook itself. During that entire period I wrote only the five texts that were added to the Denoël edition when it was brought out again by the Editions de Minuit in 1957. When I wrote them,

I aimed to include them in a second collection of short texts that would be called *Le Planétarium*.

Thus I thought that my work would be more productive if I gathered and developed these tropisms between two characters who would appear to be the most traditional characters ever, Balzacian characters. As in *Eugénie Grandet*, there would be a father, considered a miser, and his daughter, but here a narrator would try to see what goes on behind the appearances which those "characters" constituted—all these more and more complex movements that take place in them, overflow in them, that invade everything and make it impossible for a modern writer to write a novel in the traditional form.

Sartre had asked me to show him what I had already written.... He was very interested in it. I showed him what followed... and he published the beginning of this *Portrait d'un inconnu* in the *Temps modernes* that he had founded.

He thought that he would write an article on the book when it was published, or a preface. He finally decided upon the preface. From the beginning, I did not agree with him on certain points of this preface which, in other respects, helped me a lot.... I would be ungrateful not to acknowledge it.... Those points on which I disagreed with him were, first, that he seemed to consider my "tropisms"—always concealed under "la pierre des lieux communs" [the stone of commonplaces]—vague and shapeless. But for me, these movements become very exact, as precise as clockwork; there is nothing visceral or limp about them. It is a dramatic action which unfolds so scrupulously that when there is a missing link, I cannot go on without first finding it.

Another point on which I disagreed with this preface, but I saw it only completed... is that Sartre still claimed that there could be only one form for the novel, whether it be that of Meredith or of Dostoevski, with great scenes between characters who are not there just as mere appearances. Sartre considered this *Portrait d'un inconnu* an "attempt to murder the novel" reminiscent of Miró's "attempt to murder painting." For him, the *Portrait d'un inconnu* was an antinovel, whereas for me it was an attempt to murder the *traditional* novel and it alone. It was not an antinovel, but a contemporary novel, one that only a modern writer could write.

Sartre, who was very fond of Hemingway's novels... though he had advised me to read Faulkner whom he thought I would like . . . considered this *Portrait d'un inconnu* an interesting curiosity, but he told me: "Now you are going to write real novels; if not, you are making the sacrifice of your life," which really surprised me. But the future seemed to prove him right. The sacrifice appeared to be beginning. With this preface by Sartre—and it is hard to image what Sartre represented in 1947: busloads of tourists would stop in front of the Café de Flore and the Café des Deux Magots to watch Sartre working; he had to shut himself in at home and later migrate to Montparnasse. Well, with this preface, the book was first rejected by Jean Paulhan. This rejection surprised Sartre, but not me. . . . Paulhan had already refused my *Tropismes*. . . . Then Sartre gave it to a publisher, Nagel, who accepted it out of friendship for him, kept it for more than a year, and returned it to him saying that it was definitely not publishable, as he would lose too much money.

At that time, a new publishing company was founded, that of Robert Marin, where a friend of Sartre's, François Erval, was working, and it was he who published *Portrait d'un inconnu*. After he had sold 400 copies, Robert Marin disposed of the rest before the date authorized by the contract, which enabled me to have it published later by Gallimard.

I was almost sure that the book would be published one day, but nonetheless, I was worried.

This was in 1949. In 1947 I had published an article called "De Dostoievski à Kafka" ["From Dostoevski to Kafka"] in *Les Temps modernes*. These two authors were then completely disassociated from each other and their admirers were gathered on opposing sides: "Those of Dostoevsky," who believed in the existence of an inner life, in the "psychological," and "those of Kafka," for whom this inner life—even if it existed—was of no interest. *L'Etranger* by Camus was a perfect example of this absence of any "inner conscience": it was as though it had been vacuumed out of him. Although not entirely, however—only until the end of the book where psychology comes rushing back to restore it.

I tried to show in my article that psychic life had not disappeared from Kafka's characters, that without it there is no possible literature, and that Kafka had followed to the end the route on which Dostoevski had embarked.

And then, in 1950, I wrote an article entitled "L'Ere du soupçon," where I attacked the traditional forms of the novel. I think that it was the loneliness in which I found myself as far as literature was concerned—the lack of response, of interest in what I was writing—which impelled me to think about the reasons that prevented me from writing in conventional forms. It seemed to me that the imitation of the novelistic forms that had reached its peak in Balzac's work was no longer at all possible.

I never thought—as was often believed—of attacking Balzac's work. I have always admired him. I can only repeat clichés when I say that Balzac was a "visionary." And this "vision" which was his, he showed in a certain form, a form constituted by characters, very clearly and strongly drawn, characters all in one piece who move by a kind of capillarity from one layer of society to another. Those colorful characters of well-defined features remain, forever, living forms, the elements of an art that has lost none of its power. It was Balzac's effort to succeed in creating those forms, forms that were his alone, that breathed into them this life which they preserved. Cousine Bette or Père Goriot are still living.

But it was impossible to imitate them. To a modern writer's eye, the character no longer had this divine simplicity. He had little by little disintegrated. We had a tendency to look at the surrounding world through a microscope. I think that it was Bernard Shaw who wrote in the preface to one of his plays that the world which had seemed macroscopic to the writers of the past was looked at by the moderns through a microscope. I wondered what Balzacian characters would have become if Balzac had been our contemporary, which forms he would have created: certainly not those of *Eugénie Grandet* or those of *La Princesse de Cadignan*, which in my eyes is one of his masterpieces.

As I was saying earlier, in the power, in the originality, that which gave Balzac's writing all its good qualities, qualities which still now are so evident, these qualities disappear today in those copies of the ancients. In those novels the characters are the principal anchors and the plot plays the most important part and monopolizes the reader's entire attention. It was no longer there, as far as I was concerned, that the source of life was to be found.

But critics and readers continued to cling to the characters. Were they plausible? Were they "real" characters like those seen around us? They were confusing art with life as they perceived it, as classical literature, and later its imitators taught them to perceive it.

Nathalie Sarraute

For me, those "characters" that we build around us, this enormous wax museum where, for the purposes of practical life, we manage more or less to find our way, have nothing more to do with the art of the novel. This art has moved into other areas. Each writer has his own, one which belongs to him alone.

The area in which I work is that of those inner movements, those "tropisms" which pass through the characters' natures as through the large mesh of a net. They develop in anonymous consciousnesses. I have never been able to give a name to those appearances which for me are characters only when they speak of each other and see themselves as characters.

If I had given them names, I would have been situated outside, at a distance, instead of being inside within this stream of movements in constant transformation where I would like the reader to let himself be taken without worrying about where he is.

After "L'Ere du soupçon," which was published in 1950 and which evoked little interest, I wrote another article, "Conversation and sous-conversation" ["Conversation and Sub-Conversation"], which this time was rejected by *Les Temps modernes*.... It went too much against what they stood for.... It was published in the *Nouvelle Revue Française* in 1956. In this article, I attacked the form of traditional dialogue, dialogue being for me only the outer manifestation of inner movements....

And then I wrote "Ce que voient les oiseaux," where I wanted to show that it is in committed literature, modeled on old-fashioned forms, that true formalism could be found.

When, in 1956, those articles were published together under the title *L'Ere du soupçon,* they curiously evoked great interest. For the first time, a book written by me had a good press. Yet I had published in 1953, this time at Gallimard, a novel, *Martereau,* that had nothing to do with the traditional novel. It had received a certain amount of praise from the critics, for no one had noticed that it was not written in the form of the traditional novel. What in this novel was shown as a mere appearance, the character of Martereau—an appearance that was undone little by little, and this disintegration was for me the main interest of the book—this character, his nature, was what the critics saw above all else. They wanted to see only what they already knew.

But the publication of *L'Ere du soupçon* suddenly awakened

127

them. This theoretical work also drew the attention of Robbe-Grillet, and it was at that moment that we first met.

I do not want to recreate here the history, today well known, of the Nouveau Roman. All that I want to say is that Robbe-Grillet's energy and immense optimism were equal only to my passivity and my fundamental pessimism.

With regard to the circulation of my books, I owe a lot to this movement of the Nouveau Roman. I say it again and again, but I think that without it my books would not have had the audience that they have had. It is not an enormous audience, for my books are considered to be difficult books, but without the Nouveau Roman, it would have been smaller.

There has been, however, considerable diversity among us since the beginning. As has already been said, what Alain Robbe-Grillet writes and what I write are exactly the same, except entirely different. In my work, it is a stream of internal movements, and in his, it is an interplay of external stills.

But as far as the freedom of novelistic forms is concerned and the necessity of constantly transforming them in order to keep them alive, we were in agreement. It was a pleasure for me to meet writers much younger than I who shared my opinions. Alain Robbe-Grillet at that time offered to republish *Tropismes* and the five texts I had written between 1939 and 1941 at the Editions de Minuit.

The publishing house of Robert Denoël where my first *Tropismes* were published no longer existed. Robert Denoël had been murdered during the Occupation.

Tom Bishop asked me to recount the evolution of my work over the last fifteen years. I am still a good pupil and am therefore going to do what he asked of me. I have on occasion been reproached for continually writing the same thing. This is an entirely extravagant reproach in my eyes. Excuse the comparison, but will it ever be said that Balzac always wrote the same thing? No, never! Yet he always worked the same novelistic material: his own. The world he saw, he always saw with the same eyes. From book to book, all he did was show, in various forms, his own forms, the same content.

The same can be said of almost all novelists.

But in the classical novelists and in their imitators, those forms were the characters and the plot. In my books, those forms are the inner movements which, in unfolding, create a dramatic action.

Nathalie Sarraute

Having seen a few, one imagines that all the others are identical, while, in fact, they differ one from the other as much as the characters of a novel.

It is just that the reader's eye is not used to it. It is used to seeing the characters and to following their actions while being carried along by the stream of a plot. Balzac clearly distinguishes and easily differentiates Cousine Bette from Rastignac, but in my books, how can one of these undefinable movements be distinguished from the others?

Thus it is said that they are always the same. But I challenge anyone to find in my books two identical tropisms. These tropisms are my characters and their unforeseeable development is, in my work, the plot.

When I meet good readers—which is not very often—they are as interested in these movements as in characters. They wonder, in the same way, how these movements are going to evolve....

I am glad to mention those criticisms here. It makes me feel good to be able, for once, to respond to them....

The substance and the forms of my books, therefore, have evolved, though they still reside in the same regions of psychic life, in those regions where I place myself, where I work.

It has always been the same for all novelists. This is why Dostoevski used to say that he always wrote the same book. He was not working with the same material as Chekov or Tolstoy. Each time, he created from his material forms which could only be his own.

After those references—forgive me for my lack of modesty, but it is obviously not on standards of quality that I draw these comparisons—I can say that when I try to see the direction in which my books have evolved, it seems that since *Le Planétarium* and *Martereau,* they have tended to be more abstract. They are more and more often concerned with sensations of an intellectual nature.

In *Les Fruits d'or* [*The Golden Fruits*] the tropisms clustered around the rise, or it can even be said the seizing of power, immediately upon publication of a book, *Les Fruits d'or,* and then around its downfall. Readers have difficulty in establishing a direct and innocent contact with this book: a screen of conventional and frightening opinions prevents it.

In *Entre la vie et la mort* [*Between Life and Death*], I wanted to show, among other things, the inner movements produced in writers by the effort to write. It was very difficult to express, with words, work on words. I called this book *Entre la vie et la mort* because, throughout the working process, a text is always between life and death. If the initial sensation that gave rise to the text has lost its power or has disappeared, the text continues to function, but it has lost what was giving it life. It has nothing left to support it. It loses its independence and is doomed to veer toward harmony and a beauty that are perishable because they obey preestablished notions with which the text has nothing to do and which it should forget.

This harmony and this beauty at first overjoy the writer, but when he rereads his text, he realizes that this beautiful text is a dead text. He had to destroy it and come back to the source of life, to the sensation.

The writer is also between life and death, for his text, in order to live, requires both complete solitude and the presence of and adhesion to others. Herein lies a delicate balance: too much of either is equally dangerous to the life of the text.

In 1972, in *Vous les entendez?* [*Do You Hear Them?*], the language that triggered the tropisms was made of laughter. Teenagers laugh and those laughs, perhaps provoked by their father's admiration for a pre-Columbian statue, produce, punctuate all the sentences with an inner dramatic action, with a conflict that is, for the father and for the children, of a great and vital importance, although nothing, or almost nothing, appears on the outside. It is a struggle between legitimate and delightful admiration for the museum masterpieces and the need for being iconoclastic in order to create new forms. This struggle takes place among very close people, which makes it more intense.

I will now comment only very briefly on my next books, for I must stop.

Certain words . . . "C'est ce que disent les imbéciles" [That is what fools say] . . . written by a philosopher, words which I had read rather long ago and which had profoundly struck me, became the title of my novel, *Disent les imbéciles* [*Fools Say*], published in 1976.

In this novel, we witness the construction of characters, as we have always been invited by literature to do, and we witness their classification: On the very top are placed the geniuses, the infallible ones, those whose ideas, even if they happen on occasion to be stupid, are always blindly accepted.... On the very bottom—the "idiots," whose ideas, whatever they are, are dismissed as worthless. What constitutes the material of this book are the different aspects of this struggle led by he who, faced with an idea, cannot say "that is what fools say" and wants to isolate the idea from any imagination, from the taboos, and from venerations that overshadow it. This struggle, of course, always takes place on the level of inner movements.

Finally, my last book, *L'Usage de la parole* [*The Use of Speech*]... is constituted, like *Tropismes*, of separate texts, each of which radiates from a spoken word.

One single word triggers and feeds the action. This word is here what the character used to be. It is around it that waves are formed.

In all of my last books, the images, the metaphors—necessary to communicate to the reader, in magnifying them, those inner movements so difficult to perceive because they are so quick, undefinable... and I claim that those inner movements take place with great force within each of us—the metaphors are often replaced by imaginary scenes. They are the equivalents, outside, of those inner movements.

I will just say a few words about the plays which I started writing late, in 1965. There are at this time six of them. In these plays, the tropisms appear in the dialogue itself. A language is spoken which is only apparently that of conversation. It is the subconversation which constitutes the dialogue. Thus it could be said of my plays that, compared with my novels, they are like "an inside out glove."

I think that now I must stop. I have already spoken for too long.

The Place of the Action

Monique Wittig

What has been taking place in Sarraute's work since *Les Fruits d'or* is so total a transformation of the substance of the novel that it is difficult to grasp it as such. As it has the volatility of spoken words, I will call the material with which she works—in order to establish a comparison with what linguists call "locution"—"interlocution." By this word, infrequently used in linguistics, I imply all that occurs between people when they speak. It includes the phenomenon, in its entirety, which goes beyond speech proper. And as the meaning of this word derives from *interrupt,* to *cut someone short,* that which does not designate a mere speech act, I extend it to any action linked to the use of speech: to accidents of discourse (pauses, excess, lack, tone, intonation) and to effects relating to it (tropisms, gestures).

In this perspective, Nathalie Sarraute's characters are interlocutors: More anonymous even than Kafka's K., they have the tenor of Plato's Georgias, Critons, Euthyphrons. Called forth by dialogue and the same philosophical necessity, they disappear like meteorites or like people we pass in the street, people who are neither more nor less real than characters of a novel and who are bedecked with a name to satisfy the needs of our inner fiction. But what matters here over and above those interlocutors who, for the reader, are ordinary characters, ordinary propositions, is Sarraute's philosophical matter, the locution and the interlocution, what she herself, with regard to the novel, calls "l'usage de la parole" [the use of speech]. Unlike the science of linguistics, which has but one anatomical point of view on language, the point of view of the novel does not have to impose limits on itself for it can collect, gather, in a single movement, causes, effects, and actors. With Sarraute, the novel creates phenomena in literature which as yet have no name, either in science or philosophy.

It must first be noted that all those problems relating to character, to point of view, to dialogue which Sarraute developed in *L'Ere du soupçon,* have been resolved by the fact that the use of speech has become the exclusive theme of her books. The character, totally changed in its form, was still too cumbersome for the needs of the text. This form itself has disappeared. The spatiotemporal universe, which generally constitutes a pregnant element in fiction (description of places, of buildings, of precise geographical spaces) and which was already very restricted in the novels of Sarraute preceding *Les Fruits d'or,* is now the most abstract that it can be: it is any unspecified place where one speaks or else, perhaps, a mental space with imaginary interlocutors.

Sometimes an interlocutor breaks off, drops the conversation, and withdraws to undetermined places. Sometimes, too, there is a "here" and a "there," but this indication of distance does not correspond to place, but to a disparity at work in the language: Those people there and these people here are not speaking the same language. The point of view, far from being unique, is constantly and quickly shifting, according to the interlocutors' interventions, provoking changes of meaning, variations. The multiplicity of this point of view and its mobility are produced and sustained by the rhythm of the writing that is broken up by what is called discourse and its accidents. It is important to emphasize this multiplicity as far as the psychological, ethical, or political interpretation of the characters is concerned, for no interpretation is possible. It is, on the contrary, continually prevented. Not one of the spoken discourses, not even the inner dialogues or the inner discourses, is assumed by the author and, further, there is no privileged interlocutor entrusted with her point of view (contrary to Plato's Socrates), that which forces the reader to adopt them all successively, as temporary scenarios, as in *Martereau,* for example. Thus "le lecteur, sans cesse tendu, aux aguets, comme s'il était à la place de celui à qui les paroles s'adressent, mobilise tous ses instincts de défense, tous ses dons d'intuition, sa mémoire, ses facultés de jugement et de raisonnement" [the reader, who has remained intent, on the lookout, as though he were in the shoes of the person to whom the words are directed, mobilizes all his instincts of defense, all his powers of intuition, his memory, his faculties of judgment and reasoning].[1]

I would delight in speaking of the very substance of the text itself, of the rhythm, the sequences, and their mode of development, of the use of words as isolated words dispersing between interlocutors, of the spectacular oscillations of the text at moments when shifts in point of view take place, of the interlocutory sequences, of the clichés that are orchestrated around a word, as though by baton, of the birth and deployment in counterpoint of a text. This text responds like some kind of antique Greek choir, not tragic but sarcastic, commenting on the fortuities of the discourse, of the dynamic gathering of all the elements in a unique movement that carries them all away and which is the text.

But I must speak of matter that is more philosophical. That is why I mentioned Plato, although, contrary to his, Sarraute's interlocutors do not deliver it as a whole.

The use of speech, such as it is practiced everyday, is an operation that suffocates language and thus the ego, whose deadly stake is the hiding, the dissimulating, as carefully as possible, of the nature of language. What is caught unaware here and suffocates are the words between the words, before the "fathers," before the "mothers," before the "you's," before "the arising of the dead," before "structuralisma," before "capitalisma." What is smothered by all kinds of talk, whether it be that of the street or of the philosopher's study, is primary language (of which the dictionary gives us an approximate idea): the one in which meaning has not yet occurred, the one which is for all, which belongs to all, and which everyone in turn can take, use, bend toward a meaning. For this is the social pact that binds us, the exclusive contract (none other is possible), a social contract that exists just as Rousseau imagined it, one where the "right of the strongest" is a contradiction in terms, one where there are neither men nor women, neither races nor oppression, nothing but what can be named progressively, word by word, language. Here we are all free and equal or there would be no possible pact. We all learned to speak with the awareness that words can be exchanged, that language forms itself in a relation of absolute reciprocity. If not, who would be mad enough to want to talk? The tremendous power—such as linguists have made it known to us—the power to use, proceeding from oneself alone, all language, with its words of dazzling sounds and meanings, belongs to us all. Language exists as the commonplace[2] where one can revel freely and, in one stroke, through words, offer to others at arm's length the same license, one without which there would be no meaning. "Par toutes leurs voyelles, par toutes leurs consonnes [les mots] se tendent, s'ouvrent, aspirent, s'imbibent, s'emplissent, se gonflent, s'épandent à la mesure d'espaces infinis, à la mesure de bonheurs sans bornes" [With all their vowels, their consonants, (words) stretch, open up, inhale, become saturated, fill up, swell, spread over infinite space, over boundless happinesses.[3]

Language exists as a paradise made of visible, audible, palpable, palatable words:

quand le fracas des mots heurtés les uns contre les autres couvre leur sens... quand frottés les uns contre les autres, ils le recouvrent de gerbes étincelantes... quand dans chaque mot son sens réduit à un petit noyau est entouré de vastes étendues brumeuses... quand il est dissimulé par un jeu de reflets, de réverbérations, de miroitements... quand les mots entourés d'un halo semblent voguer suspendus à distance les uns des autres... quand se posant en nous un par un, ils s'implantent, s'imbibent lentement de notre plus obscure substance, nous emplissent tout entiers, se dilatent, s'épandent à notre mesure, au-delà de notre mesure, hors de toute mesure?

[when the clash of words colliding with one another drowns their meaning... when, rubbed together, they produce a shower of sparks which conceals it... when the meaning of each word is reduced to a tiny kernel surrounded by vast, misty spaces... when it is hidden under the play of reflections, of reverberations, of scintillations... when words are surrounded by a halo and seem to float, suspended at a distance from one another... when they settle into us one by one, embed themselves, slowly imbibe our most obscure substance, fill our every nook and cranny, dilate, spread to our measure, beyond our measure, beyond all measure?][4]

But even while the social contract, such as it is, guarantees the entire and exclusive disposition of langauge to everyone, and while, in accordance with this same right, it guarantees the possibility of its exchange with any interlocutor on the same terms—for the very fact that the exchange is possible guarantees reciprocity—it nevertheless appears that the two modes of relating to language have nothing in common. It is almost as though, suddenly, instead of there being one contract, there were two. In one, the explicit contract—the one where the "I" is made a human being by giving it the use of speech, the one where the practice of langauge is constitutive of the "I" who speaks it—face to face with words, "I" is a hero (*héros—héraut, Hérault, erre haut*)[5] to which the world, which it forms and deforms at will, belongs. And everyone agrees to grant this right to the "I"; it is a universal agreement. Here, I do not have to stand on ceremony, I can put my boots on the table, I am almighty, or as Pinget says in *Baga,* I am the "roi de moi" [I am my own king]. In the other contract, the implicit one, the very opposite takes place. With the appearance of an interlocutor, the poles are reversed:

> Disons que ce qui pourrait les faire céder à ce besoin de fuite... nous l'avons tous éprouvé... ce serait la perspective de ce à quoi elles seront obligées de se soumettre... cette petite opération... Petite? Mais à quoi bon essayer raisonnablement, docilement, décemment, craintivement de s'abriter derrière "petite"? Soyons francs, pas petite, pas petite du tout... le mot qui lui convient est "énorme"... une énorme opération, une véritable mue."

> [Let us say that what might make them give way to this need to escape... we have all felt it... would be the prospect of what they would be obliged to submit to... that little operation... Little? But what good is it to try—reasonably, docilely, decently, fearfully—to take refuge behind "little"? Let us be frank, not little, not little at all... the appropriate word is "enormous"... an enormous operation, a veritable molt.]⁶

That the other advances in his own words is sufficient for the "I," even before it utters a word, to be thrown a robe which is anything but a royal cloak:

> D'elle quelque chose se dégage... comme un fluide... comme des rayons... il sent que sous leur effet il subit une opération par laquelle il est mis en forme, qui lui donne un corps, un sexe, un âge, l'affuble d'un signe comme une formule mathématique résumant un long développement.

> [Something emanates from her... Something like a fluid, like rays... under whose effect he feels he is undergoing an operation which gives him a form, which gives him a body, a sex, an age, rigs him out with a sign like a mathematical formula that sums up a long development.]⁷

Even before "I" knows it, "I" is made a prisoner, it becomes the victim of a fool's deal. What it has mistaken for absolute liberty, the necessary reciprocity, without which language is impossible, is but the surrender, a deal that overthrows the "I" at the mercy of the slightest word. That this word be uttered and

> le centre, le lieu secret où se trouvait l'état-major et d'où lui, chef suprême, les cartes étalées sous les yeux, examinant la configuration du terrain, écoutant les rapports, prenant les décisions, dirigeait les opérations, une bombe l'a soufflé... il est projeté à terre, ses insignes arrachés, il s'est

secoué, contraint à se relever et à marcher, poussé à coups de crosse, à coups de pied dans le troupeau grisâtre des captifs, tous portant la même tenue, classés dans la même catégorie.

[The center, the secret spot where the General Staff is located and from where he, the Commander-in-Chief, all the maps spread out for him to see, examining the lay of the land, listening to reports, taking decisions, directing operations, a bomb hit it ... he is thrown to the ground, his insignia torn off, he is shaken, obliged to get up and walk, pushed forward, by blows from rifle butts, kicks, into the gray flock of the prisoners, all dressed alike, classified in the same category.][8]

In the second contract, the implicit one, in the interlocution no holds are barred and may the strongest win, he deserves it. To speak of one's right would be inappropriate in this case, for one is the strongest only by taking advantage of the unlimited power over the other granted by language, a power all the more unlimited because it has no recognized social existence. It is, therefore, with complete impunity that the strongest in words can become a criminal. Words, *les paroles,*

pourvu qu'elles présentent une apparence à peu près anodine et banale peuvent être et sont souvent en effet, sans que personne y trouve à redire, sans que la victime ose clairement se l'avouer, l'arme quotidienne, insidieuse et très efficace, d'innombrables petits crimes. Car rien n'égale la vitesse avec laquelle elles touchent l'interlocuteur au moment où il est le moins sur ses gardes, ne lui donnant souvent qu'une sensation de chatouillement désagreable ou de légère brûlure, la précision avec laquelle elles vont droit en lui aux points les plus secrets et les plus vulnérables, se logent dans ses replis les plus profonds, sans qu'il ait le désir, ni les moyens, ni le temps de riposter.

[provided they present a more or less harmless, commonplace appearance, can be and, in fact, without anyone's taking exception, without the victim's even daring to admit it frankly himself ... often are the daily, insidious, and very effective weapon responsible for countless minor crimes. For there is nothing to equal the rapidity with which they attain to the other person at the moment when he is least on his guard, often giving him merely the sensation of disagreeable tickling or slight burning; or the precision with which they enter straight into him at his most secret and vulnerable points, and lodge in his innermost recesses, without his having the desire, the means, or the time to retort.][9]

With the turn of a word, one is brought into line and led between two gentlemen, like the narrator in *Martereau,* for that which, in accord with the primary pact, establishes the "I" as free, now holds it bound hand and foot. Winged words are also bludgeons, language is a lure, paradise is also the hell of discourses, no longer the confusion of languages as in Babel, or discord, but the grand ordinance, the bringing into line of a strict meaning, of a social meaning.

What is taking place between the two contracts? Why is it that, at any moment, no longer almighty subject, no longer king, "I" can find itself rolling in the dust at the foot of the throne? When Sartre spoke in the preface to *Portrait d'un inconnu* of the "va et vient incessant du particulier au général" [incessant coming and going from the particular to the general], that which is the approach of any science, he was thinking of the tropisms, of this movement of consciousness, of this indicator of a reaction to one or several words, and he was imagining a particular consciousness trying to reach the general. Actually, however, it is just the contrary, since each time "I" is spoken in the singular, it is then, according to Sarraute, that "I" is the general, an "infinite," a "nebula," a "world." And one interlocutor, only one, is sufficient for the "I" to pass from the general to a simple particular in a movement that is exactly the reverse of that attributed to science.

It is there, in the interval between locution and interlocution, that the conflict emerges: the strange wrenching, the tension in the movement from particular to general, experiencd by any human being when from an "I"—unique in language, shapeless, boundless, infinite—it suddenly becomes nothing or almost nothing, "you," "he," "she," "a small, rather ugly fellow," an interlocutor. The brutal reduction (a "véritable mue" [true molt]) implies that the so-promising contract was glaringly false. And thus, for Sarraute, it implies not only that the social meaning or the contradictions between the general interest and the particular interest, in exercising a constant pressure over the exchange of language, particularly in the interlocution, are at the origin of the conflict, but also it is toward the entire system that Sarraute turns the interrogation: toward the *fundamental flaw* in the contract, the worm in the fruit, toward the fact that the contract in its very structure is an impossibility—given that, through language, "I" is at once everything, "I" has every power (as a locutor), and that, suddenly, there is the downfall wherein "I" loses all power (as an interlocutor) and is endangered by words that can cause madness, kill. The social significance, the commonplaces are not the cause: they come after, and are used. It even seems that that is what they are there for, "one has only to draw from the common stock." Moreover, they are at everyone's disposal, everyone makes fervent use of them, the weak, the strong, each, in his own way, playing the victim, the cocky one, the model young couple, the self-assured man, without there being any winners or losers. The reductive "you" which levels them, demeans them, labels them "honteuses et rougissantes dans leur ridicule nudité, esclaves anonymes enchaînées l'une à l'autre, bétail conduit pêle-mêle au marché" [ashamed and blushing in their ridiculous nudity, anonymous slaves chained one to the other, cattle led pell-mell to the market][10] can, like a boomerang, turn back on the aggressor, as is the case in *Martereau,* where the powerful one, in turn, becomes impoverished: "tendre faible transi de froid ... les gamins lui jettent des pierres.... La face peinte, affublé d'oripeaux grotesques, elle le force chaque soir à faire le pitre, à crier cocorico sur l'estrade d'un beuglant, sous les rires, les huées." [Tender, weak, numb with cold ... the street urchins throw stones at him.... With his face painted, rigged out in an absurd get-up, she forces him each evening to play the clown, to crow "cockle-doodle-do" on the stage of a cheap cabaret, while the audience howls and hoots.][11]

Any social actor makes use of this weapon of commonplaces, whatever his situation, for it is the debased form of reciprocity that has founded the exchange contract. But the conflict due to the confrontation of the two modes of relation to language (locution and interlocution) remains, nevertheless, insurmountable, from whatever point of view.

The substance of Sarraute's novels envelops this double movement, this deadly embrace, with its violent, vehement, passionate words. That is what leads me to say that the paradise of the social contract exists only in literature, where the tropisms, by their violence, are able to counter any reduction of the "I" to a common denominator, to tear open the closely woven material of the commonplaces, and to continually prevent their organization into a system of compulsory meaning.

Notes

1. Nathalie Sarraute, *L'Ere du soupçon* (Paris: Gallimard, 1956), 144. English translation: *The Age of Suspicion,* trans. Maria Jolas (New York: George Braziller, 1963), 115.

2. Translators' note: By "lieu commun," Wittig evokes here both the common place, as in a communal place, and the *commonplace,* as in a platitude of language. This desired ambiguity is lost in written English (though not in spoken English), where a choice must be made between the two.

3. Nathalie Sarraute, *Disent les imbéciles* (Paris: Gallimard, 1976), 130. English translation: *Fools Say,* trans. Maria Jolas (New York: George Braziller, 1977), 101-102.

4. Nathalie Sarraute, *L'Usage de la parole* (Paris: Gallimard, 1980), 148. English translation: *The Use of Speech,* trans. Barbara Wright, in consultation with the author (New York: George Braziller, 1983), 142.

5. Translators' note: The homonymic pun on "héros" (hero) is not translatable.

6. Sarraute, *L'Usage de la parole,* 88-89. English translation: *The Use of Speech,* 85.

7. *Ibid.,* 91. English translation: 87.

8. Sarraute, *Disent les imbéciles,* 42. English translation: 35.

9. Nathalie Sarraute, "Conversation et sous conversation," *L'Ere du soupçon,* 122-123. English translation: 97-98.

10. Nathalie Sarraute, *Martereau* (Paris: Gallimard, 1953; Le Livre de Poche, 1964), 129. English translation: *Martereau,* trans. Maria Jolas (New York: George Braziller, 1959), 127.

11. *Ibid.,* 213. English translation: 211-212.

Discussion

Tom Bishop: I am very surprised by the fact that silence in the plays and novels of Nathalie Sarraute has scarcely been mentioned this evening. In the area of modern theater, the use of silence really seems to me to be the very core of what is being done today, not by all the important playwrights, but by many. It is always an avant-garde, of course, but in that context Nathalie Sarraute seems to be situated at the very center of what is being done.

Nathalie Sarraute: No, I disagree with you on that point. In all my plays, all that can be said, that which is never said in real life, is said.

In my play *Le Silence,* I was interested in this silence only because it elicits a flow of words that externalizes the inner movements, the "tropisms." The silence acts as a catalyst. I leave as little room as possible for the unsaid. With the producer's and the actors' help, I try to lead the spectators as far as I can and then, if they go further, so much the better.

In my plays, what is normally never spoken of is spoken of. In another of my plays, for instance, someone asserts something untrue. This lie has to be harmless. It must not be one of those lies that directly involves those who hear it, that threatens their life, their feelings. Someone claims to have been in the Resistance. No one around him is directly involved. It is an untruth, that is all. In reality, when we hear an untruth, we have a disagreeable impression. We do not like to hear such things. And then the impression wears off, it is quickly forgotten. In my play *Le Mensonge,* however, this impression is precisely what impels the drama. Everyone speaks and excitedly tries to force the truth out. They try to elicit from the one who is lying this truth that is there, that exists like a living thing and that is crushed by the lie—whereas in reality no one would say anything. It would be quickly passed over.

I would like to add that all that is said in my plays is the opposite of an exchange of platitudes. There is not one word that does not externalize inner movements. That any critic could see in this mere platitudes or small talk has always seemed to me to be erroneous.

Robert Pinget

I have not a great deal to add to the remarks I made at the Cerisy conference on the New Novel a few years ago, for I have always worked along the same lines. (These remarks, incidentally, were reprinted as a postface to the translation of one of my novels published here by Red Dust, *The Libera me Domine*.) What I can do, though, is go into greater detail about the way I treat the material of my novels, and try to explain how I write them.

In fact, since what is still, I believe, called the "New Criticism"—an offshoot of the science of linguistics, with which it is even sometimes confused—since the New Criticism has seized on our work, it seems that we authors have no option but to take a stand on this discipline, whether it be to reject or to accept it. It has to some extent impugned the author, even going so far as to throw doubt on the importance of his role. These critics no longer talk of creation; they talk of production, which they see as something like the result of all the forces arising out of intertextuality as a generalized phenomenon.

The positive aspect of this way of envisaging literature is the importance the new critics attach to the study of the text as such: that is to say, as the field of interaction of signifiers.

But the risk it runs, if I understand it right, is that, if taken to extremes, any text by any writer would qualify as food for thought, as if all texts issued, and could only issue, from the same universal mechanism, and as if the only thing that mattered was to understand its functioning, without bothering any longer to ask ourselves either why, or with what aim, it functions. If that were the case, it would be the end of any scale of values.

Unless this type of criticism were to be confined to the texts of a few elite writers whose sole preoccupation was precisely to please it, and who refused themselves the flights of fancy arising, for example, from spontaneity—the *bête noire* of this criticism. In that case, however, it would have become too selective and no longer have the audience which, after the improvement of its methods and the broadening of its views, it deserves to reach.

It would be logical, as things stand at the moment, for the authors who have wholeheartedly subscribed to the spirit of this discipline, to stop signing their texts, since they admit that they do not have exclusive rights to them. Yet they continue to sign them. This, then, is a phenomenon we should keep in mind.

So far as I personally am concerned, I have taken a great interest in the work of this new school because it has helped me to a better understanding of the movement of my texts, and to become aware of an element of their significance that is not negligible. But it is ideally impossible for me to exclude from my writings the totally subjective side they contain, and the light they throw on my most secret intentions. My work does not consist solely in discovering the functioning of the text on the page, but also in trying to discover from where my choice of words comes and the relationship to my aspirations that they may signify.

What I call the *tone of voice* is nothing other than the deliberate choice of a certain vocabulary, and it is the sum total of this vocabulary that is alone responsible for breathing life into the text. This choice differs in each of my books, and is the result of a simple preoccupation with change and renewal. In the same way, it implies a different syntax from one book to the next.

This means that I only partially subscribe to the idea that a text is merely a production; in other words, a game deliberately played with the purely material interrelationship of signs. Even though, of course, my writings no longer contain any representation in the classical sense, they do still contain something eminently subjective, which is the search for a persona, an expression. It is just possible that my books may simply be exercises in the control of my creative faculty, of my sensations, of my memory. Exercises in the mastery of the tone, which may take various forms.

People today still talk a great deal about Mallarmé, and about his dream of the ideal Book—an object independent of any other concept than that of pure beauty. But they forget that, apropos of *Hérodiade,* he wrote in a letter: This poem "into which I put the whole of myself without realizing it . . . and to which I finally found the key."

This is to say that he himself, whose all-embracing consciousness has been so much praised, accepts not only the participation of the unconscious in writing, but also the fact that a poetic text reflects the temperament of the author, and that it can, therefore, be a way for him to know himself.

Mallarmé also wrote, elsewhere: "On paper, the artist creates himself," and not: "the artist creates." Here he implicitly recognizes the expressive role of the text, and he never, to my knowledge, went so far as to deny the author as a unique individual, or, consequently, the significance of writing insofar as it is concerned with other than purely functional phenomena.

On this same subject, it would be difficult to be more lucid than Baudelaire, who wrote in the preface to one of his translations of Edgar Allan Poe, *Nouvelles histoires extraordinaires:* "But above all, I want to say that, having allotted the proper share to the natural poet, to *innateness*, Poe also allotted a share to science, to work, and to analysis—which will seem exorbitant to those who are arrogant but not erudite."

And again, comparing Poe to those poets who believed solely in disorder and whose aim was to write poems with their eyes closed: "likewise, Edgar Allan Poe—one of the most inspired men I have ever known—made an effort to hide his *spontaneity*, to simulate sangfroid and deliberation."

Innateness, spontaneity, inspiration, which I assimilate with the unconscious, with its most immediate manifestations that will then be controlled: on reflection, this is self-evident.

I have great respect for the present-day critical methods. I even owe a debt of gratitude to those who employ them, since they have been good enough to turn their attention to my work. But I do not think that, given the still very new state of the science from which they are derived, these methods are the only ones capable of making an exhaustive assessment of the value of a text.

It is not solely in the light of pure deductive reasoning that my books should be approached, for insofar as it is possible, I allow them to be activated by the irrational, particularly in their sequences. Why? A question of idiosyncrasy, of temperament. In my eyes, the share allotted to the irrational is one of the ways that may help me to arrive at a personal "truth," which is only to a very limited extent present in my awareness of it. This is a kind of open provocation to the unconscious. This "truth," while it is no more important than that of anyone else, is nevertheless more valuable to me, if only because it helps me to a better-informed approach to the truths of other people. We are all, indeed, more or less dependent on the collective unconscious, whose nature we can only glimpse by examining as best we can those manifestations of it which we perceive in ourselves.

I do not know whether this proposition is orthodox: I mean, that the fact of intentionally having recourse to the irrational causes some revelation of the unconscious to emerge, but it seems to me that the magic of primitive peoples did not work otherwise. Also, the study of its practices has taught us many things, side by side, of course, with the interpretation of dreams, which does not date from today, though the irrational discourse of dreams is not released intentionally.

All this does not mean to say that the "psychological" significance of my work is more important to me than its aesthetic significance. I am merely trying to avert the error people may fall into if they consider that once my book has been closed, nothing should remain but the pleasure—or the boredom—of having read it. Something more, something indefinable, fortunately, is intended to be its distinguishing characteristic. To my mind, this characteristic can only be perceived by a kind of criticism that does not belong to any school but which dips more or less at random into the work.

In short, it is by a very personal method, and in the actual process of writing, that I criticize my manner of understanding literature, and I can only do this in terms that are not in common use. This criticism is an integral part of my work. And it is the reason why I have never felt a need to construct a theory independent of my writings.

If it is *de rigueur,* in this assembly, to speak of technique, I will very briefly say that the structure of my novels is often built on recurrences. These recurrences, or repetitions, are of four kinds.

(1) Complete recurrence, *ab initio,* or repetition of the first part of the book in the second. Bipartite structure, then. Typical examples: *No answer, Fable, The Apocrypha.* What is important here is the repetition of all the themes, but with perceptible or imperceptible modifications, distortions, variations, transfigurations, which finally destroy, or at least shake, the certainties that the reader may have fastened on in the first part. Hence the impression that the book is being composed, and decomposed, under his very eyes. The

Robert Pinget

formula I have employed to define this procedure and which applies to all my books is: *Nothing is ever said, since it can be said otherwise.*

(2) Partial and progressive recurrence, all the way through the book. After a certain number of pages, let us say, recapitulation of themes with variations, and so on with different themes. Typical examples: *Someone, The Libera me Domine, Passacaglia.* "Unipartite" structure, then.

(3) Complete but reversed recurrence, starting from the middle of the book, of the first part in the second, which thus repeats it by going back to the beginning. Bipartite structure, but disguised as "unipartite," as the book is all of a piece. This is what I have called anamnesis. Unique example: *That Voice.* Variations and hypotheses proliferate, as in (1) and (2). It is only the stimulus that differs. I would, therefore, stress the fact that in order to write, I need a positive stimulus to trigger the creative process.

(4) A fourth kind of recurrence is the pure and simple repetition of certain key phrases or *leitmotifs* throughout the book, which thus increase its resemblance to a musical composition. These repetitions, or refrains, are additional to the three other kinds of recurrences and are to be found in almost all my novels. I like to use them, because they are more effective than all the others in creating an impression of surface unity. The difficulties in reading caused by the variations on the themes are thus, in my eyes, or rather, in my ears, smoothed out. And the reason why it is these *leitmotifs* that I am the most attached to is, it seems to me, because they persuade me that in spite of my liking for combinatorial games, the most important thing to me is to convince myself, and to make the reader convince himself, that once a work of art has assimilated all possible complexities of expression, its aim must be to say only one simple thing which, I think, is called poetry.

This part of my technique, which I can describe only very succinctly here, is relatively easy to apply and to analyze. Its effects on the writing itself, on what the reader reads, is another matter. He is hindered by an abundance of assertions and negations, of alterations, second thoughts, parallels, distortions—in short, by an apparent absence of logic.

But the logic, or reasoning, of art is not that of Logic. Art is always founded in nature, but reconstitutes it in a different way, makes it into something greater, more beautiful, more true, less immediately apprehensible. Of course, the criterion of this beauty and this truth changes from century to century and from artist to artist. This is a truism.

My own way of exalting nature has been to make people discover, or to try to make them discover, its infinite variety. What I have called its *potentialities,* which are all included in a given reality. The imagination is, in fact, a constituent part of our being and is just as necessary as dreams and observation.

Every time I tackle a new book, my temperament incites me not to give it exactly the same form as its predecessor, in other words, the same language or the same tone, which are indissolubly linked to its form. The result of my way of working is that each book is different right from the outset. But very fortunately, whatever I do, my readers say that no matter which of my books they tackle, they recognize the same voice in it. I say very fortunately because, all things considered, the essential for me, in these experiments, is to explore and throw light on what my innermost depths conceal, and this I can only achieve by means of successive trial and error.

My attachment to the technique of the intermingling of themes and their variations is due to the admiration I have always felt for so-called baroque music. When I was very young I was already captivated by it, and for years I tried to exalt its spirit in rather imperfect poems. It was only later that I pursued the idea of taking inspiration from it in the novel. This may seem inconsistent, after what I have just said about the deliberate irrationality of my writings, for the type of music in question goes to great pains to set an example of the most rigorous geometry. In this connection, we should remember the accusations made in the nineteenth century against baroque music, and its grandiose and disconcerting discoveries. Invention, experimentation, and the unexpected are triumphant in this music, thanks to an exceptional mastery of means. Is there any need to mention the mirror-image technique employed by the greatest representative of this school? The irrational, controlled and measured in masterly fashion, is the very wellspring of his creative power.

It is piquant to remember that in the last century this form of art was considered to be "chaotic, cultural muck"!

But to pursue this analysis of the relation of my work to that of composers, who include one of the most formidable past masters of all time, would be to condemn it to the most inevitable shipwreck.

Robert Pinget

I would be better advised to say, merely, that for thirty years I have devoted myself to a kind of experimental writing that is intimately linked to oral expression. My exercises in vocabulary, syntax, rhythm, and punctuation have always been aimed at trying to match this writing to the voice that inspires it. My ear catches something that my pen endeavors to transcribe. My books are to be listened to, rather than to be read.

As for the subjects treated in my novels, they are taken from the most banal, apparently derisory, everyday events, *in which there is nothing that can make a novel,* but which I have chosen for my material. This is to say, given the importance I attach to every well-thought-out formulation, that I play on this appearance to the point of exhausting it in order to make anyone who listens to me admit that, beneath or beyond appearances, a drama is being played out. Now, if this drama is being played out, the game must be to give the listener a premonition of it—one must play fair. A lucid activity, in other words, gratuitous, hence necessary. Every work of art is more or less a dangerous game which may well be mortal. Let us not forget that drama is an essential act of nature which is played out in the innermost depths of the being, and hence moved by passion, moved by pathos. Once again, these are all truisms.

Their horror of passing time, of the everyday, has the paradoxical effect of making my narrators cling to these everyday events in order to reduce them to nothingness. Hence their constant, liberating repetitions, and their open access to the world of the imagination. The systematic confusion of grammatical tenses and of situations is symptomatic of this need to annihilate the obstacle. This quest to discover something else through the medium of the imagination only retains its character to the extent to which the narrators decide to forget what they are looking for, fascinated as they are by the discovery itself, and fearing more than anything else that they might glimpse the beginning of the end of their spiritual adventure. In other words, the narrators have no option but to despise death, which would be the end of the Word. This they do by flushing it out everywhere and demystifying it with humor. A task that could not be more vain, as they well know, but they accept it, once again because of their liking for the game. They are, therefore, perfectly cognizant of their extravagance, but it is the rule of this procedure, which might seem absurd to anyone who had no sense of liberty.

Let me repeat that my work belongs to the domain of art, and that I use every artifice of language in it, among which contradiction is by no means the least. Thus, to go no farther than this element of contradiction, which is the most obvious and simplistic form of variation, a casual reader may well find that contradiction is the only thing he remembers after his quick reading of my books. But this would be to amputate them of three-quarters of their content, not to say the whole.

If I do not quote any of my other books here, it is because their composition is simpler and more apparent. They are no less typical, each in its own way—I am thinking in particular of *The Inquisitory*—of my constant and primordial concern with tonality, with the exigencies of my ear, and of my declared intention, from my very first book, to extend the limits of the written word by replenishing it with the spoken word. I felt an urgent need to adopt this language deliberately, with its particularities of syntax, its inventions, and its rich vocabulary.

My first novels all reflect this fascination with these potentialities that then manifested themselves more freely. All the suggestions, refutations, prolongations, and metamorphoses of fragments of speech are deliberately expressed in them. A more rigorous disposition or composition of these fragments imposed itself later, but the material has remained the same.

But if I were to try to make this exposé more systematic, I would run the risk of falsifying or restricting the meaning of my writings, and that would be to betray them.

After thirty years of publication with Les Editions de Minuit, I am still affiliated to the New Novel and I still stand by its efforts and discoveries, which are of great diversity and undeniable present-day significance. For my part, by the choice of a method of which I have given you only the barest outline, I have attempted an approach to the dark face of language, in order to make it easier for unconscious values to break through and thus enlarge the field of my conscious activity. This has involved reconciling innateness with calculation, and often putting the accent on paradox which, as Jung said, is one of our supreme spiritual values.

To end on a more general note, I should like to read you a short paper I wrote in 1977 for the Mainz Academy, of which I am proud to be a corresponding member. This institution was conducting a little inquiry into what it entitled "Literary Baggage" [Literatur als Gepäck].

Here is my reply:

To say baggage is to say voyage. . . . The journey we undertake without a travel agency, and without having chosen it. The journey that lasts a lifetime. "Did you have a good journey?" It is the privilege of those whose baggage has been well packed to be able to answer yes. What will they have put into it? The thing that weighs the least, and whose name is: wisdom. It is vigilant, and it devours the kind of time that is always doing its utmost to prevent us from continuing our crossing: chronological time. Could there be another kind, then? Yes, that of childhood, of legend, the time of myths, of origins. *That* time has no weight, for it is a product of the Word. We have access to it when we listen to what was said in the beginning, the memory of which we have all retained in our innermost depths. *In illo tempore*, in that primordial time, which remains and does not pass, we were told truths which were soon written down. So the Word was consecrated by the Letter, and was called Legend—*that which is to be read*. All literature, whether sacred or profane, has its source in this ancient, mysterious process.

The sole "baggage" that helps us to conquer chronological time and to participate in the other, absolute time, is a bouquet of texts, an anthology which we are able to refer to at every moment of our existence. These texts may be of a different nature, but they nevertheless have the same far-distant origin. The *homo religiosus*, linked to the essential—if we admit his presence in every one of us—rebels against the lacerations produced by the succession of days, and seeks refuge in the time which knows neither succession nor laceration, that of the Word.

Light baggage, buzzing with words, which, ever since the world has been the world—and there are many legends that vouch for it—has ensured our passage, without let or hindrance, over on to the other bank.[1]

Note

1. I wish to take this opportunity to pay homage to my publisher, Joanna Gunderson, Director of Red Dust, to my various former translators, and to Barbara Wright, my English translator since 1975.

Is There a New Novel Today?

Leon S. Roudiez

Ecrire et n'être rien pour laisser passer le tout[1] [To write and be nothing in order to let everything flow through]. Is there a new novel today? What a strange question! When I proposed it as a topic, I had no idea what the answer might be. Nor did I have any inkling of the paths and byways I would be traveling in search of that answer. Consequently, what I am presenting here is not a rigorous scholarly paper. Rather, it is the summary of a somewhat random account of my peregrinations in search of a distinct new form of fiction.

I was interested in finding out if there were a significant number of writers who might be doing something similar to what the so-called New Novelists had done some twenty-five years ago. Their common, although unconcerted design, was to break with the past—and this in a most general and radical fashion—that is, by challenging the necessity for fiction to be woven around those components hitherto considered indispensable: characters, plot, verisimilitude, linear chronology, well-wrought style. You know the list as well as I do.

In other words, if there is a "new novel" today, it is written by a number of persons attempting to effect a break with the past—and this past would necessarily include the New Novel. Also rejected would be the disciples of the New Novelists, that is, disciples who write fiction in the manner of *Portrait d'un inconnu, Le Voyeur, Quelqu'un, Le Palace,* or *L'Emploi du temps*. I should probably want to leave out the present work of the New Novelists. Whatever reason or excuse there was, in the 1950s, for grouping their activities, for emphasizing what they had in common, that reason no longer exists, and today their differences stand out. If, however, I could identify another kind of "new novel" emerging now, such a fiction might well share some traits with the more recent work of the "old" New Novelists as their practice evolved over the years and acquired features that were not present in their work in the 1950s—or, at least, not detected by the critics.

My quest did not appear very promising at first. For several years now, each time I have gone to France, I have inquired abut the work of younger fiction writers. Usually, people would give me a gloomy estimate of the novelistic scene. On occasion, a name has been mentioned; the name was always new to me (and this, of course, proves nothing), and it did not show up again either in conversations, reviews, or essays (and this again proves nothing as to the quality of the person's writing). What it could demonstrate, on the other hand, is the necessity for someone—fellow-novelist or critic—to lump those solitary individuals together, assert that they share the same goals, and give their enterprise a name, as was done in the case of the New Novel. For one reason or another, that has not happened, with the exception of Jean Pierre Faye's "Collectif Change" and a number of young writers who are working under the aegis of Jean Ricardou. The latter are doing interesting things. They are very much theory conscious, but so far they have not yet broken through, they have not caught the attention of a wider audience.

Change is something else again. Three members of the group have been publishing fiction, Faye since 1958, Philippe Boyer and Jean-Claude Montel since 1970; in addition, *Change* published Danielle Collobert's *dire I-II* in 1972 and *il donc* in 1976. In March, 1978, they attempted to do precisely what I suggested a moment ago, that is, to promote a new generation of writers the way the review *Esprit* and the Editions de Minuit publisher, Jérôme Lindon, had done in the 1950s. A double issue of the *Change* collection was entitled "La Narration nouvelle," and in it Faye urged readers to hasten the demise of the novel, which he said was now a useless genre, and replace it with a new narrative that was no longer mimetic but transformational, involved in the historical process.[2] Whatever the merits of the theory and the talents of the writers published by *Change*, I see no evidence that the collective was able to convince a sizable segment of the reading public or of the critical establishment. Perhaps that issue of *Change* was too heavily theoretical. Perhaps they were seen as promoting their own people. Perhaps there were other reasons having to do with the politics of the intellectual and literary set in Paris. At any rate, as far as I can tell, the fictions were generally reviewed (and often quite favorably) as individual productions, not as components of a new, coordinated venture.

I had become acquainted with the works of Montel, Collobert, and Boyer by attending the *Change* colloquium at Cerisy-la-Salle in 1973 (actually, the "Narration nouvelle" issue called attention to several other writers: Geneviève Clancy, Agnès Rouzier, and Didier Pemerle). I was more recently led to investigate the work of two other fiction writers who are completely unrelated to the *Change* group. I was asked about one of them by people in this country, not in the field of French, and as a result I decided to look at some of the works by Tony Duvert. The other, Eugène Savitzkaya, was recommended with much enthusiasm by Alain Robbe-Grillet; it seemed appropriate to read at least two or three of his works of fiction. A curious thing about both of these writers is how few serious reviews or critical essays their works have inspired. That is especially striking in the case of Duvert, whose first novel came out in 1967, ten years earlier than Savitzkaya's first. Savitzkaya is doing a little better—but he is still getting less attention than Robbe-Grillet, for instance, five years after *Les Gommes*.

I suppose the relative silence that surrounds Duvert's novels is due to one aspect of that fiction—homosexual pornography. That, however, will not concern me here. Let me emphasize, in passing, that I am not interested in making ethical judgments, or even aesthetic ones. I do not intend to decide whether a book is good or bad. Rather, I am attempting to identify any distinctive, innovative traits it might possess as a written text.

When I read Duvert's first novel, *Récidive*,[3] it was soon clear to me that the lesson of the New Novel had been assimilated. The preliminary section is called "Exposé" [statement or report] and is divided into subdivisions that are titled: "Première narration: octobre" [First narration: October], "La même, mais qui mentionne un nom véridique" [The same, but which mentions a real name], "Rectification," "Deuxième narration, provisoirement limitée à un temps apocryphe. Décembre" [Second narration, temporarily limited to an apocryphal time. December], and finally, "Rappel succint de ce qui précède" [Brief reminder of what precedes]. (Incidentally, all those subtitles have been eliminated from the revised edition of 1976). Without reading the text itself, one surmises that the relationship between narrative and any possible referent is shaky or problematic, and it comes as no surprise when one finds out that the "brief reminder" does not at all sum up the events of the preceding pages. As the text oscillates between first- and third-person narrative, the subject of that narrative is placed in doubt, and a similar indeterminacy affects characters. Linearity also goes by the board. So much for similarities, and I have no intention of going into details about this, for I am looking for distinctive traits. What I find here is a stronger presence of the flesh; aside from the pornographic passages, where a perverse, sadomasochistic sensuality is displayed (and almost expected), a pervading sensuousness runs through the entire text. It can be positive, as in this statement, "La sueur qui indondait mes membres m'ouvrait à la nuit, que j'éprouvais comme une fraicheur"[4] [The sweat streaming down my limbs opened me to the night, which I felt as a coolness], or negative, as in the following excerpt:

Il était environné de portes, d'escaliers, de porches creux, de ruelles inégales, de gueules et de ravins prêts à le happer. Il éprouvait comme un frottement entre sa peau et lui-même. Il se serait obscurci, contracté au centre d'une baudruche, d'une caverne mobile où couraient des souffles chauds. Isolé comme un espion à l'affût, il attendait dans la nuit le choc qui devait survenir, le hurlement, les fuites, les éclats qui expliqueraient cette terreur.[5]

[He was surrounded by doors, stairways, hollow porches, by uneven alleyways with sloughs and ravines ready to snare him. He felt a sort of friction between his skin and himself. He would have darkened, contracted to the center of a balloon, of a mobile cave where warm gusts were flowing. Isolated like a spy on the lookout, he awaited in the night the shock about to take place, the scream, the flights, the outbursts that would explain this terror.]

The terror that is explicitly named at the end has been symptomatically described in bodily terms during the eight or nine preceding lines. While that is not too distant from what Claude Simon does in some of his narratives, one would agree, I think, after going over Duvert's pornographic pages, "choses qui inspirent un dégoût légitime" [things which inspire a legitimate disgust], Duvert himself writes, ironically, of course, in one of his blurbs (*Paysage de fantaisie,* back cover) that they have little in common with either Simon's sensuous eroticism or Robbe-Grillet's intellectualized sexual banter. They do bring to mind Christine Rochefort's violently ironic *Quand* *tu vas chez les femmes*⁶ or, leaving out the sadomasochistic business, Chantal Chawaf's *La Rêverie*.⁷ What I find curious is that the most advanced of his fiction from the textual point of view, that is, where there is the highest degree of scription, are the first two. His *Journal d'un innocent* (1976), for instance, harbors a far more conventional text than either *Récidive* or *Portrait d'homme couteau* (1969). There is a single, unified narrative in the first person, characters have stable referents, and so forth. The title, however, alludes to the apparently meaningless pages a penniless, retarded boy typed on the narrator's typewriter during the short period he stayed with him. The narrator is reminded of the proverbial monkey who, haphazardly hitting the keys, would, according to the law of averages, eventually reproduce all the great literary masterpieces and also produce some of his own. But the narrator is mortal, he would run out of time, and he must eat—he will therefore choose his words with care in order to communicate efficiently. He adds, "Quant au langage de l'innocent, je l'envie mais peu de gens le liraient"⁸ [As for the language of the innocent, I envy it but few people would read it]. It might be tempting to read this symbolically as representing Duvert's own evolution in writing from youthful innocence to what is generally called a more mature sense of reality. As such a statement conforms with our dominant ideology, I pepper it with irony. I also note that *Récidive* is centered on a boy of about fifteen who is seldom in control of the events that are described, is usually younger than his partners, and plays what is known as the female role in homosexual encounters. He fits the description Montel has given of the "new narrator": "Non seulement il ne maîtrise plus l'action, n'influence plus l'enchaînement des faits, mais il ne se gouverne plus lui-même. Tout lui échappe, se passe hors de lui. Il ne maîtrise ni ses désirs, ni l'ordre social qui le broie"⁹ [Not only does he no longer control the action, influence the linking of facts, but he no longer governs himself. Everything escapes him, occurs outside of him. He governs neither his desires nor the social order which grinds him]. On the other hand, the narrator of *Journal*... tries to be in control, is older than his partners, and assumes both male and female roles. Suffice it to say for the moment that the three shifts are not incompatible.

I might add that even in *Récidive,* where the relationship between text and referent is a shaky one, the referent is nevertheless recognizable—as it is, for instance, in the fiction of Claude Simon or in the earlier fiction of Robbe-Grillet. The independence of the text is far more pronounced in the works of Jean-Claude Montel and Danielle Collobert, as it has become in those of Samuel Beckett. Duvert's second novel, *Portrait d'homme couteau,* actually does move in that direction, with the text seemingly in conflict with the referent; but in subsequent novels the conflict is resolved in favor of the referent. It does become obvious that he has an ax to grind, and as a result his writing becomes more and more transparent.

Of Savitzkaya's four novels, I actually read three—those that happened to be on the bookshelves of the Paris bookstore where I inquired. Reading them was a most pleasurable experience. They do not resemble any of the works by the so-called New Novelists, except perhaps, fleetingly, some aspects of those by Marguerite Duras. Nevertheless, in matters of plot, characters, verisimilitude, and linearity, they evidence no return to the ways of conventional fiction. It seemed as though the domain of the New Novel had been swept through by winds out of Lautréamont and the Surrealists, but with results that are unlike the tests that we associate with either. On the other hand, musing over Savitzkaya's name, I wondered if he were not born in Poland and if he had not emigrated in his youth, bringing along with him the memories of fantastic tales and legends of eastern Europe, suffusing his fiction with a mixture of cruelty and naiveté. Actually, he is Belgian; were he Polish, Savitzkaya would be an unlikely name for a man—but it matters little. I mention it only to give an idea of the impression I derived from his writing. It would seem then that the texts of Savitzkaya are quite special and very different. But wait—didn't I say there was something there that made me think of Duras? What exactly was it that reminded me of her writing? Certainly nothing like what happens when one reads Renaud Camus's *Passage,*[10] for instance, where entire statements, as well as characters' names, are quoted out of Duras's novels—along with those of two or three dozen other writers. It is something much more subtle. It has to do with the way clauses and sentences are put together, the way a paragraph is brought to a close—or rather, the way it opens up on something else. It is the way meaning is generated; it constitutes poetic language, if you wish, but poetic language comes in many guises. Two short excerpts, one from each writer, will perhaps illustrate my point.

Il relève la tête et le reconnaît. Il a toujours été là, dans cet hôtel, depuis le premier jour. Il l'a toujours vu, oui, toujours, sur la route devant l'hôtel, autour du tennis, la nuit, le jour, à tourner dans cet espace, à tourner seul. Son âge n'est pas ce qui apparaît, mes ses yeux.[11]

[He lifts his head and recognizes him. He was always there, in this hotel, since the first day. He has always seen him, yes, always, on the road in front of the hotel, around the tennis court, by night, by day, walking around in that space, walking alone. His age is not what appears, but his eyes.]

That is from Duras's *Détruire dit-elle.* And now, Savitzkaya:

C'était un véhicule de très bonne qualité, il nous permettait de nombreaux déplacements sur n'importe quel sol. C'était un véhicule rouge ou blanc ou noir, avec des portières et des fenêtres, avec des roues et un toit. C'était le meilleur des véhicules, le véhicule noir, la belle machine qui brillait. En fait, il s'agissait d'un ingénieux assemblage de tôles en métal léger et souple. Il nous conduisait partout, suivant nos désirs.[12]

[It was a very good quality vehicle, it enabled us to travel often on any kind of ground. It was a red or white or black vehicle, with doors and windows, with wheels and a roof. It was the best of vehicles, the black vehicle, the beautiful machine which shined. In fact, it was an ingenious assemblage of light and supple sheet metal. It would take us everywhere we wanted.]

That paragraph, from *La Traversée de l'Afrique,* refers to something quite different, and its meaning is also dissimilar. What brings the two together is not style either—but an absence of style. Each one exhibits syntactic repetitiousness: three sentences beginning with "Il" corresponding with three beginning with "C'était." In both, there is an enumeration of obvious and unnecessary details (unnecessary, that is, from a rational point of view). And both end with a suggestive illusion that is not rationally expected.

Now this may not seem like much to go on, but I believe we are in possession of a minute but significant clue. First, we must remember that Duras is a woman, as are two of the writers that I named in connection with Duvert, and three of the five "New Narrative" writers as well. With that in mind, let us leave Savitzkaya and proceed to the dialogue between Duras and Xavière Gauthier, published under the title of *Les Parleuses.*[13]

What will concern me in *Les Parleuses* is the attempt, by the two writers, to identify what in the writings of Duras issues specifically from a woman. It was not easy for them to do so, certainly no easier than it is for me to identify what is new in fiction writing today. At one point Gauthier says of some of Duras's recent works, "Je crois qu'il y a la question du sujet, aussi, dans vos livres. Je veux dire qu'elle est complètement mise en question, le sujet de Descartes, le sujet traditionnel, complètement plein, opaque et rond; il est complètement criblé.... Oui, lézardé."[14] [I think that there is also the matter of the subject in your books. I mean that it is completely called into question, Descartes' subject, the traditional subject, completely full, opaque and round; it is completely riddled.... Yes, cracked.] That is somewhat problematic. On the one hand, among those who have contributed most toward the rejection of the concept of the unitary subject, we find the names of Freud, Lacan, Derrida—all men. On the other hand, it is a fact that both Derrida and Lacan have struck a responsive chord among a number of women. And Derrida, at Cerisy, in 1972, in response to a question from a woman, said, "J'aimerais bien écrire, aussi, comme (une) femme. J'essaie."[15] [I would very much like to write, also, like (a) woman. I am trying.] Also at Cerisy, the same year—the occasion was a colloquium on Nietzsche—Derrida read a paper later republished separately as *Eperons/spurs*,[16] supposedly a commentary on Nietzsche's style. He said, "Il n'y a pas d'essence de la femme parce que la femme écarte et s'écarte d'elle-même. Elle engloutit, envoi par le fond, sans fin, sans fond, toute essentialité, toute identité, toute propriété."[17] [There is no such thing as the essence of woman because the woman averts and she is averted of herself. Out of the depths, endless and unfathomable, she engulfs and distorts all vestige of essentiality, of identity, of property.] And later, "Si le style était ... l'homme, l'écriture serait la femme"[18] [If style were a man ... then writing would be a woman].

Let me now confront you with two questions from Lacan, the first dealing with the subject, more precisely, the discourse of the subject in analysis.

Le sujet ne s'y engage-t-il pas dans une dépossession toujours plus grande de cet être de lui-même, dont ... il finit par reconnaître que cet être n'a jamais été que son oeuvre dans l'imaginaire et que cette oeuvre déçoit en lui toute certitude. Car dans ce travail qu'il fait de la reconstruire *pour un autre*, il retrouve l'aliénation fondamentale qui la lui a fait construire *comme un autre* et qui l'a toujours destinée à lui être dérobée *par un autre*.[19]

[Does the subject not become engaged in an ever growing dispossession of that being of his, concerning which ... he ends up by recognizing that this being has never been anything more than his construct in the imaginary and that this construct disappoints all his certainties? For in this labor which he undertakes to reconstruct *for another*, he rediscovers the fundamental alienation that made him construct it *like another*, and which has always destined it to be taken from him *by another*.]

The second one is twofold. The first part displaces what Derrida stated in the quotation I just read—but the practical consequences are the same: "Il n'y a pas *La* femme, article défini pour désigner l'universel. Il n'y pas *La* femme puisque ... de son essence elle n'est pas toute."[20] [There is not *The* woman, the definite article designating the universal. There is not *The* woman since ... she is not the entirety of her essence.] The second part may sound derogatory at first reading, but it is not at all:

Il n'y a de femme qu'exclue par la nature des choses qui est la nature des mots, et il faut bien dire que s'il y a quelque chose dont elles-mêmes se plaignent assez pour l'instant, c'est bien de ça—simplement, elles ne savent pas ce qu'elles disent, c'est toute la différence entre elles et moi.[21]

[A woman exists only as excluded by the nature of things, which is the nature of words, and it must be said in fact that if there is something about which they complain enough nowadays, it is precisely that—quite simply put, they do not know what they are saying, that is the entire difference between them and me.]

Think about it for a second and put it alongside what Duras says: "ce que j'essaye, c'est le discours organique, puisque je n'ai pas de référence,"[22] [What I attempt is organic discourse, since I have no reference.] Gauthier's comment: "l'homme empêche que le silence s'entende et ... c'est tellement rare, dans vos livres le silence s'entend" [man prevents silence from being heard and ... it is so rare, in your books silence is heard].[23] Later, "il n'y a que les femmes qui écrivent complètement"[24] [only women write completely]. Or, in the words of Josette Feral, commenting on the same Lacan statement, "They do not know what they are saying because the words are given to them from elsewhere, forged outside of them, because they accept them as already constituted, already ordered, hierarchized in given structures—morphological, lexical, syntactic."[25] No wonder the narrator of Luce Irigaray's *Passions élémentaires* cries out, "Bâillonnée par ton discours, rigidifiée sous tes jugements, recouverte des attributs de ton choix, qu'attends-tu encore de moi?"[26] [Gagged by your speech, made rigid under your judgments, clothed with attributes of your choosing, what more do you want from me?]

On the other hand, it is a woman, Julia Kristeva, who has provided us with the most elaborate theory of the heterogeneous subject, and her essays on that topic are well known and easy to locate.[27] Furthermore, Kristeva has worked out the theoretical basis for something Lacan and Derrida, and Duras and Gauthier as well, are agreed upon: what one might call womanly and manly characteristics do not necessarily coincide with the biological division of the sexes but have been given those names as a consequence of prejudices imposed upon us by a long-standing aspect of dominant ideology. It is true that Duras and Gauthier, in the spontaneity of their conversations, give excessive emphasis to their own uniqueness as women and the utter otherness of men. The endnotes they have added show that they are aware of that exaggeration, and toward the end of the first dialogue, Gauthier does say, "De toute façon je pense que les écrivains-hommes, pour écrire, il faut qu'ils soient des femmes aussi. Non?"[28] [In any case I think that men writers, in order to write, must be women also. No?] To which Duras responds, "Ah, oui, ça c'est certain."[29] [Oh, yes, that is certain.] The vocabulary is awkward, and the statement contradicts the specificity Duras claims for her writing.

Perhaps, instead of talking about the man/woman dichotomy, we should adopt the phraseology found in Kristeva's theory, where the symbolic modality is opposed to the semiotic one. And you will perhaps recall that, in *La Révolution du langage poétique*, she quoted from Mallarmé's *Le Mystère dans les lettres*, where the mystery involved a "space" underlying writing, and commented: "Evoquons seulement, en ce lieu, les passages qui apparentent le fonctionnement de cet 'air ou chant sous le texte' à la femme."[30] [For now, however, we shall quote only those passages that ally the functioning of that "air or song beneath the text" with woman.] Unfortunately, the semiotic, in that context, does not have the meaning most people associate with "semiotics," that has fallen victim to a trendy situation.

Be that as it may, it should be clear now that the answer toward which I am leaning, in response to my original question, is the following: yes, there probably is a new fiction today, and it is characterized by the ever-increasing presence of something one might call a woman-text. I do not much care for that hyphenated expression, but the more accurate phrase, semiotic text, would be impractical and confusing. Let me propose gynetext, a word Naomi Schor introduced in passing, in 1976, in an essay on *Madame Bovary*[31] — and see what happens.

The gynetext does not affect what our notion of the novel is or should be. The so-called New Novelists have taken care of that adequately. It affects writing itself — and here I prefer to say scription, a term I introduced a little over ten years ago and that corresponds to the strong connotation of the French word, *écriture*.[32] In other words, I agree up to a point with what Faye was saying in 1978 in the issue of *Change* that heralded "la Narration nouvelle." There is, of course, the matter of a different vocabulary: I emphasize "text" and "scription," whereas Faye and his friends stress the "narrative." That, however, is not the crucial difference. The fundamental lack that I notice in that issue of *Change* is the general, almost complete, absence of any reference to a woman-text, a gynetext. They promote the work of several women — but they leave them out of context, the context of all the women who have been publishing fiction during the 1970s. Even Mitsou Ronat, a woman who has been a member of the collective since early 1971, has nothing to say about women in that issue. What the writers of *Change* do stress is the link of the New Narrative to history. That is the thrust of Ronat's piece on Mallarmé. Again and again, throughout that issue, the theme of a reconciliation between Marxism and psychoanalysis is brought up.

In 1974, in an interview published in *Tel Quel,* Kristeva had said:

l'enjeu est le passage de la société patriarcale de classe et à religion, c'est-à-dire de la pré-histoire, vers.... Qui le sait? Ça passe en tout cas par ce qui est refoulé dans le discours, dans les rapports de reproduction et dans les rapports de production. Appelez-ça "femme" ou "couches sociales opprimées": c'est la même lutte, et jamais l'une sans l'autre.[33]

[at stake is a shift from a patriarchal society, with classes and religion, which is to say from pre-history, toward.... Who knows what? In any case, it involves what is repressed in speech, in the relations of reproduction and in the relations of production. Call it "woman" or "oppressed social levels": it is the same struggle, and never one without the other.]

She unwittingly put her finger on what would be missing in *Change* four years later.

There is yet a problem. If my woman-text, my gynetext, can be written by a man as well as a woman, why bother with the sexual identity of the biological subject? Why not simply deal with the text, or the narrative as the *Change* people did, and let the feminists fight their own battles? Now there is a statement I have heard in this country a number of times (curiously, though, I have not heard it made in France) to the effect that the liberation of women would also, in the long run, entail the liberation of men. It would be a liberation from various aspects of the dominant ideology, and it is a statement with which I agree. We must remember that the ideology also told us what roles woman should play in literature—what they were allowed to read and what they should write. In France, as well as here, one of the results of the feminist activity was a change in the way women wrote—more precisely, an easing of the repression that prevented them from publishing certain texts and freeing them from having to pretend that they were male writers or from adapting their writing to the ideologically acceptable phallotext. It goes without saying that extensive research is needed in order to unravel the complex ways in which this could have affected the writing of men, for the presence of Lautréamont and Artaud cannot be brushed aside that easily.

On the other hand, one cannot ignore the activity of women students in Paris during the upheaval of 1968. We need more research in order to learn more about their possible influence, both on the events themselves and on the male writers of the new generation. It seems clear that 1968 gave feminism a new impetus, even though, in France, the encouragement came via the United States. One would also have to examine the part played by male homosexual writers. As I indicated earlier, the first two fictional works of Tony Duvert display the presence of what I have since identified as a gynetext. Duras, in the dialogue I have been quoting from intermittently, said, "Je connais beaucoup de femmes dans mon cas qui ne peuvent supporter . . . des hommes que lorsqu'ils sont homosexuels" [I know many women who, feeling as I do, cannot bear men unless they are homosexual]. And a few lines later, "ils vivent sur un fond de désespoir et de peur qui les ouvre./—Les homosexuels?/oui, comme nous" [they live against a background of despair and fear which opens them up./—Homosexuals?/yes, like us].[34]

All I can say at this point is that my intuition tells me that there is a connection between feminist activity since 1968 and some types of fiction that are now being published—by men as well as by women. That, aside from the fact that more women seem to be involved, is an additional reason for discarding the technically accurate phrase "semiotic text." In all honesty, I want to give women credit for what is going on, even though those women we call feminists do not necessarily produce a gynetext. The word "gynetext" signals the presence of women, even though it is a problematic one, while "women-text" might seem to tie things too closely to the biological.[35]

At this point, I want to attempt to identify some of the salient features of the gynetext. I was earlier led to mention the disintegration of the unitary subject. I have pointed out evidence of this in the fiction of Savitzkaya and in the early writings of Duvert. It can also be detected in the work of Maurice Roche, whose first novel, *Compact*,[36] was dedicated to Faye and prefaced by Sollers—a collector's item, no doubt. In that preface, Sollers accurately points out that we, as readers, "sommes simultanément ce 'tu,' ce 'je,' ce 'on,' ce 'vous,' ce 'il,' ce 'ils,' du rêve, du mythe, de l'épopée, de la tragédie"[37] [are simultaneously this "you," this "I," this "one," this "you," this "he," this "they," of dream, of myth, of epic, of tragedy], for the subject of the text is anonymous and wanders in search of a forgotten name. In his preface to Montel's *Mélencolia* (1973),[38] Faye also stressed one of the character's (perhaps the main one) losses of identity, a character recognizable only through the use of the demonstrative pronoun "ce." The same concern as to the identity of the subject is stated in the following paragraph from Philippe Boyer's *Non Lieu*:

Ou ce sont des mots tracés sur la glace en grande lettres épaisses avec les produits de maquillage (un seul mot suffisamment explicite), des lettres majuscules qui s'interposent sur la surface froide entre celle qui regarde et celle qui est regardée. Des lettres qui interrogent: de cette question que Clarisse met tant d'insistance à ne pas entendre encore, celle de savoir qui est là (nulle part, dans la béance ouverte par le jeu de glace), quand on commence à douter qu'un nom suffise à répondre.[39]

[Or they are words drawn on the mirror with lipstick in large thick letters (one single word, explicit enough), capital letters that are interposed on the cold surface between she who looks and she who is looked at. Letters that inquire: with the question that Clarisse so insistently does not want to hear again, that of asking who is there (nowhere, in the gap opened by the mirror play), when one begins to doubt whether a name is a sufficient answer.]

She has a name, but an uncertain one: when she meets a man, she first gives it as Clarissa rather than Clarisse. Here, however, the problem emerges through meaning conveyed, not through the actual working of the text.

When I look at some of the fiction written by women, I find a similar contrast—but meaning is either much more explicit, or at the other extreme, the challenge to identify seems a bit more subtle. In Collobert's *dire I-II* (1972), for instance, the initial part of the fiction is a first-person narrative that addresses itself to a second person: "je" speaks to "tu." On account of the writer's name, one expects the "je" to be feminine, the "tu" masculine; one's expectations are often fulfilled, as in the statement taken at random, "En nous cernant de la tempête pour que tu sois devant moi, debout, dressé, comme un grand résistant, dur et tendu contre tout"[40] [Ringing ourselves with the storm to have you stand before me, erect, like a strong opponent, hard and taut in the face of everything]. On the other hand, when I read, "Je reste seul possesseur de la vision"[41] [I remain the sole owner of the vision], the masculine form of "seul" comes as a surprise. A typo, perhaps? Hardly possible, for a few lines further down I read, "Je te cherche toi, vivant, vivante, sans équivoque" [I am looking for you, alive,[42] with no equivocation]. Ironically, the text stresses an equivocation that the meaning denies. I could give you a number of similar examples that, in this fiction, illustrate the uncertainty of identities. To continue the previous question: "Qui est-tu. Te transformer comment. Appartenir déjà aux contradictions. J'admets d'être trahi. L'amour sans l'autre tout fait. Donne-toi. Je dis donne-toi. Je te reçois, je t'admets à nouveau, mais toi, déjà sombre, déjà engloutie." [Who are you. How can I transform you. To belong already to contradiction I accept being betrayed. Love without the other one being completely shaped. Give yourself. I say give yourself. I receive you, I accept you again, but you, already somber, already engulfed.] In the second part of Collobert's book, personal pronouns practically disappear and the syntax disintegrates—but that is another matter.

If, with Collobert, significance and meaning occasionally converge, that happens much more frequently in a fiction like Jeanne

Hyvrard's *La Meurtritude,* which is also a first-person narrative. Early in the book is read: "Les mots se vidant hors du corps de cette femme que je ne connais pas. Cette femme aux doigts coupés. Cette femme qui écrit une histoire qu'elle ne sait pas. Le corps habité par ces mains qui ne m'appartiennent pas."[43] [The words emptying out from the body of this woman whom I do not know. This woman with severed fingers. This woman who writes a story she does not know. The body inhabited by these hands which do not belong to me.] Meaning practically overflows. There is an implicit reference to the Lacan statement I quoted earlier, but most emphatically, there is an affirmation of the split nature of the subject. There is also the mention of severed fingers, and this does not convey meaning in the same fashion. The fingers are the narrator's, as the context implicitly states. It is made explicit two pages later: "Je les croise avec mes doigts coupés"[44] [I cross them with my severed fingers]. Later, however, appears the following: "Tu me regardes avec tes doigts coupés"[45] [You are looking at me with your severed fingers]. Previously, we had a reference to "les trois doigts de grand-mère coupés dans les machines"[46] [Grandmother's three fingers severed by the machines], and we eventually come upon the following: "La femme aux doigts coupés? Comment la laisser? Tous les jours, elle attend le retour de François"[47] [The woman with severed fingers? How can I leave her? Everyday she awaits François's return]. We know that the name François was connected with is Victorine, while the narrator is specifically called Jeanne, and even Jeanne Hyvrard, in the text. It is clear that the phrase referring to severed fingers has the same function as the gender agreement had in Collobert's novel: It signifies a problematic identity. Such uncertainty, or such a splitting of the subject, is most explicit in statements such as, "Ce n'est pas moi qui écris. C'est une autre femme. Elle habite mon corps"[48] [It is not me who is writing. It is another woman. She inhabits my body]. Or, as the narrator puts it in Hélène Cixous's fiction, *Dedans,* "Personne ne sait qui je suis.... Moi-même je n'ai pas su non plus, du moins au début"[49] [No one knows who I am. Even I did not know, at least at the beginning].

A second feature of the gynetext, one to which I have alluded several times, involves questioning language itself. Not only the narrative, the relation of language to a referent, but also its syntax ("Le mot compte plus que la syntaxe"[50] [The word counts more than syntax] Duras has said), grammar, and vocabulary. By the last, I mean treating words not as if they were transparent signs but rather as elements of the material world that can be tampered with, turned around, and played with, as Cixous does at the outset of *Portrait du soleil*. She "misspells" and breaks up the word "orange" in order to produce a birthplace, the city of Oran, and the "I" of the writer: "L'oranje est mon fruit de naissance et ma fleur prophétique. La première fois que j'ai coupé un mot, c'était elle"[51] [The orange is my natal fruit and my prophetic flower. The first time I ever cut a word, that was it].

More generally speaking, the assumption is that human beings are introduced to language at the moment of the thetic, or phallic, phase of their development, and that this thoroughly coded and structured language is the privileged manifestation of the symbolic modality in Kristeva's vocabulary. Such a language represents the law of the Father, while the semiotic modality is closer to the Mother, nature, the unconscious, the real. That was stated in the form of indictment by the narrator of Monique Wittig's *Les Guérillères*:

Elles disent, malheureuse, ils t'ont chassée du monde des signes, et cependant ils t'ont donné des noms, ils t'ont appelée esclave, toi malheureuse esclave. Comme des maîtres ils ont exercé leur droit de maîtres. . . . Elles disent le langage que tu parles est fait de mots qui te tuent. Elles disent, le langage que tu parles est fait de signes qui à proprement parler désignent ce qu'ils sont appropriés.[52]

[They say, unfortunate one, they chased you from the world of signs, and yet they gave you names, they called you slave, you unfortunate slave. Like masters they exercised their right as masters. . . . They say the language you speak is made of words which kill. They say, the language you speak is made of signs which literally speaking designate what they appropriated.]

The gynetext could be said to manifest the workings of the semiotic modality within the otherness of language — an otherness that social constraints have led most of us to accept as our own. Or, in Kristeva's words, "Le langage semble être vu depuis une terre étrangère dans l'écriture des femmes"[53] [Language seems to be seen from a foreign land in the writing of women]. (Remember the foreign land I fantasied in connection with Savitzkaya's work?) And Xavière Gauthier finds it astonishing that "l'homme et la femme semblent parler à peu près le même langage, autrement dit que la femme trouve 'sa' place à l'intérieur d'un système linguistique, linéaire, grammatical, qui ordonne le symbolique, le surmoi, la loi"[54] [men and women seem to speak almost the same language, that women, in other words, find "their" place within a linguistic, linear, grammatical system which orders the symbolic, the superego, the law]. Language is so vital, so basic, and so taken-for-granted, that it is difficult for people to realize that there is a part of them that is alien to it. It is no doubt for that reason that Duras and Gauthier had such difficulty, as mentioned earlier, in identifying what there was in Duras's fiction that could only have been written by a woman. Gauthier suggested that, "Ça bouge, ça glisse et c'est peut-être ça aussi cet espace qui se développe, très particulier à vous, il me semble, un espace à la fois très épais... et puis qui est à la fois clos et puis on sait qu'il y a un extérieur"[55] [It moves, it slides, and that may also be it, the space that is elaborated, that is characteristically yours it seems to me, a space both very dense... and also closed, and then we know that there is an outside]. Later in the dialogue, Duras approached it just a bit differently: "Et puis alors, il faut bien reprendre une sorte de grammaire élémentaire de l'image, ou de... de... comment nommer ce domaine?... Je ne sais pas.... Une femme habite complètement un endroit. Un homme le traverse, il ne l'habite pas vraiment. Je ne sais pas sur quel plan nous sommes"[56] [And then, we must return to a kind of elementary grammar of the image, of the... of... what shall I call this area?... I don't know.... A woman totally inhabits a place. A man passes through it, he does not really inhabit it. I do not know what level we are on]. The word does not appear, but a feeling of alienation is implicit in both statements—or perhaps better, a feeling of imprisonment. The same feeling comes across very strongly in Jeanne Hyvrard's *La Meurtritude*:

Je viens te voir au mouroir dans le château au bord du lac. C'est là qu'ils te tiennent enfermée. Au bord d'un marais dont tu ne sais pas le nom. Au bord d'un marais au bout de ma peine. Peut-être bien qu'il a un nom. C'est la demeure de l'innommable.[57]

[I come to see you in the castle's death-parlor by the lake. It is there that they have shut you away. By a marsh whose name you do not know. By a marsh at the end of my suffering. Perhaps it does have a name. It is the home of the unnamable.]

The narrative continues for the length of three paragraphs, a little under two pages, leading up to the statement, "Puisqu'il m'ont condamné à dire ce qu'ils veulent oublier"[58] [Since they have condemned me to saying what they want to forget]. What we have in those pages is a metaphorical statement referring to one of the features of the gynetext—that it is an *other* language (*innommable*), that it has been repressed (*enfermée, condamnée*), because it would state things that we have agreed to deny (*ils veulent oublier*). That points to the thin line that sometimes separates the gynetext from the feminist statement. A nearly identical meaning emerges out of a different metaphor in Duvert's *Récidive*:

Mais la vérité sortant du puits comme un outrage à la pudeur, car elle est nue—compliqué d'un attentat aux moeurs, si elle cherche à attirer le passant. Putain sans attrait, on la rejette dans son puits, une meule au cou.[59]

[But truth emerging naked from the well commits an act of indecent exposure—aggravated by soliciting if she tries to attract the passerby. Whore of no appeal, she is thrown back in her well, with a millstone around her neck.]

There is a difference: Duvert's metaphor is a didactic one; it comes close to being a parable. *Dedans,* one of the early fictions by Cixous, while it suffuses its title with the connotation of imprisonment, deals much more with the relation of a child, who happens to be female, with her father. And yet, that same feature of the gynetext manages to work its way through:

J'ai peu de mots. Mon père qui les avait tous, est parti si précipitamment, qu'il n'a pas eu le temps de me les donner.... Depuis le silence de mon père, je vis sur mon maigre patrimoine. Pour connaître les mots, je ne dispose que des livres qui sont dans la bibliothèque noire. Ma mère ne parle guère, de plus son langage n'est pas le même que celui de mon père.... Là où elle en sait plus que moi, c'est en anatomie et en physiologie. Bien que cela ne me serve à rien ici, je retiens ces mots par dizaines, pour lui faire plaisir; quand elle énumère et dénombre, je la suis, et nous nous recontrons ainsi aux articulations secrètes du Corps Humain.[60]

[I have few words. My father, who had them all, left so quickly that he had no time to give them to me.... Since my father's silence, I have been living on my meager heritage. To know the words, I have at my disposal only books which are in the dark library. My mother hardly speaks, and her language is not the same as that of my father. What she knows more about than I do is anatomy and physiology. Although it is of no use to me here, I retain dozens of those words, to please her; when she enumerates and makes lists, I follow her, and thus we meet at the secret articulations of the Human Body.

The final clause of that Cixous quotation brings us to another, perhaps the most important, feature of the gynetext, something I had adumbrated in one of my comments on *Récidive*: an awareness of the materiality of our being, the presence of the flesh.[61] Duras and Gauthier had also pointed that out while discussing women's knowledge or awareness (the French word they used is *connaissance*); in contrast to men, they have a "connaissance plus organique, plus proche du corps"[62] [more organic knowledge, one closer to the body]: "Elle la reçoit, oui, corporellement, justement"[63] [She acquires it yes, corporally, precisely]. In order to illustrate this, I give you a paragraph out of *Retable* by Chantal Chawaf:

La brique translucide des contreforts en train de luire. Les facades bossuées à saillies, émergées des sarcophages de leur rez-de-chausée et bombées, astres, fruits, dômes, globes, mamelles indistinctes car tellement proches, donnent sur l'utérus d'eau, sur la liaison intime sous nous, ainsi s'élève la cité sans distances, la grosse joue, l'architecture fugitive d'un frôlement charnel dont nous longeons en flottant les muqueuses, la dilatation des édifices. A même le noir de la mort, une pleine lune de fertilité cherche à se recomposer, enveloppe sonique vibrante, un souffle, une haleine, une roulade, une trille montant du milieu liquidien, quelque chose chante, d'humain, de féminin, mausolées, cantique à coupoles, hauts étages au dessus des fenêtres à tabernacles, vastes galleries sur la mer, craie du lait coagulé, mélodie continue qui a perdu, si jeune, la réalité de ses bras, de la force douce de ses bras, l'humidité des lèvres chaudes tout à côté des bras, l'engorgement de ses seins, et son langage chante encore.[64]

[The translucent brick of the gleaming buttresses. The embossed facades with projections, emerged from the sarcophagi of their first floor, and bulging, stars, fruit, domes, globes, breasts indistinct because so close, look out onto the watery uterus, onto the intimate relationship beneath us, thus rises the city of no distance, the bulging cheek, the fleeting architecture of a light carnal touch along whose mucous membranes we are floating, the dilation of the buildings. In the bare black of death, a full moon of fertility tries to put itself together again, vibrating sonic envelope, a breath, a breathing, a cadence, a trill rising from the liquidous environment, something sings, something human, feminine, mausoleums, hymns with cupolas, high ceilings over windows with tabernacles, vast galleries on the sea, chalk of curdled milk, continuous melody which has lost, so young, the reality of its arms, of the soft strength of its arms, the humidity of warm lips very close to the arms, the fullness of its breasts, and its langauge still sings.]

As no doubt perceived, there is more than materiality and sensuality in this passage. There is also a shimmering relation to the referent, unorthodox syntax, use of neologisms—with the problem of identity underlying the entire fiction.

In conclusion, after having experienced the signifying process carried out by the gynetext in the fiction by those writers I have quoted—and this brief survey by no means pretends to be exhaustive—I shall restate my intuitive answer to the initial question. Yes, there is a "new novel" today, and it is a fiction that harbors a gynetext, whether it be written by men or women.

Notes

1. Michèle Perrein, "Ainsi parle une telle qui écrit," *Magazine Littéraire*, 180 (January 1982), 19. This is a special issue entitled "Femmes/Une Autre Ecriture?" I am indebted to Danielle Haase-Dubosc, Director of Reid Hall, Paris, for calling the issue to my attention.

2. Jean Pierre Faye, "La Narration nouvelle et transformationnelle," *Change*, 34-35 (March 1978), 7-8.

3. Tony Duvert, *Récidive* (Paris: Minuit, 1967; revised, 1976). Other works, all published by Minuit, include, *Portrait d'homme couteau* (1969), *Interdit de séjour* (1969), *Le Voyageur* (1970), *Paysage de fantaisie* (1973), *Journal d'un innocent* (1976), *Quand Jonathan mourut* (1978).

4. Duvert, *Récidive*, 15.

5. *Ibid.*, 107.

6. Christine Rochefort, *Quand tu vas chez les femmes* (Paris: Grasset, 1982).

7. Chantal Chawaf, *Retable, La Rêverie* (Paris: Des Femmes, 1974), *Cercoeur* (Paris: Mercure de France, 1975), *Blé de semences* (Paris: Mercure de France, 1976), *Le Soleil et la terre* (Paris: Pauvert, 1977), *Rougeâtre* (Paris: Pauvert, 1978), *Maternité* (Paris: Stock, 1979), *Landes* (Paris: Stock, 1980), *Crépusculaire* (Paris: Ramsay, 1981).

8. Duvert, *Journal d'un innocent*, 272.

9. Jean-Claude Montel, "L'Identité—le nom," *Change*, 34-35 (March 1978), 88.

10. Renaud Camus, *Passage* (Paris: Flammarion, 1975).

11. Marguerite Duras, *Détruire dit-elle* (Paris: Minuit, 1969), 15.

12. Eugène Savitzkaya, *La Traversé de l'Afrique* (Paris: Minuit, 1979), 20. Other novels, also published by Minuit, include: *Mentir* (1977), *Un Jeune homme trop gros* (1978), *La Disparition de maman* (1982).

13. Marguerite Duras and Xavière Gauthier, *Les Parleuses* (Paris: Minuit, 1974).

14. *Ibid.*, 14.

15. Jacques Derrida, "La Question du style," Discussion, in *Nietzsche aujourd'hui,* vol. I (Paris: collection 10/18, 1973), 299.

16. Jacques Derrida, *Eperons/spurs* (Venezia: Corbo e Fiore, 1976), distributed in France by Flammarion.

17. *Ibid.*, 42. This is a quadrilingual edition; the English text, 43.

18. *Ibid.*, 46. English text, 47.

19. Jacques Lacan, *Ecrits* (Paris: Seuil, 1966), 249. Translation *Ecrits/A Selection,* trans. Alan Sheridan (New York: W. W. Norton & Co., 1977), 42.

20. Lacan, *Seminaire XX* (Paris: Seuil, 1975), 68.

21. *Ibid.*

22. Duras, *Les Parleuses* (Paris: Minuit, 1974), 48.

23. Gauthier, *Les Parleuses,* 49.

24. *Ibid.*, 51.

25. Josette Feral, "Towards a Theory of Displacement," *Sub-Stance,* 32 (1981), 55.

26. Luce Irigaray, *Passions élémentaires* (Paris: Minuit, 1982), 62.

27. See Julia Kristeva, "Le Sujet en procès" and "L'Expérience et la pratique," in *Polylogue* (Paris: Seuil, 1977).

28. Gauthier, *Les Parleuses,* 51.

29. Duras, *Les Parleuses,* 51.

30. Julia Kristeva, *Revolution in Poetic Language,* trans. Margaret Waller (New York: Columbia University Press, 1984), n.p.

31. Naomi Schor, "Pour une thématique restrainte," *Littérature,* 22 (May 1976), 46.

32. See my *French Fiction Today* (New Brunswick, N.J.: Rutgers University Press, 1972), *passim.*

33. Julia Kristeva, "La Femme, ce n'est jamais ça," *Tel Quel,* 59 (Autumn 1974), 24.

34. Duras, *Les Parleuses,* 152-153.

35. I was overly optimistic on this score. When I read this paper at New York University, Monique Wittig reacted adversely and interpreted my gynetext as just another attempt at isolating "feminine writing"—as had been done in the past. John Barth suggested later that I should discard the word "gynetext" because it was likely to open up a can of worms. Having said it, however, I now find it difficult to un-say it. Perhaps someone else will come up with a better term.

36. Maurice Roche, *Compact* (Paris: Seuil, 1966). His other novels would perhaps reveal different aspects of the gynetext.

37. Philippe Sollers, Preface to *Compact,* 9.

38. Jean-Claude Mentel, *Mélencolia,* preface by Jean Pierre Faye (Paris: Seghers/Laffont, 1973).

39. Philippe Boyer, *Non Lieu* (Paris: Seuil, 1972), 15.

40. Danielle Collobert, *dire I-II* (Paris: Seghers/Laffont, 1972), 58. The same publisher brought out *il donc* in 1976.

41. *Ibid.*, 36.

42. Translators' note: "Vivant" (masculine) and "vivante" (feminine) have no real equivalents as adjectives in English.

43. Jeanne Hyvrard, *La Meurtritude* (Paris: Minuit, 1977), 17-18. Other novels by Jeanne Hyvrard, also published by Minuit, include *Les Prunes de Cythère* (1975), *Mère la mort* (1976), and *Les Doigts du figuier* (1977).

44. *Ibid.*, 19.

45. *Ibid.*, 84.

46. *Ibid.*, 46.

47. *Ibid.*, 130.

48. *Ibid.*, 21.

49. Hélène Cixous, *Dedans* (Paris: Grasset, 1969), 66-67. Her *Portrait du soleil* was published by Denoël in 1973. Other works by Cixous are too numerous (and too well known) to be listed here.

50. Duras, *Les Parleuses*, 11.

51. Cixous, *Portrait de soleil*, 5.

52. Monique Wittig, *Les Guérillères* (Paris: Minuit, 1969), 162. An earlier novel, *L'Opoponax*, was published by Minuit in 1964.

53. Julia Kristeva, "Oscillation du 'pouvoir' au 'refus,' " *Tel Quel*, 58 (Summer 1974), 100.

54. Gauthier, "Existe-t-il une écriture de femmes?," *Les Parleuses*, 96.

55. Gauthier, *Les Parleuses*, 16.

56. Duras, *Les Parleuses*, 75.

57. Hyvrard, *La Meurtritude*, 25.

58. *Ibid.*, 27.

59. Duvert, *Récidive*, 23.

60. Cixous, *Dedans*, 53-56.

61. It should go without saying that since men and women joy and suffer through differently constituted bodies, themes and intensities within their respective scription will perforce be different.

62. Gauthier, 31.

63. Duras, 31.

64. Chawaf, *Retable, La Rêverie*, 91-92.

Discussion

Tom Bishop: If this is the New Novel today, or rather tomorrow, as in reality you are really looking ahead, I find your vision to be very apocalyptic and dismal. I believe that the distinguishing of novels written by women when the description of this specificity derives from three people among whom only one has written novels—I refer here to Lacan, Kristeva, and Derrida, Derrida being the only one who wrote any—leaves us once again very long on theory and rather short on fiction. In my opinion, the phrase "Only a woman could have written that" is precisely one against which someone like Nathalie Sarraute has struggled her entire life. If there were only one thing to be said on behalf of the Nouveau Roman, I think it would be that the voice of the Nouveau Roman, whether that of Sarraute, Simon, Pinget, Ollier, or any other writer, is *one* voice and not the voice of a man or the voice of a woman. It seems to me that this is precisely one of its strengths. I had a feeling that even Monique Wittig, whom you quoted, winced rather noticeably at seeing herself bound by the kind of interpretation you offered. I may be wrong; she will have to speak for herself.

Leon Roudiez: I had no idea I was binding anybody. In the first place, I thought I made it clear—although given the nature of my talk, it may not have been clear—that I did *not* want to distinguish female writers from male writers, but rather to distinguish *one* feature in today's writing which I am calling, temporarily, the "gynetext," a feature that some men share with some women. As I pointed out, there are feminist writers who do not manifest the "gynetext" specifically. And I have in mind certain books that I recently read: *Les Variations Goldberg* by Nancy Houston, for instance, that might be called feminist. It is a good novel, but I do not find a "gynetext" in it. So, too, for *Fatima,* by Leila Sebbar, which is not the kind of novel to manifest a "gynetext." This also is a feminist novel, but not a "gynetext." Therefore I am not making this distinction which disturbs you.

Monique Wittig: I am very surprised that Leon Roudiez has fallen right into the middle of the most critical issue now taking place within the women's movement, both here and in France. This is the question of knowing whether or not there is a feminine writing. I think that it was Hélène Cixous who first used this phrase. Before responding, may I remind you that Virginia Woolf, when she wrote, used to say, "Le premier devoir de l'écrivain femme est de tuer l'ange du foyer en elle" [The first duty of the woman writer is to kill the angel of the hearth within herself].

The second thing that I would like to say is that, as a writer, since you quoted me, all that I am trying to do, all that I am trying to break down in my books, has to do with categories of sex. My effort is to go beyond categorization by gender. What I was saying yesterday about Nathalie Sarraute, in reflecting specifically on language, is that for me the basic language is a language that falls short of, or goes beyond, as you wish, categories of sex. From the moment we speak of sex, we have to speak in terms of symbols. As far as I am concerned, I come closer to a language that is much more concrete than that. When you quoted this passage from *Les Guérillères* on words that kill, I meant it literally, not at all symbolically. There *are* words that kill. Words that kill are words of oppression. And they do not kill symbolically. They kill in reality. They kill directly. Nathalie Sarraute, in her *Tropismes,* shows how the use of language can, in certain cases, really kill.

The third remark which I wish to make is that the category of the subject is, indeed, currently in jeopardy, but this is not due to women. It is historically precarious. It has been shaky since the beginning of the twentieth century. It has been shaky since 1968 for us in France. It is shaky for homosexuals and for women, but for concrete and materialist reasons, not at all for symbolic reasons. I think that it is shaky for everyone. If it is shaky for some, it is shaky for others. And if we cannot go on together, we will go nowhere.

Leon Roudiez: I really do not see any problem. Once again, as I answered Tom Bishop, I had no intention of making a gender distinction and of identifying a feminine writing. I did not use that phrase. I am well aware of the important controversy, that is more than a controversy, that is preoccupying feminist circles, mainly in France, perhaps less in the United States. There is a recent book by Jane Gallop called *The Daughters of Seduction: Feminism and Psychoanalysis* in which she specifically takes up this problem with regard to a text by Stephen Heath. This is precisely the danger encountered in identifying certain aspects of writing with *a* woman or *the* woman or *the* feminine. But despite this danger, it nevertheless remains, or so it seems to me, that there were those prejudices, let us say this oppression. It was present for so long and imposed on women a certain number of characteristics rejected by men, by the prevailing ideology. There was this association of certain characteristics with a so-called feminine writing. And the danger, obviously, is that this be revived. It is also true, however, at least this is the feeling I have for the moment, that what was rejected, and projected onto women, is something that men repressed, something that they did not want to accept. They claimed not to be like that and that it was women who were like that.

I know that many ex-feminists or feminists in France do not like being called feminists, but their struggle is nevertheless analogous to that of women called feminists in the United States. And it is thanks to the feminist movement, to the work that these women have accomplished and that they are still accomplishing, that those repressed traits, suppressed by the prevailing ideology, are surfacing again. Men, little by little, are realizing that these are not feminine traits, that they are traits common to men and women, but that they were projected onto women historically. It is also thanks to them that now, perhaps, we are coming to a time when both men and women can shoulder those repressed traits.

Monique Wittig: What do you mean by that? What are those repressed traits?

Leon Roudiez: I come back to this theoretic division between symbolic language, or at least symbolic modality, and semiotic modality and, in a way, representing the law, the father....

Monique Wittig: But language cannot be only a symbolic modality. It is not possible. Language exists materially. It is a sound, it is written, it is not *only* a symbol. And furthermore, we are facing an Anglo-Saxon audience. And to it, symbol and sign mean the same thing, whereas in France, they do not mean the same thing.

Leon Roudiez: But by symbolic modality, I mean what organizes language in an extremely rigorous way, with syntax, grammar.... And when this is impaired, it makes the repressed things reemerge. Artaud would be an example. Obviously it is a language, if you wish, but it is a language whose structure, determined by the symbolic modality, is, in a way, often destroyed in certain of Artaud's texts. Artaud was not a woman and Artaud was perhaps not influenced by women, but there is something there which goes along the same lines, it seems to me.

Monique Wittig: Yes, but there has been a tendency to completely assimilate irrationality, for instance, craziness, with women. This has always existed! It is not new! It is as old as the hills! This is precisely what men wanted women to be: crazy, foolish, moronic, not knowing what to say. "They don't know what they are saying." You said so yourself! But I thought I knew what I was saying!

Leon Roudiez: I think that we have a final point to clarify here: namely, craziness. We do know, thanks to many things and thanks to the works of Michel Foucault in particular, that craziness is an arbitrary category. It is a category which enables us to dismiss something and thereby to repress and suppress. And if women have been associated with craziness, it is not because women were crazy, but because people did not want to have anything to do with certain aspects of culture and society. Now it is time for men to reclaim craziness.

Monique Wittig: So it is no longer our fight?

Leon Roudiez: No, if you wish.

Monique Wittig: If it is no longer our fight, I agree.

Michel Rybalka: I want to thank you, Leon Roudiez, for this remarkable lecture about which I have, however, a few hesitations. Your question was: "Is there a Nouveau Roman?" I think that you have very well shown both the homosexual and feminist components of the New Novel and, personally, I would add that within the feminist framework of writing there is one very fine author, Jeanne Hyvrard, and that within the area of homosexual literature, there is also a very fine author who is now becoming well known. This is Renaud Camus. At the beginning, you wanted to describe to us one particular situation and you left out, therefore, numerous elements. This is to say that there are, I think, components to the Nouveau Roman other than those you described. Finally, you have given us a kind of thesis, a hypothesis.

Leon Roudiez: A hypothesis.

Michel Rybalka: And you left out a rather significant number of elements of reality, if you will. I am not going to enumerate right now all the elements that you failed to notice, but I would like to mention here, in this regard, Georges Perec and all those connected with the *Oulipo*. The finest author of the 1970s was perhaps Georges Perec, and it may well be he who, in a sense, has prolonged a kind of New Novel.

Leon Roudiez: I think that I said, or at least suggested, that my list was not exhaustive and that I therefore left out many things. I agree with you that it is a hypothesis, not a demonstration, and I hope that others will now be interested in this hypothesis and will try to determine whether there is, indeed, something to it, whether there is some truth in what I suggested, or rather in what my intuition suggested to me.

As for Georges Perec, okay. He is a very interesting writer. Does he manifest the features that I listed? I am not always sure, but it is possible. We should consider the example of a great many writers by studying their texts. Men or women, it does not matter.

The New Novel—
Past, Present, Future:
A Roundtable

Alain Robbe-Grillet *Monique Wittig*
Claude Simon *François Jost*
Nathalie Saurraute *Michel Rybalka*
Robert Pinget *Tom Bishop*

Tom Bishop: Personally, I was very struck by a number of things these last three days. Most notably, that we have found—that you New Novelists have found—points in common rather than elements that separate you. Robert Pinget spoke of solidarity, of writers backing together the Nouveau Roman. I think that this is what is emerging now or, in any case, what is emerging here. It may be a mere tolerance, but I think that it is rather an appreciation that you seem to have for each other, one that you have undoubtedly always had.

Perhaps it is due to the fact that for a long time people wanted to emphasize above all what separates you. In fact, for a while, for a very long while, and all this broke out around the Cerisy colloquium, there was a tendency to define you, to let you be defined by the theoreticians. It seems to me that this time has passed and that today you all speak of your own work, or you all tend to speak of your work, without first thinking of the critical point of view and of the entire theoretical picture, the entire theoretical superstructure, that actually seemed very heavy for a rather long period of time. I see in this a liberation in the way you all view your work. It may be a kind of Olympian detachment that derives from the fact that the Nouveau Roman is better established, but I would like to ask you if, indeed, you do have the feeling that you have detached yourselves from the image of you that was projected by the criticism of the 1960s and 1970s.

Claude Simon: As far as our projected image is concerned, if you are referring to day-to-day criticism which, as everyone knows, is fickle, I have never been very concerned with its most often derisive attacks. As for the more serious criticism, that which can be called "theoretical" (and I think you are alluding to Ricardou), it seems to me that it was rather he who separated from us, or at least from me. While I continue to consider his theoretical works among the most estimable, I have the feeling that he pushed to the extreme a spirit too radical and sterilizing to be "practical" and that this has worked against him.

Alain Robbe-Grillet: I think it could be said that Ricardou's role has been very positive, as the function of theory for a writer is not at all to comfort him. It is not that he first creates a work and that he is then bolstered by theoretical strongholds, by a defense of the work in question. That is perhaps how Ricardou conceived of it, but for us writers, theory has always played a very different role. It has aimed at chasing us away from ourselves rather than securing us in the positions that we have acquired. All that can be theorized, in other words, is practically of no interest to the creator. Just as the work of art begins where meaning stops, so, too, it can be said that what I am trying to do begins where the theory of what I am trying to do stops. Consequently, theory is very interesting precisely because it shows just how far meaning can go and just where the beginning of what is no longer formal or formalist meaning, but rather the work which remains to be done, may be situated. What interests the writer is the work to be done, not the work he did. And one can theorize only about what already exists.

As far as I am concerned, I do not in any way renounce Ricardou's theoretical works, even if I do consider them mad. As a matter of fact, this madness is part of something that continually fascinates the writer. "And today," Tom Bishop claims, "we have moved away from...." No! It is just that certain theories are outdated, not only the formalist theories of Ricardou, but also an entire period of theorization. This was a time when theory played a very significant role, and it often irritated Americans that theory was so important in France. I think I am very French in this respect: I like theories. Of course I do not necessarily respect them, but I was trained as a scientist and have always been fascinated by scientific theories. A scientist never thinks that a theory has to be right or wrong. This does not exist in science. A theory is not right or wrong: a theory is productive or it is not. There were theories which, at a given moment, produced or resulted in something, even if it was merely a way of chasing ourselves away from ourselves, of driving ourselves out of the texts we had written and which already could be theorized about.

Tom Bishop: But the fact that today those theories have no longer the same....

Alain Robbe-Grillet: But others are on their way. Beware!

Nathalie Sarraute: With regard to Ricardou, I have always considered his theories, or at least most of them, to be untenable. They were of no significance for writers, for when they write, writers are not thinking about theories. I do believe, however, that Ricardou's points of view were dangerous to readers—and we are all readers. If I, as a reader, had had to read books according to Ricardou's principles, I would have stopped reading. It would be impossible for me to read a book by Claude Simon, looking for the word "yellow" on page 67 and on page 126, even if this were one of the rules of the game and if Claude Simon had written his book for us to find the word, which, by the way, I do not believe to be the case. This was the danger of Ricardou's theories: they ran the risk of turning people away from reading.

Monique Wittig: I would like to remind you that Alain Robbe-Grillet, in *Pour un Nouveau Roman,* begins his book by saying that he is not a theoretician. What he does do, however, is explain the problems he has progressively faced in his writings. And the same holds true for Nathalie Sarraute. They both had to defend themselves against a certain press that was misinterpreting what was taking place. I was feeling exactly the same thing a moment ago when I reacted to feminine writing. Today, as soon as a woman writes anything, the sign "feminist writer" is tacked on her. For me, the concept of feminine writing is a paradox that is absolutely undemonstrable.

Alain Robbe-Grillet: What Monique Wittig has pointed out is very true. It is true that Nathalie Sarraute published, as did I, writings of a theoretical nature. But these writings of a theoretical nature are never considered a theory of the novel and, *a fortiori,* as *the* theory of the novel. By this I mean that a theoretician is someone who builds a totality. He is someone who ties together all his preoccupations and then decrees normative truths—about the field of literature, for instance. And it is obvious that neither Nathalie Sarraute, in *L'Ere du soupçon,* nor I myself, in *Pour un Nouveau Roman,* have ever done that.

In closing the first session here, François Jost spoke along these lines when he remarked that with Ricardou we had gone from proscription to prescription. What we first theorized about, Nathalie Sarraute and I, was the langauge of the critics in authority. We analyzed expressions, words, criteria that we found in the press. All that Nathalie Sarraute published in *L'Ere du soupçon* was, in a way, an analysis of what we were reproached for not doing. Obviously, this was proscription, and we were opposing those criteria.

On the other hand, it is true that Ricardou's period was one when suddenly people wanted to prescribe, to say "This is what has to be done." Obviously, this was the very opposite of our own idea of the Nouveau Roman, since when we got together—first Nathalie Sarraute and I and then all our friends—it was precisely under the banner of freedom. What we were claiming for every writer was the freedom to invent the novel, everyone for himself and in each novel he wrote.

For me, any writer who invents the novel is a "Nouveau Romancier." I think that it was Nathalie Sarraute who, already at the beginning, remarked that the word "formalist" was wrongly being applied to those people who were inventing new forms, because on the contrary, the formalists are those who reproduce already existing forms. There was not any prescriptive theorization here at all, only a descriptive analysis of what the critics in authority were saying.

Tom Bishop: Alain Robbe-Grillet, you said yesterday or the day before that the revolution that the Nouveau Roman was intended to be had not materialized and that ultimately literature was not profoundly changed by you, in the plural.

Alain Robbe-Grillet: No, it was changed, but the revolution did not materialize because freedom cannot be an institution. If the Nouveau Roman had succeeded, Ricardou would, in short, have taken over and our novels would have been institutionalized. This was

The New Novel: Past, Present, Future

what Stalin did, if you will, with Marxism. He dogmatically transformed what in the beginning was a movement toward, a movement of, something unknown. I am talking about a kind of project which is not even clearly defined for itself and which ventures in a direction that it itself propels. The revolution did not succeed, therefore, fortunately, for if it had, we would have stopped writing. Everyone would have stopped writing. I say fortunately because this movement of continually chasing ourselves away from ourselves must be endless. The greatest danger for a writer is to rest on his laurels, to say that he wrote such and such a book that people liked and that he is now going to write another one just like it.

You know that I, personally, have always been reproached for not writing as well as I did the year before. Those critics who had authoritatively scorned *La Jalousie,* for instance, claimed, when I published *Projet pour une révolution à New York,* that it was a pity that I had not continued to write along the same wonderful lines as *La Jalousie.* But what precisely is important for an artist is that he disappoint his public in order to prevent it from becoming tranquilized. And the fact that the Nouveau Roman has not become institutionalized, I phrased as the fact that the Nouveau Roman has not succeeded, but this failure is its very life.

Tom Bishop: This question of succeeding or not succeeding, of revolutionizing or not revolutionizing, does it not also imply the existence of another generation, one following yours, in which there would be novels linked, in some way, to what you did? Do you have the impression that there are writers who have, in one way or another, followed what you tried to do?

Alain Robbe-Grillet: There are writers all over the world who admit to having been influenced by the Nouveau Roman. I am thinking of Peter Henke, for instance, in Austria or of Julio Cortázar in South America, as well as many others around the world. But to create epigones is not the artist's goal. What I fear most are the numerous pseudo-Simons, pseudo–Robbe-Grillets, the pseudo-Durases. If someone has to write following in our footsteps, it will not be to our glory, but "against us." This is exactly how I consider my having been influenced by Sartre, for I wanted to write "against him." And when people stand up to someone whom they admire, then there is creation: in standing up to, and not at all in following.

François Jost: I do not want to return to the madness of certain theoreticians whom you mentioned a moment ago, but while hearing you speak, I asked myself various questions. These really amount to only one that I will formulate at the end.

I wondered, first, when you were speaking of Ricardou, about the relation of the theoretician to the writer. This relation is, in fact, rather new insofar as, except for Mallarmé's or Proust's drawing-room conversations, few writers have continually found themselves confronted by their critics. This seems to me to be something rather peculiar to the New Novel and something rather new. When a critic speaks of the New Novel, he often experiences a feeling of embarrassment insofar as there is always a New Novelist facing him who tells him, "This can no longer be said because it is no longer fashionable" or "This has to do with linguistics," and so on.

Robbe-Grillet often asks: "What impels a writer to write?" Now I would ask him the question, or I would ask myself the question: "What impels a critic to write?" By this I mean, why does a critic choose to speak about the Nouveau Roman rather than about Balzac or Flaubert? There must be a reason why he has chosen one area rather than another. The critic is often supposed to be a kind of angel: not only should he not speak of himself, but of someone else. He should speak, moreover, of someone else in a way that accommodates this someone else. This is something which is difficult to ask of the critic. The critic, when he writes criticism, is looking for something in the writer of which he is unaware. If Ricardou sees exactly the same thing in Flaubert, Roussel, Mallarmé, Poe, Robbe-Grillet, and Claude Simon, it is because, in fact, he is looking for something that he does not manage to find and not merely because he is interested in Robbe-Grillet, Flaubert, Poe, Mallarmé, or Simon. To a certain extent, he tries to understand a little about what is taking place in his head.

Thus the question that a critic may have to face—and it is an agonizing question, a question that always causes anxiety when one is writing, I think—is that of knowing whether, when he speaks about a writer, what he is saying has any chance of corresponding to the texts of which he is speaking. It is a question that we sometimes ask ourselves in all honesty, but then we prefer to go out for a walk! But what I am wondering, with regard to the criticism that has accompanied the New Novel, is whether it did not have at a certain time a certain element of truth. Of course, today, it is very easy to reject a certain kind of criticism, one which, as far as

The New Novel: Past, Present, Future

I am concerned, I have always rejected, but is this not simply due to the fact that the New Novel has completely evolved? If it were possible to find generators, or to say in 1970 that a novel was made from, entirely from, the word "yellow" or the word "red," did this not, after all, correspond more or less to something?

It seems to me that what is interesting in this movement of the New Novel is precisely that in practice it has really called into question that on which it was leaning ten years ago. What renders ten-year-old theories obsolete is not the fact that ten years ago the thinking was more stupid than that of today, but mainly that today's novel is no longer yesterday's (and when I say today's and yesterday's novels, I am still situating myself within the New Novel). What Nathalie Sarraute or Claude Simon, Robert Pinget or Alain Robbe-Grillet are producing is, of course, characteristic of Sarraute, Simon, Pinget, and Robbe-Grillet, but it is no longer truly characteristic of the Nouveau Roman, if by Nouveau Roman one means a unique and homogeneous school. This is why it is really stupid for a critic to cling to yesterday's theories and to try to construct a unifying theory like those of the 1970s. But the question I would like to ask of all these New Novelists before us is, specifically, do you not feel that if, in 1970, there was a completely formalistic, and a little too rigoristic criticism, this was due in part to the fact that it could disclose much more easily than today various things that were calling for as structural analysis?

Claude Simon: We must agree on the meaning of this "more easily" and the phrase "structural analysis." I do not have the impression that my last novels are less "structured" than those of ten or fifteen years ago. But of course I may be wrong. In any case, is persisting in constructing endless anagrams from the words of the text really undertaking a structural analysis (to say nothing of claiming to find in them the keys to the text)? Sometimes this produces interesting results; sometimes it does not. For instance, when Ricardou transforms *La Route des Flandres* [*The Road to Flanders*] into "La Route des flancs" ["The Road of the Flanks"], I remain perplexed. The transformation of *La Bataille de Pharsale* into "la bataille de la phrase" [the battle of the phrase] is much more successful. But where does this lead? The Geneva library owns millions of anagrams by Saussure. He stopped, I think, when he realized that he could also find some on postcards written by a soldier. But what can I answer Ricardou when he tells me: "Perhaps this was not your intent, but, nevertheless, it is there!"? Well, fine. And the same goes for the color yellow which, as he noticed, reappears often in this novel. That, too, is a fact. So what? I think I remember that someone worked with might and main at a similar interpretation of the violet or the mauve in Proust. Once again, all this leaves me rather cold and, in any case, it does not seem to in any way resolve the question of the structures in a novel. At a certain moment, in emphasizing the primacy of the text, Ricardou acted in the interest of the public health. But in overdoing, one falls from one excess into another. On the other hand, I see developing here and there today, notably with Lucien Dällenbach, a criticism which, while continuing to give the text the attention it merits, also makes use of other criteria to open out onto wide and more substantial horizons.

François Jost: I wrote an article in *Poétique* six years ago about *Leçon de choses* in which I said that I found this book very funny and extremely interesting, but that your first part, "Génériques," was somewhat of a let-down as far as the well-known theory of the "generators" was concerned. By this I meant that you began with any number of things—the description of a ceiling, of plants, of waves—and then, at the end of three pages, what could possibly have developed out of a certain number of words came to a sudden end with your saying that one could go on indefinitely, and the novel continued along another line.

Claude Simon: I am sorry, Franççis Jost, but it is just the contrary. Perhaps I should explain the genesis of this novel. In reponse to a request from the Maeght Gallery, which had had the idea of a series of posters composed of short texts illustrated by painters, I wrote a short description of a room in my country house that was being renovated by masons. This text ended with these lines:

La description (la composition) peut se continuer (ou être complétée) à peu près indéfiniment selon la minutie apportée à son exécution, l'entraînement des métaphores proposées, l'addition d'autres objets visibles dans leur entier ou fragmentés par l'usure, le temps, un choc (soit encore qu'ils n'apparaissent qu'en partie dans le cadre du tableau), sans compter les diverses hypothèses que peut susciter le spectacle. Ainsi il n'a pas été dit, etc."

[The description (the composition) can go on (or be supplemented) almost indefinitely, depending on the meticulousness exercised in the execution, the yielding to proposed metaphors, the addition of other objects entirely visible or fragmented by wear, time, a shock (or that only part of them appear in the frame of the painting), not taking into account the various hypotheses which may emerge from this sight. Thus it was not said that, etc.]

And then, once this text was sent to Maeght, I told myself: "Now that you've written that, do it! Prove that it's possible, go on!" And that is what I did. If the title of the first pages is "Génériques," what follows is entitled "Expansion." It is from the elements of the first description that three short stories develop: One recounting the mason's work, another, an episode of war (Soldiers fortifying themselves in a ruined house waiting for an enemy attack), and the third, showing the figures of a reproduction of a painting by Renoir still tacked on one of the walls of the room. I composed the novel, interweaving these three stories a little like the themes of a fugue follow from and overlap each other. So I was delighted when a while ago I heard Pinget speak of music.

One detail might be of interest. When I had almost finished writing this novel, I realized that, in fact, I had only been developing all the connotations of the word "chute" [fall], such as they appear in the dictionary of Littré: *chute d'un mur* [the fall of a wall], *chute de cheval* [the falling off a horse], *chute d'obus* [the falling of shells (military)], *chute d'une femme* [the downfall of a woman], *chute d'une place forte* [the fall of a fortified town], *chute du jour* [nightfall], and so on. But there was nothing premeditated in this. This was just how things happened.

François Jost: This is precisely what I tried to show.

Claude Simon: But you just said that the novel went on with something other than "Génériques"! I do not understand.

François Jost: There was a kind of play with criticism: Calling the first chapter of *Leçon de choses* "Génériques" was at the same time a joke and a kind of play on structure as a whole. I specifically tried to show that this novel was a disillusionment for the "nouveau lecteur" [new reader], the reader who thought he had understood everything about the functioning of the Nouveau Roman once and for all. The problem has really to do with the relation between the critical commentaries that you come across every day and your practice of writing.

Claude Simon: It is possible that after having read *Leçon de choses*, a reader might not easily understand how I went on from there to write *Les Géorgiques*. And yet, while these two texts are very different, their principles are not. Perhaps I would not even have been able to write *Les Géorgiques* without having written *Leçon de choses*. But all this requires long explanations and I am not, at this point, going to begin another lecture.

Alain Robbe-Grillet: Actually, what Ricardou did very well was to de-Ricardolize you!

Robert Pinget: I very much appreciate François Jost's intervention. I find it very honest. Everyone is ganging up on Ricardou. I think that at a given moment this intelligent critic shed a certain light on our works, and suddenly, though no one knows why, he is no longer spoken of. We ought to acknowledge that he is someone of value.

Claude Simon: Our friend Pinget is Christianly making himself the defender of the poor and the orphan. It is touching and very charitable, although I wonder whether true charity would not rather be to warn someone that he is treading on thin ice. No one has said here that Ricardou's writings are worthless. The problem, if I must repeat myself, is that, like all theses pushed to the extreme, those that he developed have, in practice, led him to a dead end, and his followers along with him. In this regard, he is dangerous. Moreover, he seems to have been suffering, for some time now, from a pathological megalomania, which is of no help either. Just as I did not spare him my public approbation when I found what he was doing interesting, I have told him very frankly (and in writing) what I think today. That is all.

Alain Robbe-Grillet: I would like to extend this debate to the more general topic of the relation between the writer or the creator and critics in general. The New Novel is a good example because it has been widely considered. A lot has been written about the Nouveau Roman, and with great diversity. Personally, I have always been very interested in what was being written about it and, of course, in what was being written about me in particular. The first thing that I realized is that a critic is not a scientist. The critic develops his own fantasies and he can do only that. The critic is a kind of minor writer in some cases, major in other cases. I am thinking of Barthes, for instance. Yet he remains one who does nothing but develop his own fantasies. Though I spoke of academic criticism as having been unreceptive to the Nouveau Roman, that criticism was still very interesting. There were many lessons to be learned from it, precisely because the fantasies of an ideology were present within the criticism and it was very interesting to get to know them. Of course, the interest was not for the purpose of revising our writings, but to enable us to situate our own efforts. As far as university-related or high-level criticism is concerned, people such as Blanchot or Barthes, for example, were interested in me. But I understood from the start that their effort was not really to speak about me, for Blanchot could never speak about anyone but Blanchot and Barthes could speak only of Roland Barthes.

The funniest thing is that they both wrote articles on *Le Voyeur* at a time when I was almost unknown. These two articles are extraordinary! One would think that they are not about the same book. In one, called "Littérature littérale," Roland Barthes spoke of *Le Voyeur* as if there were no sexual crime in the book. He never mentions it. His article is written entirely on the level of things: objectivity and a kind of realism which, of course, was not simple, for Barthes had a shrewd mind. Blanchot, on the other hand, saw only the sexual crime. In fact, Blanchot's text started with this sentence: "Where does the light illuminating *Le Voyeur* come from?" This light was the crime itself. So why is it that this light which illuminates *Le Voyeur* was never seen by Barthes?

You know, for three years after publication of *Les Gommes*, I never said that this text was linked with Sophocles' *Oedipus Rex*. For three years, no one mentioned it. Not one critic ever said it, not even Barthes, who wrote a text on *Les Gommes* in which he never mentioned either Sophocles or Oedipus. Does this mean that Barthes's texts were uninteresting? Of course not! They were fascinating! But what is most fascinating is that it is possible to write two such different things. And soon it was three, because when Goldmann got involved, there was an entirely different point of view. In other words, the value of this very Barthesian notion of the polysemy of the text must be affirmed, not by *one* critic, for probably he himself would be able to develop only his own fantasy, but by *several* critics.

I was very fond of Ricardou. He was fascinating. For me, his only mistake was in not acknowledging this polysemy. At the colloquia devoted to us in Cerisy, he had a tendency first to rectify the mistakes of other critics and then our own mistakes. He has a dogmatic mind, a normative mind, but theory is not always normative. A scientist using the particle theory to study light would never say that the wave theory is wrong. He would easily admit to another physicist working on the wave theory. Now you know that these two theories are incompatible. They cannot go together. A coherent world where light would be both waves and particles is not possible. Nevertheless, physicists of light are not at all bothered by this contradiction. And what I ask of this supposedly scientific criticism is that it function like modern science, like this science which knows that it is never true, but merely interesting. And this, I think, was the case with Barthes, with Blanchot, and to a great extent, with Ricardou as well.

Monique Wittig: But for one who is working either on the wave or the particle theory, both are legitimate, both are right, is that not so?

Alain Robbe-Grillet: How can they be legitimate if the two are incompatible and are mutually destructive? If light is made of particles, it cannot be made of waves.

Monique Wittig: And yet, it is so for both theories.

Alain Robbe-Grillet: No, there has never been any experiment up to now, though we keep trying, where the two theories would work together. People have to consider either one or the other. They are as mutually exclusive as Goldmann and Barthes.

Tom Bishop: And with respect to criticism, Monique Wittig, does one critical point of view on a particular writer not exclude another?

Monique Wittig: No, because they are what I call heterogeneous elements. It is possible to have a heterogeneous point of view where two points of view do not negate each other, where each is right from its own perspective.

Alain Robbe-Grillet: I think it is much more interesting if the two points of view negate each other, if the two poles are irreconcilable. You know, in the translation of Hegel's dialectic, the equivalents of thesis, antithesis, and synthesis were used in French and "synthesis" clearly showed that the French mind could not tolerate this contradiction. *Aufebung* does not at all mean that there is a synthesis of the two, but only a level of going beyond where the two converge

The New Novel: Past, Present, Future

on something else. And the fact that in the dialectic, thesis and antithesis are incompatible, that they are at odds with each other, is, in my opinion, essential. And this is all the more so when we speak of literature, for literature is precisely the place where those struggles between incompatible poles take place.

It has been much debated, for example, whether the Nouveau Roman is objective or subjective. What is more interesting is that it cannot be both and, nevertheless, both are there. You can read the Nouveau Roman objectively, as Barthes did, or subjectively, as Blanchot did. The two are there operating in the text. And the text is precisely the place, the site, of this contradiction between irreconcilable things. Both are not true for if they were, they would tolerate each other, but not tolerating each other, they are mutually exclusive. In Hegel's description, one of them has to die, it is completely out of the question that both survive.

I would also like to make a brief point relevant to the problem of consciousness because problems of consciousness—the hero's consciousness, the other characters' consciousnesses, the narrator's consciousness, the writer's and the reader's consciousnesses—are very important problems because they have given rise to numerous misunderstandings. The misunderstanding very often in question is that the public imagines that the writer is hiding something, that the writer knows what is taking place in his character's consciousness, but that he is not saying what it is. This was true to a certain extent of *L'Etranger* [*The Stranger*] by Camus insofar as "the stranger," Meursault, appears as an empty consciousness only in the first part of the book, his consciousness overflowing—as Nathalie Sarraute has often remarked, both in her theoretical essays and here—at the end. Unlike *L'Etranger*, one of the basic characteristics of the Nouveau Roman, one which has profoundly shocked the reader, is what has been called the dehumanization of the characters. With the New Novel, the reader was said to be facing heroes who were no longer human beings because they no longer possessed a consciousness. In fact, while they did not have a *humanist* consciousness, they did possess another kind of consciousness.

What is strange is that readers remain completely conditioned by a transcendental philosophy which maintains that consciousness is full and that it diffuses fullness and meaning around itself, while what we call a modern consciousness, or a Husserlian consciousness, is an empty consciousness. There is nothing within consciousness,

Husserl claims. Consciousness is simply a movement of outward projection, what he calls phenomenology. What is very bizarre is that the word "phenomenology" has very often been used by the critics, and most often it is misused. For some of them, in other words, phenomena were things in themselves which existed outside the consciousness of the subject, and consequently, man was said to have been replaced in Robbbe-Grillet's books by objects. This has been widely maintained. Others, on the other hand, supposed that in this phenomenology, the notion of intentionality was, despite everything, an intention which issued from a fullness within consciousness.

Now, what is a modern consciousness? What is there in the characters of the New Novel that unites us so well, Pinget, Simon, Sarraute, and all the others? It is precisely that the consciousnesses are no longer full consciousnesses. They are consciousnesses which exist only in this movement of outward projection. The question that we might ask ourselves is whether the writer is such a consciousness. Also, I think that we are obliged to say that the consciousness of the novelist is a struggling consciousness. By that I mean that no one can really claim to be a Husserlian consciousness. This does not exist. We continue to be transcendent consciousnesses, humanist consciousnesses, while within our consciousness there takes place, as well, this struggle between the old human consciousness—God, truth, and so on—and this purely Husserlian consciousness. This consciousness never has anything inside itself, but is unceasingly projecting itself out of itself, away from this self in which there is nothing, toward the world where there is nothing either.

Nathalie Sarraute: I think that my friends will agree that the New Novel was most useful as a total liberation of the forms and the content of the novel. When I wrote *L'Ere du soupçon* in 1950, people asked me what I meant by "traditional." This was a word that was not used. People did not even know its application. New novels are published which are not written in the traditional form: writers may completely suppress chronological time, not use proper nouns, organize the dialogue as they wish. They are not judged on these things.

This freedom derives, I think, from the movement of the Nouveau Roman. Young writers are not even aware of the freedom they are enjoying. And the same holds true for their private lives. The new generations have no knowledge of the tyranny to which preceding generations were subjugated. I believe that it is one of the advantages, one of the successes, of the Nouveau Roman that the forms of the novel have become free. All liberations are slow, and it is not possible to determine their effects on the basis of a few years.

Robert Pinget: I would like to say that I disagree with Robbe-Grillet as far as Husserl is concerned and the rejection of any religious significance, for I have always been a believer. I do not write of it in my work, but to deny the divine presence....

Alain Robbe-Grillet: I have just said the contrary.

Robert Pinget: This is not true.

Alain Robbe-Grillet: I have just said that a Husserlian consciousness does not exist. I just said yesterday that there is no pure revolutionary and that God is always within us. This was precisely my whole point. We are the place of those contradictions and the New Novel is no longer the novel of conquered freedom, because freedom cannot be conquered for once and for all since it, too, is a movement of conquest. We need God to be atheists.

Claude Simon: This whole discussion is completely beyond me. For example, we have mentioned the characters of the Nouveau Roman. What does this mean? Which characters? And which New Novels? We are getting bogged down in total confusion. The status of the character in Robbe-Grillet, Butor, Pinget, Nathalie Sarraute, or myself is as different as a carp from a rabbit, a hummingbird, or a cauliflower. So what are we speaking about? I would like to know, and to know what I am doing here. My little contribution to this colloquium denounced the danger, a deadly one in my opinion, faced by art when from time to time a certain scientism is introduced, and I have just listened, apropos of the novel, to a passionate discussion on theories of physics.

Personally, I could care less. I tried to say yesterday that I am a simple craftsman and that the expression which I think best suits a description of my work is "puttering about." The entire question for me consists of starting a sentence, seeing it through, and finishing it. Already on this level, very complex problems of structure are faced which are very hard to resolve, and I succeed only by a good deal of erasing and by trial and error. The same holds true for paragraphs, chapters, and the totality of the novel. This is trouble enough, believe me. So when I hear people speaking of higher philosophy, laws of physics, "Husserlian consciousness," or other matters, I ask you to excuse me, but I must humbly confess that this is completely beyond my competence and my preoccupations.

Nathalie Sarraute: As for me, when I write, I never think of any consciousness, whether Husserlian, full, outwardly projected, or remaining within. This would completely prevent me from writing.

American Parallels: An Afterword

John Barth   *Robert Coover*
Jonathan Baumbach   *John Hawkes*

The final session of the conference consisted of a round-table discussion among four American novelists whose innovative fictions, representative of this country's evolutionary (experimental) novelistic climate for some twenty years, have been likened to the achievements of the Nouveaux Romanciers. John Barth, Jonathan Baumbach, Robert Coover, and John Hawkes participated in this session not for the purpose of adding to the critical commentary on the French New Novelists, but rather to pay homage to a group of writers with whom they all feel, to a greater or lesser degree, a sense of community and shared purposes. The attack on establishment fiction that occurred in this country in the 1960s and 1970s bore an implicit relation to that which had begun somewhat earlier in France, and thus the effort was to explore the ways writers in America had responded, both to the established dogma and to the example set by the French New Novelists. This acknowledgment of the American writers of their appreciation of the French achievements was what drew them to the colloquium, and it was in tribute to their visiting colleagues that the Americans, by invitation, read from their own work, allowing their texts, in and of themselves, to reveal and celebrate the kinship.

The readings, which allowed for a synoptic view of the imaginative territories investigated by these writers, illustrated common concerns and consistent strategies within an arena of extraordinary diversity. And the dialogue that accompanied these readings, focusing not on the question of influence but on that of affinities, revealed aesthetic and technical complementary counterpositions and related efforts. Jonathan Baumbach, for example, in introducing the session, offered the following list of concerns shared by "some or all" of the Americans with the Nouveaux Romanciers:

1. Words. Sentences.

2. The hostility of certain readers who believe the novel must abide by certain rules, rules that have been inductively arrived at by myopic observation of the nineteenth-century novel.

3. A romantic refusal to believe that everything has already been done.

4. A sometime compulsion to devise a work of fiction that determinedly breaks the rules—or as Robert Bresson puts it in his *Notes on Cinematography*—"to bring together things that have never yet been brought together and did not seem predisposed to be so."

5. A certain rebelliousness against received notions. A turning of received notions against themselves. Orneriness.

6. A refusal to take literally such dichotomies as intellect and feeling, form and content.

7. An attempt to revise the notion of what is possible.

8. Investigating ways of telling a story and ways of not telling a story.

9. A withholding of empathy—an engendering of distance. A refusal to allow the reader to be passive.

10. The novel as self-contained object separate from the reader's life.

11. A refusal to create the illusion (or the convention of the illusion) of reality.

12. An involvement with cinema—with cinema as dream, with dream as cinema.

"Many of the items on this list," noted Baumbach, "are the same item: a restructuring of the same statement."

A variety of other parallels were indicated by other participants, such as that contained in a comment by Coover.

Robert Coover: Listening to John Hawkes read, bringing his text so alive there for the moment, reminded me of one quality a lot of contemporary American writers share, I think—both with each other and with many of the so-called Nouveau Roman writers— and that is a renewed interest in oral forms, literature that can be spoken as well as read. Here in the United States and in France, as well as almost everywhere else, there has been a reaction against the old ossified novelistic forms, which just do not seem to be telling the truth anymore, and as a kind of by-product of this, we have all been going back to some of the forms that had fallen out of

American Parallels: An Afterword

favor with the rise of the novel, including those of oral storytelling. It has been an attempt, you might say, to recover the mainstream, and in that sense I feel that one thing we share with the French writers here is a return to that mainstream, even as, in our ambition, we seek to carve out new channels for it.

It was not the intention of the American novelists, however, "to describe or invest connections to the Nouveau Roman, nor to claim they exist, nor to claim they don't exist," as Baumbach remarked, "but to give some indication of our concerns as writers." Indeed, John Barth went so far as to question the very notion of a new American Fiction (referring to the title of the American roundtable), reminding us that contemporary writers in this country are as different from one another as they are from their French colleagues. Barth, in fact, offered what was perhaps the most comprehensive overview of the current American literary scene, with his characteristic and inimitable wit.

John Barth: The announced topic of our roundtable presentation is "Fiction: The New Americans." It should not be imagined that there is any such animal as an American New Novel, in the sense that this conference celebrates justly the French Nouveau Roman of the late 1950s and 1960s. Whether there are certain meaningful parallels between what we in America have been doing and what we are celebrating here remains to be discussed by my colleagues. But I have come all the way from Baltimore to New York to reassure you that at least among American novels I see no disturbing signs of an American New Novel. I myself published a new American novel in this calendar year, and as is my custom when that occurs, I have kept a little list of who else has done likewise among those of my countrymen upon whom I maintain a watchful eye. That little list includes all three of my fellow panelists: Mr. Baumbach, Mr. Coover, and Mr. Hawkes. It includes, in chronological order, Saul Bellow, Paul Theroux, John Cheever, Jerzy Kosinski, Thomas McGuane, Anne Tyler, John Gardner, Bernard Malamud, Joyce Carol Oates, Don DeLillo, John Updike, Kurt Vonnegut, and Stanley Elkin; also story collections by I. B. Singer, Mark Helprin, and Anne Beattie. It has been a bountiful American literary year, and there is still a whole quarter of it yet to go. But I do not detect among those books, several of which are surely both good and important, anything resembling a noteworthy new general direction in the U.S. novel.

Nor do I, for that matter, when I think about what we U.S. novelists have been up to over these last dozen years or so. I suppose that the term "black humor" described something reasonably real and reasonably significant back in the American 1950s. Later labels, such as "fabulatore" and "metafictionists," have some descriptive power, but what they describe strikes me as comparatively more special and minor, rather than a general energizing spirit—though some individual works tagged with those labels are no doubt good works.

Then there is the adjective "Postmodern," which I have done my bit to help confuse. I continue to believe that that adjective describes a very approximately shared inclination among numerous writers and other artists in the second half of our Western twentieth century; an inclination to work out in their individual ways not the next best thing after Modernism, but the *best next* thing after Modernism. However, that inclination cuts across national lines, and what is more, people smarter about such matters than myself have assured me that what *I* mean by postmodern fiction is not what the term really means at all. So forget it.

What else is there? In conversation recently with a newly notable, younger U.S. realist writer who happens moreover to be an ex-alcoholic, I learned that yet another younger U.S. newly notable, minimalist realist short-story writer of whom we then spoke is also a former alcoholic. We turned then to speaking of a third, an ex-student of mine, now similarly a younger ex-alcoholic minimalist, et cetera, and since I had seen the names of these three writers lumped together now and then in the *Times,* I was moved to coin the term "Post-Alcoholic Blue-Collar Minimalist Hyperrealism" to describe this potentially significant new literary phenomenon. I suppose Gore Vidal would be pleased: he has more than once sneered at what he calls the Alcoholic American Republic of Letters. But pleasing Gore Vidal is not my mission in life. Anyhow, one of those three gifted authors-on-the-wagon, or on the bandwagon, has since unfortunately relapsed, and anyhow, they are all mainly short-story writers, not novelists. So there goes that. (In fact—setting aside the alcohol, the "hyper," and the hype—I believe the new flowering of the American realist short story, as represented by the likes of Frederick Barthelme, Ann Beattie, Raymond Carver, Stephen Dixon,

American Parallels: An Afterword

Barry Hannah, Mark Helprin, Bobbie Ann Mason, and Mary Robison, to be the most noteworthy recent development in American fiction. But so rapidly does the literary weather change, I feel impelled to date this observation 3 P.M., October 2, 1982, and fix the latitude and longitude as well.)

My friends, what I believe is this: that when it comes to movements, coherent literary ideologies, and the issuing of lucid position papers, the French arrange these things better. I have read and reread for my own pleasure, and for the edification of my students, Alain Robbe-Grillet's collection of position papers, *For a New Novel*, dozens of times I am sure. A marvelously lucid exposition. I believe that from time to time an authentic aesthetic phenomenon like the French New Novel appears, even in non-Gallic literatures, interesting and homogenous enough about which to make a few nonridiculous generalizations. Such phenomena make life easier for teachers, art historians, culture watchers—for anyone interested in understanding and registering what is going on around us, since we can think and talk only with the aid of categories. But I take the tragic view of categories; and I believe further that inhomogenous, nondescript ideological interregnums, such as novelistic North America may be enjoying presently, can also be fecund for the production of fine individual works of art, which are at least as valuable as coherent aesthetic movements. Since the novel is of all the genres of literature—perhaps of all the forms of art—the least categorizable, the most anarchical and flexible, the most hospitable to amateurs and naifs and to fruitful contamination of every unlikely sort, I believe that it is as likely to thrive in an incoherent period as in a coherent one.

Therefore I advise the culture not to worry if there is no American New Novel. The culture has more important things to worry about. More to the personal point, I believe that the odds against my writing an excellent new American novel, which I quite aspire to do, are not worsened in such an interregnum, if we are in fact in one. Those odds may even be improved.

And I wish the old French New Novel good luck and good health, as I wish the newer Latino novelistic "boom" good luck and good health. My admiration is uncontaminated by envy.

Questions from the audience provided further impetus for the timely consideration of such issues as the presence of women writers on the horizon of recent American fiction, the conscious versus intuitive renovation of narrative forms, the categorization of fiction (experimental, avant-garde, postmodern, and so on), and the engagement of "new" fiction with new political realities. As in the discussions with Robbe-Grillet, Sarraute, Simon, and Pinget, what surfaced readily in this segment of the American roundtable was the distinction between a spirit of rebelliousness and a true ideological determinism, a radical will to reform, which appeared in the essays of the French writers as the single most important unifying trope. This consistency, alluded to in the introduction of this book, should alert the reader to the celebration of creative process, to the commemoration of the innovative consciousness, which, over and above any theoretical point of departure grounded in a negative valorization of antecedent literary practice, impelled the practitioners of Modernism to extend the boundaries of artistic praxis beyond those historically maintained. It is here that the true cultural—and political—value of this literature resides, a value to which the discussion that follows clearly attests.

Question: Among the themes you used as metaphors for talking about what you are doing, there were the usual male sexual fantasies. And when Mr. Barth read the list of novelists who have published in America this year, which is an incredible list, they were mostly men. Where are the women in the New American Novel?

John Barth: Be it remembered first that I did mention Joyce Carol Oates. There's three women, I suppose, right there. I also mentioned Anne Tyler, Ann Beattie, and Mary Robison, and should have mentioned Alice Walker but forgot to. It may be that others of the excellent American writers who happen to be women did not happen to be publishing books this year.

John Hawkes: Another response to that question: Within the last five years, say, the number of novels written by women has increased enormously. There is an extraordinary amount of fiction being written in this country by women. Among them is at least one who is indeed creating new forms of fiction—my former student, Marilynne Robinson. Her novel *Housekeeping* is drastically her own, extraordinarily poetic, and very much to be included in any discussion of serious fiction in the United States today. As I say, there are as many if not more current works of American fiction written

American Parallels: An Afterword

by women as by men. But, except for Marilynne Robinson, I cannot think of any American woman writer working beyond the realistic tradition.

Jonathan Baumbach: I do not know that this is a question that we really ought to pursue. To break down writers in terms of sex leads to other kinds of chauvinism. There are a lot of extraordinary women writers around, but to talk about them as being women writers as opposed to writers is pointless, it seems to me. Pointless and demeaning.

Question: My question has to do with the story, and the element of story in your work. Thomas Bernhard, the Austrian writer, once mentioned that as soon as he tries to tell a story he backs off and tries to subvert it. Do you consciously attempt to do that? Also, when you are reading your contemporaries, do you find traditional work mechanical or old-fashioned? Are you able to appreciate people like Bellow and Updike or do you react against them?

Robert Coover: As for the reaction against realism and the traditional novel, I have the feeling that this has been a worldwide phenomenon, having to do with general intellectual and social currents, not just fiction itself. When I started reading and writing seriously, looking for a voice of my own, thinking about models, forms that might properly reflect the world I found myself living in, and so on, I tended to react rather negatively to further elaborations of the old novelistic forms, and that included Bellow and Updike, whom you mentioned. It was not simply that these forms seemed played out, but rather that they seemed to distort somehow the reality that surrounded us: thus a kind of fantasy, masquerading as so-called realism, and presented to us as a kind of establishment dogma. In fact, they seemed to have much the same relationship to the established social structures of our time that ancient myths had to theirs, and it seemed to me that if you were going to question the structures of one, you had to question the structures of the other. I felt them to be in collusion somehow, deep down, at the level of form, and I found myself drawn to writing that was rebelling against them both at the same time. If I had to name the French writer who had the most influence on me at that time, for example, I would have to say it was the Irishman Samuel Beckett—that may sound discourteous, but, in fact, our French colleagues being honored here like to claim him as their own, and many of them have publicly acknowledged their debt to him. I think this reaction against form was happening simultaneously all around the world—in France, in Germany, in Italy, certainly in Latin America. And without any of us reading each other until our ideas were already pretty well formed. Thus, we all seem to be, like other generations of writers before us, hapless children of our own age, a prospect as disturbing in its own way perhaps as that of being a mere imitator of dead forms from the past.

Jonathan Baumbach: A number of the writers that were mentioned have done books that were fairly risky and might even be talked about if there were such a category as "New Novels." Bellow wrote *Henderson the Rain King* and Malamud started out writing *The Natural*. It is hard to know why a career goes in a certain way and hard to determine from the outside, although there is a tendency in America to somehow compromise with what the public apparently wants or with what booksellers think the public wants or with what publishers think the booksellers think the public wants. I do not think that it is a conscious selling out. I think that it is like imminent will in fascist countries. One assumes certain values that may really belong to a society, or at least the culture attributes to itself, and so people begin creating books for an audience that they believe is out there waiting for them. Inevitably, books that are created out of that impulse lack surprise. I think that in many cases writers who were very interesting at one point have been caught somehow, not only imitating themselves, but also imitating the kind of idea of success that was generated by the books they have written in the past.

John Hawkes: To respond to that general question about realism, in the late 1940s, when I was working on my first novel, a comical nightmarish story about a mythical neo-Nazi party in an imaginary Germany, it never occurred to me that this novel was not "realistic." However, when critics insisted that *The Cannibal* was more dream than document, I found myself in need of a theory about unconventional fiction. That is when I discovered that the enemies of fiction are plot, character, setting, and theme. Since then I have learned a lesson from Barth and have exempted "plot" from the dangerous canon. However, all the rest are still the enemies of fiction. On the other hand, I do not quite share my friend Bob

American Parallels: An Afterword

Coover's feeling about realism. For instance, I admire Bellow's short novel *Seize the Day* nearly as much as his splendidly inventive *Henderson the Rain King*. In fact, there is a resurgence of realistic writing in the United States today. Last night we were talking about one young writer—maybe John Barth will say more about him—Mark Helprin, who is a remarkable fictionist. It seems to me that, in the realistic tradition, David Plante is an amazingly fine writer, as is Edmund White. I myself do value the new purities and possibilities of realism, despite my allegiance to visionary forms of fiction.

John Barth: The list of good U.S. novels published this year includes more items of a traditional realistic sort than not, and this has no doubt been the case with every other year in the history of American fiction, even in the twentieth century. One is impressed once again, for what the lesson is worth, by what a relatively small impact not only the French New Novel, but also the whole phenomenon of modernism has had on English-language writing compared with its influence on European and, for that matter, South American writing. I try to say that nonjudgmentally. I am impressed by it.

As to the question of story raised by the gentleman in the audience and of backing off from story: that story is my subject matter. Stories about stories are as characteristic of my fiction as anything I can think of. This fact has been deplored by some readers and critics and praised by others, but never mind that. It is an accurate enough description of a preoccupation. As to the character of those stories, I think M. Robbe-Grillet said it best in one of those position papers I mentioned earlier. It is not the anecdote that is missing from the New Novel, let us say, but its character of innocence, the innocent anecdote. If that is what you meant by backing off from the story, okay. On the other hand, I am impressed with how very ancient that backing off is. What has been called self-reflexivity in narration is, I am convinced, as old as the narrative imagination itself. My intuitions tell me that if the first story ever told began with the words "Once upon a time . . ." the second story ever told probably began with "Once upon a time there was a story that began 'Once upon a time,'" and so on. One of the oldest literary fragments known, I understand, is an Egyptian papyrus from about 2000 B.C. by the scribe Khakheperresenb, which goes something like this: "Would that I had three words that have not already been used by other writers before me; that there were a fresh new way to say things." It is a literary statement about literary statements, and my intuitions tell me that even by 2000 B.C., "Khakheperresenb's Complaint" was probably a venerable literary genre. I imagine him saying "I'm going to do a complaint today and see if I can't do it better than the old chaps." Our contemporary "self-reflexivity" is just the foreground of a characteristic of very much earlier narrative.

Robert Coover: Let me add a note, too, about self-reflective fictions—stories about stories—because John Barth mentioned how ancient this device really is. I think our interest in stories about stories does return from time to time, and it tends to happen precisely when we begin to question not only story itself, but also who the teller is and what his interests are in telling the story, and what the interests of society are in presenting that story or in celebrating it—in our case in publishing and advertising that story. Stories about stories draw attention to process itself, such that the story stops being a kind of dogmatic presence and becomes something one can question even as he listens to it. A lot of contemporary stories about stories have, it seems to me, this sort of subversive intent.

Question: If one believes, as has been implied, that there really is no coherent way of discussing or classifying what is called the New American Novel, is there any way to discuss avant-garde or experimental fiction? Is there any on-going tradition through people like Thomas Pynchon?

Jonathan Baumbach: The terms are very hard to deal with: "avant-garde" and "experimental" in American journalism tend to be somewhat perjorative, so we are always up against what is meant by them. And I think it comes down again to writers who are not writing in a realistic tradition and, as John Barth pointed out, the very things that so-called new writers are doing are as old as storytelling. One might talk about a kind of nonrealistic tradition in American fiction, but—unlike the French, in which there does seem to be a connection of some coherence among the writers of the so-called Nouveau Roman—among fantasists, metanovelists, and postmodern American fiction writers, there is more diversion than similarity. There tends to be very little communication among us. It is only at conferences like this where we get to see each other.

American Parallels: An Afterword

I met John Barth really for the first time just a little bit ago. Pynchon, particularly, who is a kind of invisible man (it seems to me, there is as much myth going on about him as about the novels), works in a very private and distinct way and he is very much his own man. I think it is true about American writers that we determinedly—almost cussedly—go our own way. We do have things in common. I think that John Barth's talking about stories about stories may connect the four of us in certain ways. But I think the differences are more profound, and I think that is true about the so-called experimental or avant-garde. I do not think that avant-garde or experimentalism is a very useful way of describing certain tendencies in American fiction. It is very hard to find the right descriptive generalities, and the categories (avant-garde, experimental, postmodern, metanovel) all become, if not perjorative, limiting and reductive.

John Barth: I would like to add to that. Among the American literary experiments that have moved or impressed me most in the last few years, some are not of an *Experimental* character. Two short-story writers whom I admire considerably, and who are as different from one another as is imaginable, Raymond Carver and Mark Helprin, are both experimenting in an interesting way. I prefer them to what is called metafiction for the homely reason that they touch my passions. They deal with what Aristotle says is the subject of literature: human life, its happiness and its misery. Not that you cannot do that in formally radical ways; the best of the innovators are those who deploy their radical means to bring us freshly back to the old subjects. But look at these two younger writers whom I have just mentioned. Carver is a kind of burned-out elliptical realist who, at first glance, seems to be doing things much like the early Hemingway and, on second glance, is remarkably different from the early Hemingway. There are experiments in the tuning and tightening up of a rather familiar kind of realistic, elliptical realism, and at the same time, experiments in the delineation of areas of the heart that are less familiar in contemporary literature than perhaps they might be.

Helprin is a kind of John Singer Sargent romantic—some combination of D. H. Lawrence and John Singer Sargent, I suppose. The sheer excessiveness of sentiment and emotion in that young man's work impresses me enormously.

Joyce Carol Oates once said to my student writers at Johns Hopkins that she has always had trouble reconciling to her own satisfaction the fact that she admires equally D. H. Lawrence and James Joyce, who, of course, had no use for each other. I told her that I thought that was no more unusual than the problem most of us have of reconciling a socialist brain, an anarchist heart, and a capitalist stomach. These are at best negotiated truces, and the areas keep changing.

Ron Sukenick: You mentioned before, John Barth, that the Nouveau Roman or the New American Novel, or whatever you want to call it, has had very little effect on Anglo-Saxon culture. I just want to remind you that America is not an Anglo-Saxon country nor an Anglo-Saxon culture, although—and I think this is the more important point—if you read *The New York Review of Books,* you get that impression. As we know, *The New York Review of Books* has certain literary political tastes, and the kinds of attack on metafiction or nonconventional fiction often have a quasi-political tack. One is accused, for example, of trying to dismantle the culture, of trying to be antihumanist, of being drunk with chaos, of trying to stir up trouble in general. I wonder if you, gentlemen, ever think of the political implications of the various shifts in style that fiction goes through.

John Barth: I stand immediately corrected.

Question: I would like to ask something related to the previous question. I am reminded of Jonathan Schell, who has recently given us a grim warning against nuclear holocaust. He says, to paraphrase, "Since we have not made a positive decision to exterminate ourselves but instead have chosen to live on the edge of extinction, periodically lunging toward the abyss only to draw back at the last second, our situation is one of uncertainty and nervous insecurity rather than absolute hopelessness." Do you think that American novels represent this reality more accurately and acutely than the fiction that is being written on the Continent?

Robert Coover: No, I do not. On the whole, I feel closer to certain European and Latin American writers than I do to most of my American colleagues, present company very emphatically excepted. I believe what links all of us, including what few Asian and Eastern bloc writers are available to me in translation (the paucity of good

American Parallels: An Afterword

translations is a scandal in this country), is the coincidence of living in a time when basic underlying principles are being questioned. The reasons for that, the reasons we are going back to ask fundamental questions once again, are very complex. Certainly one of them has to do with a widespread feeling that the worldview which made possible Nazism, World War II, and the current very real threat of nuclear annihilation, no longer makes much sense to us. Worldviews, like personal histories or newspaper reports, are stories of a sort. We all tell stores. It is how we get on in the world. And somehow we seem to have told the wrong stories and have ended up with all these nuclear warheads, set to go off. That is at least one reason why we are so interested in the processes of narrative. We want to try to get the story right. Now a lot of us, unfortunately, are too ignorant to be of much use. We are too self-enclosed, too self-indulgent with our private little interests. We do not reach out into the world enough, bring enough of it into our heads, so that as a story is transformed it might have some hope of making serious sense to others. That would be a cautionary remark I would make to all young writers: not to give up on the world, not to pull back entirely into your own heads. You should know everything the tribe knows, or try to. I am reminded of this in part because there is another novelist in the audience today who has not been mentioned and who has always, by example and by direct badgering, reminded me of this—Sol Yurick. Sol published *Richard A* this year, on the surface a kind of generic spy novel, but one informed by a deep knowledge of current communication theory. Well, this is right at the heart of the present problem, isn't it? The way that a certain communication and information technology is advancing and leaving the majority behind, helplessly illiterate, future victims, in effect, of an elite who will be controlling this new exchange mechanism. And who but narrative artists, themselves communicators, informers, can best confront and, if necessary, undermine this new power structure?

Jonathan Baumbach: One thing struck me while Robert Coover was talking, and I think it is also in partial response to Ron Sukenick's question. I mentioned in the beginning a sense of rebelliousness that may inform a lot of writing in America, not only what is thought of as nonrealist. I think that a lot of the rebelliousness comes from a sense of the mess the world has gotten itself into and in which we are implicitly collaborating, and the sense of not wanting to collaborate any further with what seems to me the accepted forms, the recognizable forms. This is apart from our intuition as writers. We reject what seems to us the establishment way of perceiving the world because that represents also to us a world which seems set upon self-destruction.

As a kind of sideline to that question—it is an interesting phenomenon that I have some theories about which I am not going to discuss here—is how the radical press of the left... I don't know if *The New York Review* can be talked about in those terms any more, but during the Vietnam War... it spoke to the left in its antiwar sentiments... has always been fairly reactionary in terms of literature. Jack talked about Gore Vidal... *The New York Review* covers the New Novel by having Gore Vidal make dismissive fun of Donald Barthelme's favorite writers, as if that is all there is to say. There seems to be an odd disjunction there between wanting to resist political reaction internationally and wanting to foster it in terms of literary concerns. I have a complicated theory which I am not going to bring up now. Oddly, sometimes there are right-wing journals that are much more sympathetic to radical literature, maybe because literature in America has never seemed to have the same kind of impact that it has in European countries. It does not seem to be able to change the way people think politically.

Question: I would like to say something more about Ron Sukenick's reference to *The New York Review of Books* and literary politics. I do not know anything about literary politics, but I do occasionally see *The New York Review of Books,* only on very special occasions, and the poison fairly drips. It is laughable. I really do not like it, I will say that. There does seem to be a consistency in that publication aimed at whatever we call—and there is no such thing as what we call—the New American Fiction, except in individual writers. They are really out to get a few of them.

Question: We have been trying to button up those categories—novel, poetry, essay, and so on—but the fact is that the buttons have fallen off. Simply said, the New Novel is a work which is approaching the condition of poetry. This was beautifully exemplified in Alain Robbe-Grillet's title *La Jalousie* which was untranslatable. In French, a "jalousie" is both a venetian blind and that emotion which eats us alive all the time. It could not be translated, but there is the poet's touch in that he came up with this kind of a pun. In all the new writing, Continental or American, the language is approaching the function of poetry. The language itself is the hero and the protagonist of the work.

There is something so illuminating that Alain Robbe-Grillet said the night he spoke. He gave a marvelous formula for what the New Novel or the contemporary novel is: He said that in the Middle Ages the narrator told a story he knew to an audience which knew the story. Then came the Renaissance, when the story was a novelty, something new. It was something which the narrator knew and the audience did not, and the audience was waiting for him to tell the story. The catch is that as it came toward the *fin de siècle,* tremendous novels were written, like *War and Peace,* that told how catastrophic life was for all the protagonists. This novel is full of wars, miserable marriages, and disastrous errors in living, and yet the reader finishes the work feeling fine because the structure of the novel has been an orderly progression from A to Z. It gives the impression, subliminally, that society is all of a piece and the world makes sense. One could almost disregard the misery that was going on inside the story, for if the protagonist suffered, it was that he was merely a misfit, like Pierre. Then it became necessary to break up this cozy situation where the very form of the novel gave the idea that all was well with the world. This was an illusion provided by the form of the work. And so along came Benjy, the idiot in *The Sound and the Fury.* Here the reader is told the story by someone who does not know the story and who is telling it to someone who can never understand it. That is contemporary!

Jonathan Baumbach: I took pains at the outset to understate the connection, to understate, evade, and deny the connection between the Nouveau Roman and this panel called, for the sake of parallelism, The New Americans. That was a strategy, not wholly conscious, to permit us to define our oeuvre, in its wide range of variations, without preconception. It strikes me that the very act of denying our relationship to the French has made that relationship more insistently evident. The connection between us is real. We have learned from their explorations; we have admired the audacity of their work. Like the French, in their image, so to speak, we still pretend to ourselves that there are discoveries to be made, that language and form are still open to unexpected configurations, that not only some things of surprise still remain to be done, but also — and this is the most serious aspect of our debt — everything remains.

Index

Abe, Kobo, 66, 67
Amant, L', 11
Année dernière à Marienbad, L', 34
Apocryphe, 18
Autobiography, 11, 12, 36, 37, 38, 39
Avant-garde, 13, 18, 34, 35

Baga, 14
Balzac, Honoré de, 3, 14, 22, 23, 66, 73, 77, 80, 106, 109, 119, 124, 126, 128, 129, 184
Barth, John, 9, 18, 64, 195, 202, 205
Barthes, Roland, 11, 22, 32, 33, 34, 37, 38, 60, 99, 115, 188, 189, 190
Bataille, Georges, 22, 33
Bataille de Pharsale, La, 45, 95, 113, 185
Baumbach, Jonathan, 9, 18, 195, 197
Beckett, Samuel, 8, 57, 58, 61, 75, 157, 201. *See also Molloy, L'Innomable*
Belle Captive, La, 32, 36, 49, 51, 53, 67
Biography, 36, 38
Bishop, Tom, 12, 21, 24, 32, 44, 87, 180
Blanchot, Maurice, 22, 26, 33, 64, 189, 190
Boyer, Philippe, 153, 154, 164
Butor, Michel, 17, 19, 39, 93, 193. *See also* individual titles

Camus, Renaud, 157, 177
Cerisy-la-Salle (Conference in), 6, 9, 17, 19, 32, 35, 38, 40, 44, 47, 48, 49, 83, 143, 154, 159, 179, 189
Character(s), 3, 11, 14, 22, 23, 25, 27, 53, 127
Château, Dominique, 32, 38
Chawaf, Chantal, 156, 170
Chronology, 3, 14, 28
"Collectif Change," 153, 163
Collobert, Danielle, 153, 154, 157, 165, 166

Coover, Robert, 9, 18, 64, 195, 197, 203, 207

Dans le labyrinthe, 14, 27, 33, 34, 49, 50
Degrés, 14
Dialogue, 14, 132
Disent les imbéciles, 130
Djinn, 4, 18, 27, 28, 29, 30, 32, 37, 39, 48, 49, 53, 57, 62
Dostoevski, Feodor, 73, 75, 105, 125
Duras, Marguerite, 104, 157, 158, 161, 167, 168. *See also L'Amant*
Duvert, Tony, 154, 155, 157, 158, 169

"École du regard, L'," 15, 33, 48
Eden et après, L', 36, 38
Editions de Minuit, Les, 13, 14, 123, 128, 150
Emploi du temps, L', 16, 152
Entre la vie et la mort, 129
Ère du soupçon, L', 14, 24, 127, 133, 182
Etranger, L', 14, 24, 191

Faulkner, William, 21, 23, 64, 75, 81
Faye, Jean Pierre, 153
Fiston, Le, 14
Flaubert, Gustave, 3, 40, 65, 66, 78, 105, 185
Fruits d'or, Les, 16, 129, 132, 133

Gallimard, 14, 123, 125, 127
Gauthier, Xaviere, 158, 160, 161, 167, 168, 170
Genette, Gerard, 53, 56 n22, 56 n23, 89, 96, 113, 118 n5
Géorgiques, Les, 18, 48, 76, 82, 113, 188
Glissement progressifs du plaisir, 36, 38, 49, 51, 53

Index

Goldman, Lucien, 33
Gommes, Les, 13, 16, 24, 25, 32, 33, 34, 49, 57, 59, 60, 154, 189
Graal Filibuste, 14
Grove Press, 16, 27, 57, 60, 62
"Gynetext" ("woman text"), 8, 162, 164, 166, 167, 172 n35, 174

Hawkes, John, 9, 18, 64, 195, 196, 197
Hegel, Georg Wilhelm Friedrich, 108
Heidegger, Martin, 29, 108
Herbe, L', 14
Histoire, 16
Homme qui ment, L', 35, 51
Howard, Richard, 16
Husserl, Edmund, 108, 191, 192, 193, 194
Hyvrard, Jeanne, 166, 168, 177

Immortelle, L', 34
Innomable, L', 66
Inquisitoire, L', 16
Instantanés, 33

Jalousie, La, 10, 14, 25, 26, 27, 28, 33, 34, 39, 59, 62, 183, 208
Jeu avec le feu, Le, 36, 49
Jolas, Maria, 16
Jost, Francois, 7, 114, 116, 182, 188
Joyce, James, 10, 21, 40, 75, 81, 121

Kafka, Franz, 21, 64, 125, 132
Kristeva, Julia, 161, 162, 167, 174

Leçon de choses, 187
Lenard, Yvonne, 28
Libera me Domine, The, 143, 147
Lindon, Jerome, 13, 14, 153

Mahu ou le matériau, 13, 24
Maison de rendez-vous, La, 27, 35, 49
Martereau, 13, 129, 133, 135
Meaning, 8, 11, 23, 24, 34, 63, 96
Mensonge, Le, 141
Mimesis, 87, 88, 89, 90, 113, 114
Mimetic, 8, 92, 96, 97, 110
Mimetism, 90, 91, 93, 94, 95, 96, 97, 98, 111
Miroir qui revient, Le, 11
"Mise en abyme," 115, 116
Mise en scène, La, 14, 16
Modification, La, 10, 14, 16
Molloy, 14. See also Beckett, Samuel

Montel, Jean-Claude, 153, 154, 157
Morrissette, Bruce, 25, 32, 34, 35, 36

Nabokov, Vladimir, 64
Narration, 5, 24, 27, 28, 51, 53
Narrative, 3, 4, 6, 7, 8, 14, 15, 27, 28, 53
Narrator, 22
Nausée, La, 14, 24
New York University, 3, 6, 9, 13, 17, 18, 19, 32, 83
Nouveau Nouveau Roman, 10, 17

Ollier, Claude, 15, 16, 17, 19, 174
Orions Aveugle, 82, 95

Palace, Le, 152
Passacaglia, 147
Passage de Milan, 13
Phenomenology, 10, 15, 33. See also Heidegger, Husserl
Pinget, Robert, 5, 12, 15, 19, 47, 48, 55, 104, 174, 179, 185, 186, 193, 200. See also individual titles
Planétarium, Le, 10, 129
Portrait d'un inconnu, 14, 125, 138, 152
Pour un Nouveau Roman, 33, 182
Prise de Constantinople, La, 16
Projet pour une révolution à New York, 27, 28, 35, 46, 48, 49, 50, 183
Proust, Marcel, 10, 21, 66, 75, 81, 82, 83, 121, 186

Quelqu'un, 16, 147, 152

Rauschenberg, Robert, 64, 65, 68, 69, 80, 95
Realism, 3, 4, 6, 10, 15, 34, 76, 77, 110, 111, 115, 203
Régicide, Un, 38
Ricardou, Jean, 10, 16, 17, 19, 35, 40, 44, 45, 46, 106, 107, 108, 112, 113, 153, 180, 181, 182, 185, 186, 188, 189, 190
Robbe-Grillet, Alain, 4, 5, 7, 8, 15, 19, 31, 32, 33, 34, 35, 36, 37, 38, 39, 40, 41, 44, 45, 46, 47, 48, 49, 51, 53, 54, 58, 61, 65, 66, 75, 77, 83, 104, 108, 117, 120, 128, 154, 155, 184, 185, 192, 193, 200, 203, 209. See also individual titles
Rochefort, Christine, 155
Rosset, Barney, 8, 12
Roudiez, Leon S., 8, 12
Roussel, Raymond, 33, 46

Route des Flandres, La, 14, 16, 185
Rybalka, Michel, 7, 45, 75

Sarkonak, Ralph, 110, 114
Sarraute, Nathalie, 4, 5, 8, 15, 19, 24, 45, 55, 75, 104, 107, 108, 132, 133, 134, 138, 139, 141, 174, 175, 181, 182, 185, 191, 193, 200. *See also* individual titles
Sartre, Jean-Paul, 32, 33, 35, 38, 40, 41, 75, 107, 108, 109, 110, 123, 124, 138. *See also La Nausée.*
Savitzkaya, Eugene, 154, 157, 158, 164, 167
Silence, Le, 141
Simon, Claude, 5, 15, 19, 44, 46, 47, 48, 55, 87, 88, 94, 96, 98, 99, 104, 105, 106, 108, 109, 111, 112, 113, 114, 115, 155, 156, 174, 181, 184, 185, 200. *See also* individual titles.
Souvenirs d'un triangle d'or, 27, 49, 51, 54
Stendhal (Marie Henri Beyle), 3, 73, 77, 78
Structuralism, 35

Temps modernes, Les, 24
Topologie d'une cité fantome, 27, 36
Trans-Europ-Express, 35
Tropismes, 13, 24, 122, 123, 128, 131
Tropisms, 131, 141

Usage de la parole, L', 18, 131

Veillon, Olivier, 31, 39, 41
Vent, Le, 14, 25
Vous les entendez?, 130
Voyeur, Le, 13, 16, 25, 27, 33, 34, 59, 152, 189

Waiting for Godot, 57, 58. *See also* Beckett, Samuel
Wittig, Monique, 7, 167, 181
Wright, Barbara, 12, 16

Zola, Émile, 22, 23, 73

LIBRARY OF DAVIDSON COLLEGE

Books on regular loan may be checked out for **two weeks**. Books must be presented at the Circulation Desk in order to be renewed.

A fine is charged after date due.

Special books are subject to special regulations at the discretion of the library staff.

DEC. 15, 1969			
DEC. 15, 1969			
JAN. 1, 1970			